HUNTING THE
AMERICAN WEREWOLF

Beast Men in Wisconsin and Beyond

Linda S. Godfrey

TRAILS BOOKS
Madison, Wisconsin

Library of Congress Control Number: 2005911293
ISBN: 1-931599-66-1

Editor: Mark Knickelbine
Cover Designer: Colin Harrington

Printed in the United States of America by Versa Press.

11 10 09 08 07 06   6 5 4 3 2 1

Trails Books, a division of Big Earth Publishing
923 Williamson Street • Madison, WI 53703
(800) 258-5830
www.trailsbooks.com

DEDICATION

To my husband, Steven, and sons Ben and Nate, for their
good humor and support when Mom was out
hunting werewolves.

TABLE OF CONTENTS

FOREWORD

by Nick Redfern

IT IS VERY SELDOM THAT I say to people, "If you only buy one book this year, make it this one." But I'm saying it now. Following in the footsteps (or perhaps that should be the wolf-tracks?) of her book, *The Beast of Bray Road*, which detailed her personal quest to determine the truth about the unholy critter that roams the small town of Elkhorn, Wisconsin, Linda Godfrey's latest title, *Hunting the American Werewolf*, is definitive reading for anyone and everyone interested in all things hairy, monstrous, and, of course, wolfish.

If you thought that werewolves were simply the imaginative product of horror novelists and Hollywood scriptwriters out to make a few quick bucks, then think again. As Linda reveals, there really may be diabolical man-beasts roaming by moonlight the woods, the forests, and the landscape of the more remote parts of North America—and a considerable number of the not-so-remote parts, too. But they may not be all that they appear to be. In fact, they just might be your worst nightmare come to life.

While many people are inclined to accept the idea that a giant ape may possibly inhabit some of the larger forests of the Pacific Northwest, and that a still-surviving plesiosaur swims within the icy depths of Scotland's Loch Ness, the idea that real-life werewolves might actually live among us is invariably treated with hoots of derision and the rolling of eyes. But, make no mistake, as Linda demonstrates time and again, something *is* with us…something evil, and something very, very strange. Science and our own logic tell us that werewolves do not exist; and that same science and logic tells us that these creatures *cannot* exist. But try telling that to the countless witnesses to the beasts that Linda has interviewed. And, if you dare, try telling it to the werewolves, too.

What sets *Hunting the American Werewolf* apart from so many other titles that focus their attention upon the mysterious beasts that may exist alongside us is that it is written by someone with not just a keen appreciation of the subject matter and (thank goodness) a fine sense of humor, but by someone who has no personal agenda or theory that she is trying to force down the collective throats of her audience.

Rather, as an award-winning journalist, Linda approaches the world of the werewolf with an open mind, a mind that is willing to go purely and simply where the evidence takes it. And, unlike the increasing number of authors who take the highly annoying approach of simply sitting within the sterile confines of their offices, cutting and pasting reams of material from the Internet, and then have the gall to present it as "research," Linda actually goes out into the field (literally!) and undertakes her own personal studies of the witnesses and their amazing accounts.

But if you thought Linda's latest title was going to reveal to you that people really are bursting out of their clothes, Incredible Hulk-style, at the sight of the full moon, sprouting hair and fangs, and feeding on the hapless folk of some little hamlet in the fashion of those old black-and-white horror movies, you would be very wrong. As is often the case, the truth is far stranger than fiction.

Linda's book reveals startling encounters with werewolves from such widespread and diverse locations as New York, Missouri, Illinois, Wisconsin, Pennsylvania, Georgia, and Canada. *Hunting the American Werewolf* also provides the reader with a dizzying number and variety of descriptions of beasts seen by an equally varied body of witnesses across several centuries. And while it is entirely possible that some of the reports are the result of actual encounters with flesh-and-blood animals that are believed to be extinct or that are simply not catalogued by mainstream science, many of the cases seem to fall into a distinctly different category.

For reasons that I have never really been able to fathom, many researchers and writers with an interest in mysterious animals are openly hostile to the idea that the creatures they seek—Bigfoot, Nessie, Ogopogo, or any number of the veritable menagerie of beasts that co-exist with us—could possibly have paranormal origins. And yet, those same people are acutely aware that many reports of such "things" do have paranormal overtones to them, even if that is something that they choose to ignore. Linda, however, chooses not to ignore this factor, and she deserves our admiration and thanks for not taking the easy route.

One of the reasons why I agreed to write the foreword to this book is because I have had my own run-ins with the beasts of the nether-world, and I know that they are not what they appear to be. As a very young child in the late 1960s, my parents took me to Loch Ness, and I can still vaguely recall that heady day, standing on the shores as my dad told me that there just might be a dinosaur lurking within its darkened depths. My mouth dropped in awe.

And from that moment, I was determined to seek out the truth. Today, I run the U.S. office of the British-based Center for Fortean Zoology and have undertaken numerous quests in search of strange and mysterious creatures, some of which were chronicled in my 2004 book, *Three Men Seeking Monsters*.

I will be the first to admit that when, as a child, I began delving into the weird world of mystery animals, I was of the opinion that everything was black-and-white and straightforward: Bigfoot was a giant primate, lake monsters were dinosaurs, and the Yeti was a still-surviving example of that monster-ape, Gigantopithecus. But the further I delved into the subject, the more I came to realize that these creatures were not just strange: *they were too strange.* They defied logic. They didn't act like normal animals act. They couldn't be caught. And as investigators of the puzzle began to delve ever deeper into this realm of high strangeness, the more they themselves would begin to experience bizarre synchronicities and strange events in their lives—even sightings of the wretched things that they were pursuing.

For me, one of the most unsettling experiences occurred in August 2002 when I was enmeshed in the writing of *Three Men Seeking Monsters* and had a bedroom encounter with an entity dressed in a long cape and a wolf-like head. Uttering strange, rapid growling noises, it positively oozed pure evil and hatred. The skeptics would say—and indeed *did* say—that I was merely suffering from something known as sleep-paralysis. And yet, encounters of this type plagued me—and still do. Personally, I suspect that this has more to do with the fact that I routinely take part in rituals and rites to try to summon up such entities.

You'd think I would have learned my lesson by now. But, as Linda reveals in her book, I am far from being alone when it comes to positing a link between diabolical wolflike animals and the paranormal, the otherworldly, the supernatural, or however you want to describe it.

Hunting the American Werewolf is packed with accounts that suggest that those of us with a yearning desire to understand what werewolves really are should look beyond just the physical (although certainly not ignore it) and into other, stranger realms. Witches and Wicca, spirit-guides, ancient folklore, hellhounds, Native American burial mounds, supernatural doggy-doors, the realm of the dead, strange lights in the sky, and sinister characters roaming the landscape are all part and parcel of Linda's story as she separates fact from fiction and belief from reality—all the time with a rational, careful head on her shoulders.

I will not, of course, spoil things for you by revealing Linda's conclusions; but I will say that you will not be disappointed by her book. And if *Hunting the American Werewolf* encourages you to seek out these bizarre beasts for yourself, take note of the fact that, as some of Linda's witnesses reveal, when they went looking, *something* came calling. Keep that silver bullet handy....

Nick Redfern is the author of Three Men Seeking Monsters: Six Weeks in Pursuit of Werewolves, Lake Monsters, Giant Cats, Ghostly Devil Dogs, and Ape-Men *(Paraview-Pocket Books, 2004) and* On the Trail of the Saucer Spies *(Anomalist Books 2006).*

INTRODUCTION

As soon as anyone belongs to a narrow creed in science,
every unprejudiced and true perception is gone.

— Goethe, 1824

EVERYONE WANTS TO believe in something. Texas millionaire Stanley Marsh III wanted to meet Bigfoot so badly that his main goal in life was to find one of the hairy, good ol' boys and personally fly him home to Texas while sharing a few dry martinis from the bar on his private plane. Yes, Marsh actually said that. In fact, his desire for this Sasquatch *tête-à-tête* was so impassioned that he footed the bill for a $5,000 Bigfoot hunt... one that was ultimately unsuccessful.

Of course, Marsh also built a hill comprised entirely of old cowboy boots, and tattooed green wings on the flanks of his dog in case the Mexican Hairless ever had a yen to fly. And he's probably best known for his "Cadillac Ranch," consisting of ten vintage Cadillacs sunk into the ground just outside Amarillo, Texas, at the same angle as Egypt's Great Pyramid of Cheops.

Not everyone who wants to witness the mysterious feels compelled to enact such grandiose schemes, however. Most of the hundreds of people who have made the trip to Walworth County and taken a slow drive down the now-legendary Bray Road hoped for nothing more than a glimpse of something furred and furtive ducking between the farmhouses and the plowed fields. Undaunted by the fact that most sightings have occurred in other parts of the county and in surrounding areas of the state, the monster-hunters still flock with binoculars and videocams, some even clad in camouflage. They make this pilgrimage to witness one of those creatures that renowned researcher of the strange, John Keel, called "Impossibles and Unbelievables"; they seek an experience that will blow their minds.

They leave with minds mostly intact. As far as I know, no one who has wanted to see the creature has actually managed to, not even one man who claimed the beast had been spotted by the owner of a deer farm in eastern Walworth County twice, and that he had a sure system

The Indigenous Dogman—
aka, the Manwolf.

worked out for catching it on film with multiple infrared werewolf-cams. He was going to let me know when he got his pictures. I'm still waiting.

The creature remains nothing if not elusive.

The strange thing is that unlike the Texas millionaire who lusted for a brush with a real, live, fur-being, most of the people who actually have seen "the Beast" wish they had never laid eyes on it. It shakes their world too harshly. The even stranger thing is that there are many more of these people than I ever suspected. That's why this book is not a rehash of the same two dozen or so incidents I reported in the first book. It couldn't be. I have so many more to tell. Dozens of additional people have come to me in one way or another since then with their own tales, and that's just the Wisconsin crowd. Folks in other states from Georgia to Pennsylvania have also weighed in with intriguing, similar sightings, and I've gleaned others from a variety of sources.

It's quite possible not all the sightings are related; it's entirely likely that they are not even all the same type of phenomenon. But for the sake of thoroughness, we are going to inspect every one of them and look for the bigger picture. It's the only way to sort the red herrings from the real keepers. Besides, they are ripping good stories on their own terms.

And while the big question has always been whether this is an as-yet unidentified flesh-and-blood animal or something not quite of this world, a few of the newer sightings now point to the latter. I realize that not everyone believes in the existence of a "spirit world" or supernatural creatures, but then most people in this century don't believe in creatures that look and act like werewolves, either. Yet a growing crowd of witnesses swears that they are here.

Only a minority, however, say that they believe what they saw was a werewolf in the traditional sense—a shape-shifting human. It's just that there is no other universally understood word to describe this being. Some call it a Dog Man, others Wolf Man. Those of French heritage call it *loup-garou*. South Americans call it *Lobizon*. Many confuse it with Bigfoot, which it most emphatically is not. And so, while many of these names (including werewolf) are sometimes appropriate and I use them for variety's sake, I realized I needed a specific word to denote exactly the creature of the type formerly seen around Bray Road. That is, a creature that stands five to seven feet tall, covered with dark shaggy fur, that can walk and even run erect yet retains dog-shaped legs and footprints, with a manlike body and a head like a wolf or German shepherd. A long muzzle, fangs, and pointed ears on top of the head complete the picture of one truly unique entity, deserving of its own moniker.

I tried a lot of combinations, and finally turned to author and researcher Richard D. Hendricks' Weird Wisconsin Yahoo group for some help. Members came up with many brilliant suggestions, including Bipcan (bipedal canid), Anthrocan (manlike canid), and the amusing Dogsquatch. Member Kim del Rio provided a list of some Native American names for doglike beings, such as the Huron-Iroquois *agaua* (doglike one). After much deliberation, I finally decided that to be as descriptive as possible with the least amount of implied reference to Hollywood or other associations, I would stick with Manwolf. I will use this word to refer to any creature that fits the above profile. The standard Manwolf would probably look almost exactly like my illustration from the first book that I entitled "Indigenous Dogman," since this is the drawing that most witnesses say hits what they saw dead-on. And I will capitalize the word, following cryptozoologist Loren Coleman's reasoning that the title of "Bigfoot" should be capitalized until the creature is officially entered into the scientific world's taxonomy charts, at which time it earns lower case status and becomes a "regular" animal like a giraffe or wombat. (I have a feeling that Manwolf is a long way from achieving such a distinction.)

So, I'm plunging into these roiling waters and attempting to define something that is probably indefinable, even though it now has its own name. Searching for the Manwolf among Keel's "Incomprehensibles," I will observe and reflect from distances both safe and completely foolhardy.

The chief hazard in this sort of investigation is always the chance of being sucked into the murky undertow of unfounded speculation, but those dark eddies will always swirl around us when we confront the seemingly irrational. That is the main reason no reasonable scientist or reputation-conscious journalist would write this book. Weirdness-by-association is bound to occur. As the ancient Greeks used to say, "He who lies down with dogs shall arise with fleas." I'm scratching already.

George P. Hansen, in his excellent work, *The Trickster and the Paranormal,* notes that writers who cover topics such as UFOs and Bigfoot don't exactly enhance their street cred among their peers. As he writes in his preface, "The study of sexuality, in all its forms, is established in universities and medical schools. Sizeable industries and well-funded research labs are organized around cloning, artificial insemination, and genetic manipulation, despite ethical qualms. The lowly ghost researcher receives only sneers."

Of course, this is not a book about ghosts. But some of the sightings told here do have an air of ambiguity about them, and as I said earlier, some contain frankly supernatural aspects. I won't censor these stories from the mix. My aim is still to give the accounts as straight up as they are told to me, and then to try to sort them out and see what—or who—might be staring back into our wondering eyes.

But even if every sighting could be easily classified into a "solid animal" category, writing about fauna resembling werewolves would still be considered iffy. Luckily for me, I don't care. I have no scientific reputation to besmirch. As a former newspaper reporter, I do try to adhere to basic research guidelines as much as possible, and I do not augment or embroider upon any of the witness experiences. But the

Skeptic Police could order me never to write another book after this one and I wouldn't mind, as long as I felt I had set the gist of the Manwolf phenomenon out there for the open-minded to consider.

I simply want to know why so many otherwise ordinary people are seeing Manwolves, Bigfoot, and other associated upright Furries, and what this fact might mean. If you are similarly intrigued, welcome to my world.

Warning: If you have no ability to momentarily suspend belief in the world as you think you know it, this book may not be for you. We will be hunting monsters, after all, luring them from their fusty dens and ancient caves to have a long, hard spy at them from tooth to claw. But what will we use for bait, you may ask?

We will set out the only morsel that tempts them.

And that would be ourselves.

Acknowledgments

SO MANY PEOPLE were kind enough to their share their sightings stories to make this book possible. I need to thank each and every brave witness, first of all. Their eyewitness accounts are the basis for any research I've been able to do. My friends and colleagues "Summerwind" Todd Roll, "Unexplainable" Chad Lewis and his co-author Terry Fisk along with Richard "Crimson" Hendricks were key supporters in the writing of this book and generously shared much crucial information. I'd also like to thank independent researchers Richard Heiden, William Kingsley, Rick Fisher, J. R. Van Hoose, and Robert Schneck for their equally invaluable research. Author Nicholas Redfern was extremely kind to take the time to read my book and write a foreword, and Loren Coleman generously allowed me to pick his considerable brain a few times on different subjects. The Internet community has been most helpful, particularly the excellent Web site cryptozoology.com and members of the Weird Wisconsin Yahoo Group, you all know who you are…my gratitude for the conversation and inspiration. I also appreciate members of the Ho Chunk Nation who allowed me to interview them, and Wisconsin's Department of Natural Resources for thoughtful opinions offered by their wardens.

Kevin "Wiz" Nelson, Chris Chung, Sean Bindley, Brandon St. Germaine and Noah Voss, Special Deputy Werewolf Investigators, also deserve my thanks for their literal field service. It really does take a village to raise a Manwolf.

– Linda Godfrey

CHAPTER ONE

BREAK DANCING IN THE DARK

In the darkness dwelt a demon-sprite,
Whose heart was filled with fury and hate.

—Beowulf

Sullen clouds slouched low over Madison's State Street on an overcast day in May 2004. Trailing like a wagon spoke from the city's capitol building to the University of Wisconsin-Madison campus, the pedestrian mall swarmed with its usual mix of career hippies, homegrown and imported university students, and dawdling tourists. A couple of young men with heavily beaded dreadlocks banged on homemade drums in a green space between two buildings, while an earnest woman in black stood on a box shouting something about God as she flung neon-yellow leaflets at passersby. No one paid much attention to the drummers, the insistent woman, or the clouds, but the mounting clamminess in the late spring air told me that rain was imminent.

I didn't really mind; I was spending the day bumming with an old friend, Dixie, with whom I'd shared a lot of strange adventures over the years. But rather than wait for a drenching, we ducked into a small used bookstore and began to rummage the musty stacks.

After about an hour of successful hunting, I set my stack of paperbacks on the counter and noticed the checkout clerk, an average-sized fellow in his late twenties, maybe early thirties, clean-cut by Madison standards, raising an eyebrow ever so slightly at my selections. That day, they were mostly books on shamanism and metaphysics, topics I needed to bone up on for a novel I was writing at the time.

"Research," I told him, and he nodded and smiled, a little embarrassed to be caught perusing a customer's titles. "I write books," I added, feeling the need to chat a little to let him know that I didn't mind. "Maybe you have them here."

He asked me their titles, and since like any writer I'm always interested to see who's carrying my books, I told him that *The Poison Widow* was my first. His face lit up with recognition. "Oh yes, we have several of those."

"And do you have *The Beast of Bray Road*, too?" I asked. His face did not light up this time. In fact, no sooner had the title of my second book left my lips than his jaw dropped and he turned white as a—well, since most sheets aren't white anymore, and ghosts seem to come in a diverse palette these days, I'll say he turned white as a stalk of pale, gourmet asparagus, his face draining itself of blood as if he had been decapitated. Both Dixie and I were staring at him by then.

"You, *you* wrote that book?" he finally managed to sputter in a half-strangled voice.

"Yes, I did." I had never received such an emotional reaction to one of my books before and was feeling a bit unnerved.

"I need to talk to you," he said, looking around over his shoulder and behind him. "Can you wait just a minute while I get this next customer?" I nodded and moved to the side, pulling my bag of purchases off the counter.

He still looked nervous as he rang up the man's sale, although the color was starting to return to his face. Dixie had been observing in silent amusement. "Did you see how white he got?" she asked.

"Yes, and it's freaking me out," I whispered. "I have no idea what he wants." The other customer was leaving the store, and the young man turned back to me. Again he glanced quickly over both his shoulders, and I saw that now his face had gone tomato-colored beneath his dark hair. "OK," he said. "I have to tell you this. And first, I have to say that I'm not crazy!"

At that, my senses went on red alert. I'd heard that line before. And it was almost always followed by the words, "But I saw...."

Sure enough. "But I saw...this *thing*," he continued, "and I don't know what it was. I'm a graduate student, I have two undergrad degrees in science fields, I work, and I'm not some nut case. I'm not a druggie, none of those things. I don't have weird experiences. But I did have one just last week, and since you wrote that book, maybe you can tell me what it was."

There was a pleading desperation in his voice. I had a sudden feeling that this was going to be good. Not that I lacked empathy for the man's obvious, strong emotion. But I hunt stories for a living, and this situation, with the angst he was displaying, had all the earmarks of a trophy tale about to be told. I tried not to look as though I was mentally rubbing my hands in glee, although I admit that I was. "Please, tell me what happened," I said, trying to sound nonthreatening as I scrabbled in my purse for a pen and something to write on.

"Well, it happened one night last week," he said, "about 1:30 in the morning."

"Where?" I asked, scribbling as fast as I could.

"By my ex's house, right on the Isthmus, in a residential neighborhood."

That was surprising. Madison is a town built in between two large and several smaller lakes, and the narrow strip of land between the two biggest lakes is referred to as the Isthmus. There is even a weekly newspaper named after it. But it is densely populated and not the sort of isolated area in which unknown creatures are usually spotted. Still, I nodded so that he would keep going.

"I was there trying to get back together with her, my ex," he said, talking faster to get the words out, "and I was hoping to stay overnight. We were upstairs in bed when I just felt like I had to get out of there and go for a walk. She didn't understand that too well and wasn't happy about it, and so she locked me out when I went. Anyway, I was walking around when I saw what looked at first to me like a human, a man, trying to walk on all fours. But he wasn't walking on all fours the way a person would. It was weird. I was thinking it must be some crazy person so I was starting to move away, and then he started changing."

"Changing?" I almost dropped my pen.

"Yes," he said, licking his dry lips. "You're going to think this is nuts, I know. But it appeared then to be an overly large dog, or something like that. And then, its legs started moving real fast. The closest thing I can think of to describe it is when you see a person break-dancing, where they're spinning and kicking. And I was standing there trying to make sense of that, and I wondered if it was two dogs, uh, fornicating. And then, the only way I can describe it is that it was…morphing, and when it stopped, it turned and looked at me, and it had this dark, hairy body but the head and face of a gorilla." He stopped for a moment to gauge my reaction, still checking nervously to be sure that no one else was listening.

"So were you afraid?" I asked. "What did you do?"

"Well, this street wasn't that isolated," he answered. "There were cars going by during this whole process, but I felt it wasn't afraid of the cars or of me. It was about twenty yards away, and there were streetlights, so I could see it pretty well. And I wasn't exactly afraid of it, because I wasn't sure it wanted to hurt me, but I didn't know what to do or what it was going to do, so I got out of there. The bad part was, I had to go back to my ex's and get her to let me back in. I was out there ringing the doorbell for a while until she finally did, and then when she saw me, she said I looked like death."

The Madison Morpher, author's interpretation.

I glanced at Dixie; her eyes were round in amazement. The young man, whom I'll call Preston, had the same look I'd once seen in the eye of a wounded baby robin—fear, mixed with a certain knowledge of his own vulnerability. He was afraid I'd make fun of him, I knew. I'd seen that expression in so many others trying to tell me similar things.

"Wow," I said. "It sounds like some of the descriptions I've had from other people in some ways, the dark hairy fur, the huge dog or ape face. But I've never had anyone say they saw it *morphing* before. You're the first one for that!"

Preston was visibly relieved when he realized that I wasn't laughing, although I was probably turning colors myself at that point from my own excitement. And I did feel that he was telling what he believed to be a true story. The physical manifestations of the emotions that he'd exhibited—the blanching, the extreme jitteriness—would have been difficult to fake. He couldn't have planned it ahead of time, either; he had no idea who I was before I introduced myself. I'd never been in that particular store before, and even if he had read my book, he had no reason to think I'd be stopping by that day or any other day. I felt no sense that he was improvising as he talked. And despite his claim that he hadn't been afraid of the creature, he visibly relived his fright as he described what he had seen on that shadowy street.

He gave me his phone number so that I could call him for more details, and then had to return to dealing with customers waiting to pay. I left the store smiling, having totally forgotten about the weather. Although I'd interviewed dozens of people who had seen large, hairy bipeds doing one thing or another, this was the first time I'd talked with anyone who had caught something in the act of transforming!

That previous lack of witnesses who had seen the creature behave as anything other than a natural animal was one reason why, in my first book about the "Beast," I'd been reluctant to entertain at length the thought that this creature might have otherworldly origins, although I did discuss the various possibilities.

Uppermost in everyone's mind is always the traditional werewolf—that is, a human that transmutes to an animal shape. Variations on the theme include a demon manifesting as an animal-like entity or a creature that is actually a human thought-form that has coalesced into a physical manifestation. Tibetans call these thought-forms *tulpas*, but they are known by many other names around the world.

People who prefer a supernatural explanation will often choose one that aligns with their own belief systems. Christians think of demons, New Agers will cite earth spirits or thought-forms, and Native Americans will usually relate it to one of their traditional spirit creatures. Many people have expressed their beliefs to me along these lines. And yet no one I'd talked to had ever witnessed paranormal characteristics that might support an extramundane origin of the Beast. Until now.

But morphing and break-dancing? Preston's sighting was so bizarre, so out-there, I wasn't sure how I would even classify it. Plenty of people call themselves lycanthropes and claim that they bodily transform into wolfen shapes (see my interview with one in Chapter 15), but I've yet to see a videotape to document that. And in these days of high-tech, low-cost film production and editing, it would be hard to believe that such a tape hadn't been doctored, if ever one was produced as evidence.

Not that I was ruling out the possibility that this creature still could be flesh and blood; some type of strange hybrid, an out-of-place animal, or perhaps an unknown remnant of the plethora of Ice Age carnivores that once walked this land. Those who study cryptozoology would call it a cryptid, or hidden, animal. How could I make any definite assumptions when so many new sightings of all types had come to light?

Sightings by the Score

In the months since *The Beast of Bray Road* first hit store shelves, I'd been astounded at how many people had e-mailed, phoned, or approached me at book signings or library talks to tell me that they, too, had seen a similar creature but had always thought they were the only one. Now, they said, they felt that if others could speak up about their experiences, they should be able to confess theirs, too. And they wanted to tell someone, if only to finally corral the shadowy forms that had niggled at the back of their minds for years, sometimes decades, and yank them out into the open where they could be hogtied and knelt upon.

As with the first several dozen witnesses, there was no typical person coming forth for the second round, either. Men, women, young, elderly, from the very educated to the barely schooled; they approached my creature confessional in all shapes and sizes. Their one common denominator was that they had seen something big and hairy that they knew was not natural…something that shocked them as surely as if a spaceship had landed at their feet from which tiny, chartreuse men swarmed to sing a chorus of *Who Let the Dogs Out.*

Imagine seeing that, and then try to envision telling your family or co-workers about it. You know that you'd be hooted out the door. That's exactly how all these people felt after their encounters, though, and the few who did confide in a husband or wife or friend often came to regret it. Consequently, most of them just decided to keep their mouths shut, because who on God's green earth would believe them? However, seeing my first book changed that for them, most of them told me. They finally felt that they could spill what they'd been keeping inside them, and spill they did, so that I soon had a very thick folder filled with their reports.

But before I get into the details of these often-chilling experiences, a bit of backtracking for those who haven't read the first book is probably necessary. *The Beast of Bray Road: Tailing Wisconsin's Werewolf,* is about decades of sightings, from 1936 to the present, of an elusive creature that is usually described as roughly the size of a man, but with shaggy fur and the head of a wolf or a German shepherd. It's been seen moving about on two legs just as often as on four, and some have observed it traveling both ways. It happened to be christened the Beast of Bray Road because the first witnesses to come forward (though not the first to have seen it) all spied the creature on or near Bray Road, a rural lane just east of Elkhorn. The story broke with a news article I wrote in December 1991, for *The Week,* a publication distributed to all of Walworth County and some surrounding communities.

Although some wondered at that time whether it was indeed a werewolf, and even though our local animal control officer actually labeled his manila file folder "werewolf" because he didn't know what else to call this animal that people had begun to ask him about, I preferred the more neutral term, "beast." After all, we didn't really know what it was, and calling it a werewolf seemed like unnecessary hype. To my way of thinking, a story about a wolf-headed man is sensational enough on its own terms and hardly needed pumping up. Besides, there was that nice alliteration with all the *b*s.

So Beast of Bray Road it became, except for the T-shirts the newspaper began selling. They went for a *w* alliteration, with the title "Werewolf of the Week" pasted over my original sketch of a wolf man kneeling with a hunk of road kill in its upturned paws. (No matter that, as a few wags pointed out, the phrase "Werewolf of the Week" left the false impression that the paper selected a different werewolf to promote every seven days from a wide variety of applicants.) The "Werewolf of the Week" T-shirts became best sellers for the paper, but somehow "Beast of Bray Road" was the name that stuck.

The story filtered out to the mainstream media, and werewolf mania ensued. The *Inside Edition* and *Sightings* TV shows sent crews, every radio station in the country called, and to my surprise, other witnesses began coming forward. As they shared their own stories, I came to the shocking realization that the sightings were not confined to Bray Road and that they had been going on for a long time over a wide area of southeastern Wisconsin.

And now I know that the creature's territory is even larger. Much larger. It also seems likely that there may be more than one creature and possibly more than one *kind* of creature. That is, if you can believe over fifty sane and sober eyewitnesses. More to the point, how can you not believe them? Could this many people be delusional, all suffering from the same lupine vision? As bizarre as the experience of my new Madison acquaintance, Preston, sounded, he was just one more link in a long chain of shocked eyewitnesses.

But what *was* Preston's experience? Again, it was like nothing I'd ever heard before, not even in fiction about werewolves. Was it even related to the Bray Road creature? It bore some of the same hallmarks; staring the man full in the face, lack of fear at being seen, some doglike characteristics…but no one I'd talked to before had ever witnessed the Bray Road beast in the act of shape shifting to an ape or hominid. Preston's sighting also exhibited characteristics of a dog/ape hybrid, something that is supposed to be genetically impossible in the natural world.

Then there was the question of locale. Although it wasn't the first sighting reported in an urban setting (Milwaukee and Appleton also had their witnesses), it did seem strange that such a creature would appear on a residential street in the state capital. Of course, many Wisconsinites would smile at that, shrug, and ask where else in this state would a shape-shifting dog/ape show up? Of all Wisconsin's cities, Madison is well-known for its freewheeling and liberal atmosphere, especially near the campus. The town, known as the "Berkeley of the Midwest," boasts a vast range of cultures and religions due largely to its world-renowned university. My intention is not to associate the liberal atmosphere with werewolfism, but Madison has always been the kind of place where someone with a few unusual habits could blend right in. Still, I knew I would have to do some digging to figure out exactly what had manifested in the Isthmus.

Of course, it was possible that this was just a large dog and Preston's eyes had been playing tricks on him in the dim light. He'd admitted being in a rather emotional state after the problems with his girlfriend. Following that line of thought, and given the street shadows, it's possible that the creature he saw could also have been some sort of out-of-place or unknown animal—a true cryptozoological encounter. Madison has a zoo, and many apes might exhibit a posture between a dog's and a man's, a stance that would look startling when the apelike face was finally observed. Besides, I had on file another Madison sighting of a creature that acted more like a natural animal (see Chapter 7).

But since Preston claimed to have seen something so out of the ordinary, I felt that I had to at least consider some other options. Strangely, I discovered a possible answer in one of the tomes I carried out of the bookstore that day. *The Eagle's Quest: A Physicist's Search for Truth in the Heart of the Shamanic World* by, no kidding, Fred Alan Wolf, was the first of my new purchases that I picked up to read when I got home, and it didn't take long to find a chapter with a subtitle, "Shape-Shifting and Animism," that set me back on my heels.

Wolf, a Seattle author with a Ph.D. in theoretical physics, had traveled the world in search of shamanistic societies, from Druidic priests to South American tribesmen, to see whether the seemingly supernatural events that were part of their rituals could be explained by modern quantum physics. While studying in Lima, Peru, with a native shaman, he began to wonder whether werewolf stories had any basis in reality. It occurred to him that perhaps a shaman who could leave his body at will could also change into animal form, and he remembered a story told him by a shamanic researcher named Chris Hall. I'll quote the paragraph that stopped me cold.

"Chris told me that he had actually seen a shape-changing event. It was witnessed on a hill outside of Brighton, in February 1988. Someone who was heavily involved in neopaganism had taken LSD. *He actually began to resemble a four-legged animal* (italics mine).

"Other people, as well, saw this happen. And they all agreed on what they saw. But Chris couldn't describe what kind of animal it was. It was to him a kind of mythical *beast* (again, italics mine)."

That was certainly a very close description of what the young book clerk had witnessed. With Madison's religious diversity, there were probably dozens of people who considered themselves shamans living in the city, and they would have no problem finding appropriate drugs. I had to wonder, then, whether there were enough ritual-performing, hallucinogen-swigging individuals in Walworth County and other parts of the state to have caused the other sightings, too?

That's a pretty big leap. If it's a long-jump just to go from seeking natural explanations to looking at paranormal causes, it's a record-setting pole vault to go from acknowledging the existence of a spirit world that can possibly manifest in our dimension, to accepting that tangible animal forms can be conjured up by sorcery for the average person to stumble upon. And it would seem fairly ridiculous to attach this particular supernatural explanation to all of the sightings I've now documented from around the rest of the state and country. And yet I'm going to consider it for a moment, partly to explain what Alan Wolf was talking about and partly because shamanic manifestation is a possibility that many people take very seriously.

Give Me that (Very) Old-Time Religion

There are definitely people who would identify themselves as pagans or neopagans living throughout the state, but it's probably safe to say that the great majority aren't trying to turn themselves into werewolves. Neopaganism (the word could be thought of as meaning pagan revival) is a far-ranging umbrella term used to describe any number of belief systems that generally hark back to pre-Christian times. Neopagans often have a strong bent toward Celtic beliefs, especially in this country, but can include a myriad of other traditions from Sumerian to Native American. Wiccans are one major sub-set, for example.

And adherents are all over the map both literally and as to what kind of practices they've adopted. This very wide spectrum can range from a fairly simple sense of communion with nature and earth spirits, perhaps combined with celebrations of ancient holidays such as the vernal and autumnal solstices, to enactment of dark rituals including blood sacrifice. There are an endless variety of groups, sub-groups, sub-sub-groups, and independent individuals. But all of them generally spell magic as "magick" and feel there are supernatural forces they can work with to enhance their lives on this earth.

None of this, of course, means that we can say with certainty that some occult practitioner dropped a little acid that May evening in Madison and subsequently bent not only his mind but his body into the shape of a dog/ape break-dancer. In fact, there is no way to know for sure whether anyone anywhere outside of Brighton, England, is spending any time or life force whatsoever trying to enact such a feat.

Nor does it mean that anyone calling him- or herself a pagan or neopagan necessarily gets more involved than to dress creatively, commune with nature, and read a lot of fantasy literature. Of course, for many, paganism is a serious religion and they do get far more involved than that. But exactly what all of these groups and individuals do on their own time for fun or worship is far beyond the scope of this book and probably irrelevant to the Manimal spotted by most of my witnesses.

Besides, people practicing self-described pagan religions are found worldwide, yet southern Wisconsin has ended up with the biggest concentration of reported Beast sightings. And Wisconsin is populated by many more Lutherans, Catholics, Methodists, and perhaps even Buddhists than neopagans. There wouldn't seem to be much logical cause for linking the sightings with neopaganism, then, other than that one incident from Wolf's book.

Still, my eyes had been opened in a new direction. I decided that since Pandora's box had become unhinged, I was now obliged to take a hard look at whatever might come winging out. And so I began looking for other correlations. I found one amazing relationship to the ancient animal effigy mounds that are mostly peculiar to Wisconsin. Some similarities to ancient Egyptian lore also became clear, and more possibilities for "natural" explanations began popping up, as well. Preston's enigmatic experience had started me back down a familiar highway that promised many new side roads to explore if I wanted to get to the bottom of the creature mystery. Little did I know that I would soon have an even stranger witness adventure to contemplate.

CHAPTER TWO

OF WITCHES
AND WATER SPIRITS

St. Agnes! Ah! It is St. Agnes Eve—
Yet men will murder upon holy days:
Thou must hold water in a witch's sieve,
And be liege-lord of all the Elves and Fays…
— John Keats, *The Eve of St. Agnes*

Edgerton is a small town in Rock County known more for its surrounding tobacco fields and annual Tobacco Festival than for werewolves. It lies along a twisty section of the Rock River just below the spot where the Rock widens into Lake Koshkonong, famous for its panfish.

The name "Koshkonong" is Native American, of course, although its meaning varies according to which tribe you ask. The Ojibwe say it means "shut in, close in, or where there is a heavy fog," according to Gard and Soren's *Romance of Wisconsin Place Names*. The Potawatomi called it "Place of the Hog." And according to traditions of the Winnebago, now known as Ho-Chunk, who inhabited several villages along the lake's western shores, Koshkonong was once the home of a fearsome water monster that kept them wary as they gathered the wild rice that once covered most of the lake's surface like a meadow.

The days of pristine lakeshore and wild rice are gone with the bark huts of the Indian villages, however, and the shallow, 10,000-acre lake's shoreline is now plastered with hundreds of year-round houses and tiny, old frame cottages. On any good fishing day, boats pack the lake's surface, jostling for the best angling spots. Its water monster now largely forgotten, Koshkonong has been touted as a prime family vacation area since the early decades of the twentieth century. It was in these modern times that a second monster made its appearance.

Back in the summer of 1972, two high school girls I'll call Jenny and Sue (they've asked me to withhold their real names) were staying at a home owned by Sue's parents in what is called the Highland section of the lake neighborhood, near Highwood Street. The girls, both fifteen, had heard some intriguing gossip about two cottages on the nearby lakeshore. The small white houses, one trimmed in red and the other in green, were purportedly owned by "witches" who had for some reason abandoned their homes but left behind many of their belongings. The elements for adventure were all there: a warm summer evening, teenagers, and abandoned witch homes. A raid was inevitable.

The girls called four other friends, another girl and three boys, and under cover of darkness the six teens stealthily made their way to the small houses. Sure enough, the cottages appeared conveniently deserted. Peering into the windows with a flashlight, they decided the red-trimmed house offered the best pickings. To their surprise and delight, the cottage was also unlocked! One by one, the group slipped inside the creaky old wooden door, each jaw dropping at the first glimpse of the interior.

"The inside of the witch's house looked like everything was in place, like it was from the 1930s," remembered Jenny. "There was some light coming in from the streetlight outside, and it was like someone just left and time stood still. All old furniture and old rugs. It had very old wallpaper with flowers on it. Even a wind-up record player that looked like the one in the old RCA ads. Then we saw magazines and papers from the thirties in boxes and on the table. Strange! Like no one wanted to stir things up! I know we stirred things up."

Along with the magazines, the teens decided that an old brass bed would make a cool souvenir, and they wrestled it apart so each could carry a section. But their most astounding find was a small book, bound in black leather, in which the former inhabitant had recorded a number of spells and potion recipes. While many older women are mistakenly branded "witches" and harassed by area teens (such as the folk artist Mary Nohl of Fox Point, Wisconsin, whose strange artistic creations were taken as "proof" of paranormal intent, to cite one famous example), it appeared that there really was some reason to believe this home's owner had at least dabbled in occult practices. Sue nabbed the spell book and made ready to leave.

It was just about that time, said Jenny, that they heard a scratchy tinkling from the living room and realized that the old RCA Victrola had begun to play all by itself. They had noticed a "record" already on its turntable when they entered, she said, but thought that since the house had been left unlocked, it was likely that someone had recently been there listening to tunes. But when the Victrola spontaneously started cranking, the six decided that it was time to skedaddle. "We wanted to get the hell out of there," Jenny said.

Once they had grabbed all the loot they could carry, they struggled back out the front door and headed for the hill they had to climb to return to Sue's house. They had barely closed the front door of the cottage and taken a few steps when they received the shock of their lives. A movement in the dark space between the two cottages caught their attention, and as they all turned their heads to look, a dark, looming form began to materialize out of thin air. Horrified, they watched it assume the shape of an upright wolf that appeared to be coming right at them. Apart from their own fear, they all felt an immediate extreme sense of menace emanating from the creature.

"I screamed, 'What's that?'" said Jenny. The others couldn't answer her because they didn't know what the apparition was either, but began screaming themselves. They all took off running toward the woods that led up to Sue's house. Somehow, the teens managed to keep their brass bed parts, old magazines, and the spell book clutched tightly under their arms as they stumbled through the dark woods, branches tearing at their bare legs, huffing in panicked gasps as they willed their legs to move faster. None dared to look behind to see whether the shape had followed, but they felt safe once they had reached Sue's house. They hurriedly crowded inside with their loot.

"We took off running before it fully materialized to make out the face or see any eyes," Jenny explains now, still shuddering at the memory. "Sue and I think this thing is evil and tied in with the witches in that area. I think because we raided this one house, the white one with the red trim, and took her spell book, that this 'thing' was trying to scare us more than harm us. Or it would have followed us up the hill and through the woods. We all had our hands full with things we took. The brass bed in sections was hard to move through the woods. I believe this thing is seen when it wants to be seen! It's not human."

Sue's mother took possession of the spell book, Jenny remembers, but she's lost track of what happened to the other souvenirs of the evening. She hasn't kept in touch with the other four teens either, but she and Sue still talk regularly. Both women recall the whole incident with crystal clarity, although Sue doesn't like to talk about it any more. Jenny lives in a Western state now, and e-mailed in June 2004 after seeing me on one of the national TV shows that have produced documentary segments on the Beast phenomenon. She noted the similarity between my sketch shown on TV and what she remembered of the Lake Koshkonong creature. And I was excited about her story, because here was another implication that something more than an unknown, natural animal might be at work.

I also felt that this incident was important because there were multiple witnesses and because it extended the range of the sightings map. Edgerton is farther west than many of the other sightings but not so far from the general range as to seem unrelated. It's about seventeen miles west of Whitewater, and about twenty miles southwest of Jefferson, site of the well-known St. Coletta appearance of 1936 and many other incidents.

Like Preston's sighting in Madison, however, pinning down the exact nature of this experience is not easy. If Jenny had been the only one there to see it, the incident could be passed off as shadows playing tricks on the mind of one excited teenage girl. But six people had seen the same thing, all at the same time. Could a huge dog of some kind have sneaked between the buildings and then reared up on its hind legs? That's possible, but it seems unlikely that one of the six wouldn't have recognized it as a dog or that the dog would have just stopped silently without barking or even snarling. Also, Jenny states that they saw it "materialize."

There are, however, two important connections to local super-natural lore here. The first is the area's history of the Native American "water monster," otherwise known in Ojibwe and Ho-Chunk stories as a water panther or water spirit. This is a very different creature than the serpentine sea monster said to inhabit other lakes, and we'll be talking about it in later chapters. Interestingly, the very area where these "witch houses" existed was once the site of both an important Ho-Chunk village and the location of a group of the five hundred or so Indian mounds, many of them rare animal effigy mounds that surrounded Lake Koshkonong before its settlement by whites. Many but not all of the mounds contained burials, and most of them had probably been leveled and desecrated by settlers' plows and the spades of artifact seekers. But on that same ridge, which the teens had to climb, lay one of the largest and finest specimens of water panther spirit mounds anywhere, according to the reports of early Koshkonong archaeologists A.B. Stout and H.L. Skavlem. This bit of shoreline had to have been important ground to the ancient Amerindians, indeed.

Could there be a connection between the mysterious, predator-shaped animal that appeared to the six teens and that ancient water spirit monster? Again, I'll cover this in more detail in Chapter 18, but the mounds were already considered relics of the distant past when the settlers arrived. They may have had many uses, from markers for the different tribal clan totem animals to ceremonial locations. Might they have been integral to the creation of guardian spirit figures meant to watch over the burial grounds? Could the creature that appeared between the two cottages in 1972 have been a remnant of such a guardian? This incident certainly made me start looking more seriously at the old effigy mounds, and I would later make some surprising discoveries. Incidentally, the Isthmus area of Madison was also the site of numerous important mound groups.

But to complicate the matter, we have a second angle to examine: a book of "spells" on the premises and the alleged habitation by a practicing "witch" from modern times. Why the former owner and her neighbor deserted their homes remains a mystery. Maybe the houses weren't truly abandoned, just seldom used. The fact that so many items were left there would make this scenario a little more likely. And what self-respecting witch would leave her book of spells lying around for anyone to find? Jenny's personal theory, in essence, was that the woman had somehow conjured up some kind of spiritual security system that would be set off whenever human activity tripped its otherworldly wires to display a shadowy Bogeyman—or Bogeywolf—to scare away the trespassers. This is not too far from the Indian spirit guardian theory or the conjured *tulpa* theory I touched upon in the first chapter.

Whatever its explanation, the incident impressed Jenny and Sue for a lifetime. And needless to say, it forever cured them of raiding supposedly abandoned cottages.

As many others have learned, however, you don't necessarily have to be someplace you don't belong in order to have a scary experience. Most other witnesses were either driving down some darkened road, going about their day-to-day business, or sitting in their own back yards when they encountered an unknown hairy creature. Unsettlingly, it seems that Mohammad doesn't necessarily have to go to the monster, because the monster will come to Mohammad whenever it feels the urge.

CHAPTER THREE

HOTEL HELL AND BEARWOLVES

"Things do not pass for what they are but for what they seem."

— Baltasar Gracian, *The Oracle*

Portrait of a Fey Terrain and Hotel Hell

Underground springs have long been venerated by Native Americans as places where denizens of the spirit world can flit between their zone and the physical plane. A sort of supernatural doggy-door, if you will. Wisconsin is covered with these bubbling earth-fonts, which eventually became centers of tribal myth and legend. The springs, in native lore, are the underworld's most versatile agents, able to swallow up beautiful maidens who've succumbed to various tragedies or spew forth water panthers and sea serpents to wreak vengeful havoc upon those who enter their domain.

Caves, the gaping maws that allow us to enter the body of our planet, are another natural feature considered almost universally sacred by older societies worldwide. The dark interior spaces represent the womb of Mother Earth and, in many Native American tribes, are also believed to be places where master spirits of earth animals dwell. Sacred cave drawings are found in most every continent, and the remnants of Stone Age societies still include legends of cave magic in their storytelling traditions.

It's only logical then, that wherever nature puts springs and caves together, it creates a landscape dynamic that predestines supernatural hotspots.

Such a place is the seventy-five-acre nature area between Maribel and Denmark in Manitowoc County called Cherney Maribel Caves County Park. With a fifty-foot limestone cliff and a honeycomb of caves eroded from the ancient black dolomite, the Maribel hiking trails are a popular attraction for adventurous types, although a one-hundred-pound steel door now seals off the major "New Hope" cave with its "Halloween Room," so-named because it was first opened by cavers on October 31. (It also contained precisely twenty-two bats.) Industrious vandals have occasionally wrenched the door from its casing to get inside despite the precautions, however, and the surrounding rock is marred by painted and carved graffiti.

Springs abound in the Maribel Caves area, too. In fact, the Maribel mineral waters led to the construction of a luxurious limestone spa and resort in 1900 by two sons of an Austrian immigrant. The waters were fed into a special pool for bathers and also bottled to sell as a health tonic. The building, named the Maribel Caves Hotel, fell into hard times during the Prohibition era, however. It was rumored to serve as one of Al Capone's many hideouts and became frequented by a decidedly sleazier clientele. Its condition eventually deteriorated until it burned in 1985, resulting in the hollow shell that today attracts hikers and thrill-seekers alike, despite large signs promising doom to trespassers. The privately owned property is widely known on the Internet these days as Hotel Hell, and its old front door is reputed to serve as a portal leading straight down to the lair of Beelzebub himself.

Rumors about Hotel Hell run rampant. A quick Web survey will tell you that people believe that objects inside the building jump around by themselves, the walls drip with blood, unseen clammy hands seek to warm themselves on the backs of explorers, various people died there from assorted fires and mass murders, and that a little boy who died in a fire at the water-bottling plant next door still haunts the place. Paranormal investigators Chad Lewis and Terry Fisk debunk many of these claims on their Web site, *Unexplainedresearch.com*. And *Milwaukee Journal Sentinel* reporter Dennis McCann noted that when he visited, the nasty warning sign had been altered to read, "If you are found trespassing, you will be…given a cookie and soda."

Still, where a landmark is blanketed with this many rumors, some kernel of truth often supports its otherworldly reputation. There is the nearby Devil's River, for instance, so-named for its frisky whitewater rapids but also, like most Wisconsin place names with the word "devil" in them, hearkening back to a mistranslated Indian word for "spirit" that was applied by the indigenous people to many natural features they considered sacred.

And finally, there are the two young farm girls who lived only a quarter mile from Hotel Hell and witnessed first-hand what may have been one of those mysterious creatures believed by Indians to pop in and out of the ethereal Maribel subway system of sacred springs.

It's a Wolf! It's a Bear! It's a …?

In April 1994, the sisters, ages ten and seven, were playing behind the barn on their farm. Their father, who wishes to keep the family names private, told me that the girls were near a lane that led through some fields then used as a cow pasture. The lane was protected on either side by a live, two-strand electric fence, with the strands situated two feet and three feet above the ground. Beyond the grassy fields lay a wooded area with a natural spring.

To the girls' amazement, a dark shape suddenly began to materialize or form in that lane, until it appeared to be a very large, dark-furred wolf. On all fours, the creature took no notice of the girls, and they watched dumbstruck as it proceeded to walk directly through the electric wires. It was headed for the woods, they said, and as it walked, they told their father that it changed its shape to that of a bear. And then, for the bizarre grand finale in this short, three-act play, the creature disappeared entirely before it quite reached the trees.

The older girl mentioned that she thought it strange that the family border collie accompanying them appeared not to notice anything unusual. (The father added that the collie was never much of a watchdog, however.) And the girls still stick by their story, although they don't like to talk about it, the father said.

He wonders about the possible Native American connections, too. "They claim the road that runs past our farm was once an old Indian trail," he said. To complete the area's paranormal inventory, the girls' mother says that she saw a UFO while driving with the children in her car just a few miles down the road.

**The Bearwolf,
author's interpretation.**

With all that going on, it seems that some type of anomalous creature simply had to show up sooner or later to seal the supernatural deal. Admittedly, this incident happened a hundred miles or so north of the southern Wisconsin area where most of the sightings are clustered. But the materialization aspect and the wolflike shape are so very reminiscent of the Koshkonong sighting that it seems worth examining. And whether the little girls spied a supernaturally generated creature or a natural but unidentifiable Big Furry, one hundred miles would still not render a connection between the two locations impossible. Especially since, again, we find the sacred native sites (the father stated that he believed there were mounds in the area along with the venerated springs and caves) so close to the entity's appearance.

Besides, there is the intriguing combination of wolf and bear to ponder. In the first chapter, we looked at an apparently supernatural creature that combined wolf and ape, a mammalian blend that had already been thought of by the ancient Egyptians (more about that later). And while, as I have noted, in the physical world there are definite genetic limits to mating different species of animals, in the spirit world anything goes. Besides, there seems to be some precedent for dancing the Bearwolf two-step.

Wausau paranormal investigator Todd Roll has been on the lookout for what he calls the Bearwolf since October 2004 when, after giving a talk at a junior high school in Mosinee, a student told him that his older brother and sister had seen a strange creature near a paintball course north of Hatley, a small town east of Wausau and about ninety miles northwest of Maribel. They thought that it looked like a cross between a wolf and a bear, with a mane, a bushy tale, and yellow eyes. They estimated it to be the size of a small deer. Digging further, Roll learned that others had also claimed to see it, although he couldn't uncover any first-hand stories. Part of the reason Roll was so interested was that he had heard similar stories around Wausau himself when he was a teenager in the late seventies and early eighties. He had a friend who lived in the country on what he and his friends dubbed "Bearwolf Road." (The street's actual name is Burek Avenue as it heads north out of Wausau, then it changes to Decator Drive.)

Roll's friend had cousins who hunted in the woods around that area, and they often told her of seeing a strange creature "much bigger than a large dog," with fur that was black like a bear's. It usually was seen on all fours but had been observed on its hind legs at least once. "The hunter who saw this said that it didn't look at all like a bear," said Roll. "The face was 'different.' At least two of her cousins had separate sightings of this creature."

As often happens in such instances, Roll was unable to persuade the cousins to talk to him about it. And although when he asked others around his high school whether anyone else had heard of Bearwolves, people admitted that they had but no one there would talk about it, either. The same thing occurred a decade later when a co-worker confided that the Bearwolves were common knowledge in the Antigo area and that her brother had seen one. But to Roll's frustration, the brother also clammed up. It was almost as if there was a planned conspiracy of silence about the creature.

Bearwalkers

However, in March 2004, someone posted a story to a forum at *Crypto-zoology.com* about seeing a very strange creature about thirty minutes' drive from Green Bay, although the writer did not say in which direction. She did respond to an e-mail I sent her and told me that the spot was actually about twenty-five miles northeast of Green Bay, which puts it up in Oconto County. The Michikauee Flowage, a lake and large natural area, is located not far from there, with many densely wooded areas. It's very close to Lake Michigan, too, and just to the west lies the

Menominee Reservation. The writer gave me permission to use her name, Summer Theobald.

It was 2:00 AM in the spring of 1998, when Theobald spotted a movement in some tall grass near a farmhouse as she and her aunt drove past it. She said that she thought it was a dog, until it "reared up on its hind legs and stared right at the car. I only saw it for a minute, but it looked almost like a cross between a wolf and a bear. It was covered in this dark, coarse-looking fur and was bulky. It stood about seven to eight feet tall and followed the car for a few feet. Then it lifted its head, sniffed, and ran off in the other direction."

Apart from location, this story bears (no pun intended) a much closer relationship to the wolf-headed, fuzzy upright guy known as the Beast of Bray Road than did the wraith of the electric-fence encounter. The height, dark fur, and the actions of standing up to stare at the car and even follow it are all characteristics very consistent with the Walworth County character.

She added later that although the lower body was "fairly thick," it was not the same shape as a bear's. The ears were long and pointed upward, and the eyes seemed to glow green in the reflection of the headlights. "The beast was only about ten feet from the car, so I got a pretty good look at it," wrote Theobald. When I later sent her my illustration of a Bearwolf, she said that the drawing is very close to what she saw, with a few minor changes such as narrower shoulders.

This particular sighting did not claim any noticeable supernatural aspects, but as one friend said to me, isn't something that looks like a wolf or bear but stands up and follows you on two feet automatically supernatural? Casting about for something that might at least tie the northern sacred areas with some kind of previously described creature, I found a small cache of lore about an Ojibwe "bearwalker" legend in a book called *Bloodstoppers and Bearwalkers: Folk Traditions of the Upper Peninsula*, by Richard Dorson. Dorson had interviewed Ojibwe tribal members in Michigan's Upper Peninsula whose kinsmen in Wisconsin had the same stories. It seemed that these critters had been roaming the northern woods for untold centuries.

The bearwalkers were considered witches by their fellow tribal members, and while they would usually appear in the shape of bear-like animals, they sent out "bad magic" that often looked like balls of light to sicken or kill their intended victims.

"There were five or six bearwalkers here from Wisconsin," recounted one man named Archie Megenuph. "They can't kill a white man, but they can kill an Indian so we had to get them first. We wait until they come out on the road and then shoot at their light—they make a big blare of light.... If you don't have the right medicine, they put you to sleep, even if you have a gun, and walk right past you to the patient."

The "patient," Archie explained, would be killed, and on the fourth night after the death, the bearwalker would go to the person's grave and take a finger from the corpse along with the tip of its tongue. The bearwalkers all kept a collection of these grisly souvenirs from every victim.

The bearwalkers could be shot with the right medicine, Archie explained, "but you don't find anything when you shoot them either, but they die off some distance."

Why the creatures can't kill white people is not discussed in the book, but it could help explain why, as is the case with the Beast of Bray Road, the animals never seem to do anything more menacing than perhaps give a half-hearted car chase. To my knowledge, none of the witnesses I've talked to so far are members of any indigenous tribe. If they were, they might tell a different tale.

Todd Roll also has pointed out to me that Native American tribal communities are located in Shawano, which is about thirty miles northwest of Green Bay and "right in the heart of Bearwolf country." Roll also knew someone from the small town of Tilleda, halfway between Shawano and Hatley, who claimed that a coven of Wiccans often held ceremonies in the Tilleda woods to keep away the "evil spirits."

One more possible Bearwolf story did turn up, an e-mail that fortuitously arrived just as I was about to wind up this chapter. A person who wished to remain unidentified wrote,

Back in approximately 1959, my parents and I were visiting my grandparents in Pittsville, Wisconsin. They lived
about five miles north of town. One day during the visit,
another farmer came speeding up to the house and
jumped out of the car. His wife, I assume, stayed in the car.
He was all excited. He and his wife had just seen some
weird creature. The description that he gave was a huge
misshaped dog, big hump on its back, deformed face with
big teeth. When he saw it on the road, he tried to run it
over. He also said that some other farmer in the area had
seen it and took a shot at it. One of his cows had also died
the past night. (I don't recall that the creature and the dead
cow were related.)

This farmer was badly shaken up, which to me as a
youngster was upsetting since all of the farmers that I knew
were very stoic. It would take a lot to unnerve one of these
farmers. He was making the rounds of farms in the area
to see if anyone else had seen the creature.

From time to time I would think about that event and
wonder if the creature was ever seen again. A while ago
with some idle time at work, I did a search for Wisconsin
on Google…and one of the topics was the Bray Road creature or monster. I read the paragraph and it reminded me
of the event those years ago.

The person later added that the time of year was early July, and
that he also remembered the creature was said to have gray or gray-
brown fur. He assumed that it was on all fours because of the description as doglike. It's too bad he didn't have anything more precise to
describe its size than the adjective "huge," but whatever this was must
have been much larger than an average farm pooch to get the old farm
neighbor so worked up. I personally have a lot of older farm relatives,
and to say that, as a group, they are not too excitable, would be putting it mildly.

One thing I find most interesting is the year this occurred, 1959, which places it much earlier on the timeline. Incidentally, Pittsville is about fifty miles directly southwest of Hatley. Again, this is well within the roaming range of any large carnivore, and certainly within the evident Bearwolf 'hood of mid-northern Wisconsin. The terrain south and west of Pittsville is mostly large tracts of state or national forest, and a tributary of the Yellow River flows right past Pittsville and the contributor's family farm. It should be noted, too, that this seemed to be a solid animal, no transmogrifying or walking through fences. Or was it just that no one happened to observe it doing so?

Flesh or Flash: Amphicyons and Waheela

Perhaps it seems that I'm again giving far more weight in this chapter to theories from the Twilight Zone than to the wide range of other possibilities, such as hybrid wolf dogs or the oft-mentioned idea that all these creatures are just variations of Bigfoot (though many people would consider Bigfoot just as controversial). And the truth is that in these first three chapters of high strangeness, I probably am paying a bit more attention to "alternative" explanations. However, the circumstances seem to demand it.

But here's something that points us back to fleshier creature origins. A recent fossil find highlighted in a February 2005 story in the *Los Angeles Times* had scientists agog at what they described as a "cross between a bear and a pit bull." The dig site near Fresno yielded the most complete skeleton yet found of the animal estimated to have weighed about two hundred pounds, comparable to a good-sized human male.

There is also the well-known fossil record of a group of creatures that were much bigger in size, more bearlike, and probably a few notches down the evolutionary tree. From all around the northern hemisphere, paleontologists have dug up ancient skeletal remains of bear/dog-like creatures called *Amphycyonidae,* which means "dogs of doubtful origin." One of these creatures that lived 14 million years ago is known as *Amphicyon.* While it isn't hard to find basic information on *Amphicyon* on various museum Web sites, a correspondent of mine from Michigan named Bill Kingsley was kind enough to send me a copy of an article by noted cryptozoologist Ivan Sanderson, written for *Pursuit Magazine* in October 1974 about possible contemporary sightings of it.

Amphicyon may have been known anecdotally as the *Waheela* by Native Americans in northern Michigan, according to Sanderson's source, Loren Coleman, and despite its supposedly extinct condition, was said to have been encountered in modern times by a number of trappers and other explorers in Canada and northern Michigan. They described it as larger than any timber wolf, with smaller ears and a much wider head. One seen in Canada was described as about three and a half feet tall at the shoulder. (This article also refers to it as a dire wolf, which is somewhat misleading since that is a smaller, later animal more closely related to the wolf, and is classified as *canis dirus*. More on that in Chapter 7).

Amphicyon was roughly the size of a grizzly and looked much more like a bear than a dog or wolf. Its teeth, however, were very lupine. It was a ferocious hunter, with short, muscular legs that probably enabled it to rush its prey in a

The Amphicyon, author's interpretation.

quick, powerful surge. Its sturdy jaws were well-suited for crunching bone. Indeed, according to Sanderson's article, the *Waheela* was found in a place called "Headless Valley" because those foolish enough to camp there were often found with their heads bitten clean off their bodies.

Waheela stories notwithstanding, the *Amphicyon* is widely assumed to be long extinct. Whether a remnant survives or not, at least it provides some evidence that a creature combining apparent bear and canine traits did once exist. And suddenly, the idea of a Bearwolf pops out of the world of fantasy and takes its place in the parade of known North American mammals.

But how to explain phantom Bearwolves? We probably can't, but here's one stab at it, anyway. As mentioned earlier, Native Americans believe that each animal species has a "master spirit" responsible for maintaining survival. Could the master spirit of *Amphicyon* still walk the northern Wisconsin woods, searching for its long-lost corporeal cousins? If so, I've managed to craft an answer that combines crypto-zoology, paleontology, and supernaturalology (I made that last word up). And that giant sucking sound you just heard is millions of root follicles suddenly departing the scalps of devotees of all three of those official branches of inquiry as they shred the hair from their heads in agony at the very idea. But let sales of Rogaine skyrocket and schools of thought be damned; I simply make connections where I see them.

And regarding all the possible theories in these first three chapters, the point is not whether you or I believe that master spirits exist or whether it is even possible to create magical entities to go forth and guard graves, caves, or witch houses. The crux of the matter, and what interests me, is that we have this combination of factors to consider thus far:

- There are people living among us who believe that they can whip up creatures that will scare the adenoids out of anyone who sees them.
- There have been indigenous people believing and practicing the very same traditions of spirit-conjuring for untold eons.
- Where this is happening, we seem to end up with sightings of creatures that cannot be consistently explained by any rational means.

Does this prove that one is causing the other? Honestly, it doesn't, no more than someone who sees a strange light in the sky near the vicinity of a werewolf sighting proves that the werewolf came out of the UFO. All is circumstantial. But as any courtroom lawyer will tell you, while circumstantial evidence may not always win convictions, it can and does usually enter into the weight of the total argument.

Todd Roll likes to think that unnamed "earth spirits" may be involved in the case of the Bearwolf. "I have often wondered if all paranormal phenomena weren't just the spirit of the earth having a good time with us," he said. "Bearwolves, Bigfoot, UFOs, ghosts, etc., really aren't anything other than the earth wanting to rattle our cage every once in a while. One day you're driving to work when BAM, an eight-foot tall, hairy, foul-smelling, dead-goat-carrying, ape-thing shambles across the road and flashes a glowing red eye your way. You're shocked, but good old Mother Earth is chuckling in the background."

Maybe so. After being confronted with Preston's Madison chimera, the Koshkonong witch-house guardian, and the little girls' appearing/disappearing Bearwolf, I decided to look at all hairy Man-beasts—even those with a wolf/bear/ape trifecta of characteristics—in order to better look for an overall pattern to the sightings in this state. Other states will also get their turn, along with the implications of coast-to-coast sightings. But once that door to supernatural explanations is opened, very unexpected things can come lumbering out into the night, even when a sighting seems on the surface to be something as mundane as a snaggle-toothed, overgrown coyote.

CHAPTER FOUR

VAGUE APPREHENSIONS: THE PRELUDE

"If you do not expect it, you will not find out the unexpected, for it is trackless and unexplored."

— Heraclitus, *Fragments*

Back in Time

One of the questions I'm asked most frequently is how long the Bray Road sightings have been going on. I usually point to the now well-known incident in 1936 when the night watchman, Mark Schackelman, at St. Coletta Institute in Jefferson, Wisconsin, saw a tall, hairy creature digging on an Indian mound near the Catholic home for the developmentally disabled. The creature stood up and uttered in a primitive-sounding voice a word that sounded like "Gadarrah" to Schackelman. He told his son later that he felt the creature was a "demon straight from hell."

That was the earliest documented sighting I have in Wisconsin of something close in appearance to the Bray Road creature and also one of the most concrete and detailed. From there, things get a little fuzzy for a while, but not in a warm and fuzzy way. The forties through the sixties were more like an ominous prelude to the later spate of eye-witness accounts, almost like the foreshadowing you find in a well-planned work of literature.

For instance, people were seeing other weird things around the state in the thirties. A woman from Black River Falls who asked that her name be withheld told me a strange tale she had heard from her uncle. Near that city is an area called Irish Valley, and it was widely rumored that a woman who lived there was a practicing witch. She was supposed to have given birth to three children with "snake heads," who did not survive and who were buried near her home, causing the surrounding grounds to grow desolate. A friend of the woman's uncle claimed that he was walking home past this "witch's area" one night when he saw a large, shaggy creature with a head that reminded him of a goat crossing the road. It was on all fours but did not appear to be any known animal he could think of. Bears and timber wolves spring immediately to mind, but the gentleman swore that this was neither. What made the woman's uncle consider the story a serious one was his opinion that the witness was one of the most honest men he had ever known, and the uncle believed that this man would not make up tales.

It's interesting to note the connection with the witch, as in the Koshkonong sighting. And while "goat head" is not the same as a wolf or dog head, from a distance the two might be hard to distinguish, especially if the head was connected to a body that apparently didn't belong with it. Some occultists might point out that the goat is a symbol more often connected with the devil or devil worship and thus has a logical connection with occult sources. Because of deviations from the standard characteristics, though, I don't include this incident as one of the reported sightings, on the same level as most of the others in this book. I merely offer it as an example of another well-respected citizen seeing some type of furry mammal that was like nothing he had ever seen before.

I have another report from 1941 that is rather ambiguous but bears many hallmarks of a true sighting. The witness is now in his 80s, but experienced something as a high schooler that he still ponders. He asked that I withhold his name, so I'll call him Ray. The sighting occurred in the western part of the state, near Muscoda, a city of about 1,500, which is located just south of the Wisconsin River and between the Blue River and Avoca units of the Lower Wisconsin River State Wildlife Area. Marshes abound, and winding creeks twine along between Highway 80 and Richland Center. The land is hilly, a combination of farms and woods. Nearby is a large effigy mound park.

Young Ray, then a senior in high school, and his best friend Al were en route from Richland Center to a late movie in Muscoda. It was after 9:30 PM on a crisp fall evening, the dark sky lit by an almost-full moon. Ray was driving his family's new 1941 pickup truck. The boys were only a few miles north of Muscoda when they came to the foot of a small hill on the two-lane asphalt road. Ray's attention was immediately drawn to an automobile just descending the hill, heading north, because it was flashing its lights insistently and slowing up as if it wanted him to stop. Not knowing what the driver of the other car could possibly want, Ray decided to keep going.

As he ascended the hill, the road flanked by deep woods on either side, Ray remained a little worried about why the people in that car had tried to get him to stop. And then, about halfway up what was then called Paul's Hill, both boys suddenly realized what they were probably trying to communicate. Some sort of dark-furred creature was standing right in the middle of the road, partially illuminated by the headlights. Worst of all, it was standing right next to his car window. "We both saw it; it scared the hell out of me, so I took off," said Ray. "It was as high as the top of the window of my truck, so it had to be probably five and a half feet. It was a pretty moonlit night."

Ray and Al never even looked back.

Ray still isn't sure what it was. "It wasn't a cow," he said. "I suppose it could have been a bear, but there weren't any bears around there in the forties." He agreed that standing in the middle of a road next to a speeding automobile isn't typical bear behavior, either. He didn't even consider a deer as a possibility; the color, shape, and behavior were all wrong. "I know it was something," he added. He asked around his high school and town but couldn't find anyone else who would own up to spotting the creature. "Over the years, I've thought of it a lot of times," he said, "and it kind of makes me feel creepy when I think of it."

Ray did not get a good enough look at the head to positively identify what he saw, but the smaller size and the fact that he didn't notice an odor argue against a Bigfoot. The height does fall within the parameters for a Manwolf, however, and the behavior and sudden roadside appearance are very consistent with Manwolf sightings. Ditto the admittedly more subjective "creepy" feeling so often associated with Manwolf encounters. And the terrain, a marshy, river-fed area covered with woods, is classic Manwolf territory. It's interesting that the site, about a forty-five mile prowl west of Madison, is probably almost eighty miles from Jefferson and around one hundred miles to Bray Road. However, in the forties it would have been easy to find a woodsy, water-fed corridor between all three areas, particularly in the fall when cornfields were still up.

One final note: Ray's twenty-something granddaughter, who first tipped me off to the story, remembers him saying that the creature had a big dog head and a man's body. She also said that he always told her that it ran alongside the vehicle for a bit. But since he wouldn't swear to either of those details himself, either because he really didn't remember it that way or just was reluctant to say the words to someone who wasn't family, we'll have to leave it in the interesting-but-ambiguous Big Furry category. And like Ray said, "It was something."

Sneaking into the Sixties

We have to jump forward three to four decades, however, for the sightings to begin in earnest. In *The Beast of Bray Road*, there were only a few sightings from the sixties, and none of them were definitely of something wolf- or dog-headed. There was the Delavan-area sighting by Dennis F. of what he called a Bigfoot, the Wadsworth, Illinois, sighting of what was perceived to be more like a giant black panther than a wolfen form, and rumors about the Eddy, an amorphous, hairy creature that was known for haunting isolated spots in the East Troy area. In Chapter 3 of this book, we covered the 1959 sighting of what may have been the creature known around the middle belt of the state as the Bearwolf.

And again, the only other "new" reported sighting of the sixties is too indistinct to be definitively considered a wolfman or dogman. But it did happen near Bray Road!

In 1964 or 1965, Linda Bladel lived with her family on a farm on Bowers Road, which runs parallel with Bray Road, about a half mile away. One night, she and her siblings were camping out on the lawn, guarded by the family's German shepherd, Penny. As the children played in the night shadows of the yard, they saw "something big and dark" near their woods. It was larger than a dog or any other animal they might have expected to see on their farm, Linda recalled.

Frightened, the children scampered into the relative safety of their tent, and listened fearfully as the animal stomped toward them, growling and grunting. The brave dog, Penny, ran forth to defend her charges, and none of the children dared look as they listened to Penny and the unknown creature snarling and yowling over the muffled sounds of bodies tumbling on the grass. Eventually, Penny succeeded in chasing the animal away, despite suffering serious scratches and wounds, said Linda. Although everyone survived, this incident did put a real damper on the family's lawn camping adventures from that point on.

Something big and black. Of course, at night, on a shadowy, forested lawn, almost anything would appear black. But we can assume that it was probably not very light in color or it might have been more identifiable. Bear? Wolf? A coyote wouldn't have appeared larger than a dog to the children. Although a few stray bears and even wolves have been sighted within the past couple of years in southern Wisconsin as the northern part of the state becomes more and more developed, they were unheard of around here in the sixties. No one reported seeing them, and timber wolf populations were not large even in the few isolated northern areas where they still survived. And I've been unable to find any evidence that people were seeing either of these animals, both of which are usually easy to recognize, at that time in Walworth County.

This leaves us with something unknown and ferocious, and something very near where many other sightings would surface. Whatever this creature was, it also seems to have been skilled at staying out of sight for the most part. And yet, five years later, farmers on Bray Road began to grow aware of something unidentifiable skulking around the edges of their fields.

The Seventies: Balking Horses and the Bluff Monster Revealed

In February 2004, I received an e-mail from Joyce Sheard Backus, niece of Earl and Olive Sheard Bray, for whom Bray Road was named. Backus recalled hearing these first uneasy stirrings.

"I distinctly remember my cousin, their daughter, tell me of her brother who lived on the old Bray homestead, riding his horse on the property and having the horse abruptly stop near a wooded area, refusing to enter it. He was an avid horseman, and he was never able to coax the horse into that area. The horse would demonstrate obvious signs of distress and fear when they neared it. I couldn't help but wonder if that was not the Beast of Bray Road. She told me this story about twenty years ago. Her brother has since died."

Backus estimated that her uncle's skittish horse incident was in the early seventies. Although still not a full-fledged sighting, it appeared highly unusual to someone who had lived near Bray Road woods all his life.

Something was actually showing itself about twenty miles north, however, near the northern Walworth County line. In *The Beast of Bray Road*, I told about a legend I'd heard from several people in the Palmyra area about an unknown creature that was called the Bluff Monster because of its proximity to Bluff Road. The problem was, I hadn't been able to find anyone who had seen it. That's no longer the case.

Bluff Road runs east and west through the Kettle Moraine Forest, a few miles south of Palmyra. I've often noted, when mapping out sightings, that the Kettle Moraine seems to be a central location for the largest concentration of sightings, almost as if something lived in there and made regular forays out into the surrounding counties. The Kettle Moraine, named for its scoop-shaped depressions and adjoining ridges left by glaciers, is thickly wooded. Although criss-crossed with hiking, biking, ski, and horse trails, large tracts in between remain inaccessible to park users. I noted its many sacred Native American sites, such as the deep kettle known as the "Spirit Washbowl" and the strangely shaped "stone elephant" rock, in the *The Beast of Bray Road*.

But a later addition to the area's spiritual heritage remains largely unknown.

Bluff Road was named for the tall bluff used for centuries as a ceremonial site and lookout point by Native Americans, and another road to its north was named after Irvin L. Young, an engineer, inventor, and founder of a medical missionary organization. His company was located along Highway H between Bluff and Young roads, and sharp-eyed observers will notice the remains of his unfinished lifetime project in an adjacent field. What looks like the ruins of bizarre artifacts is, in fact, what remains of Young's planned sculpture park that was to serve as the focal point for a retreat for retired missionaries. The modernistic, welded sculptures were all inspired by Biblical subjects; a chapel in the very center was approached by a short bridge and fronted with a now-defaced statue of the Virgin Mary. They were all built with scavenged materials, according to Young's own designs, but he died before he was able to complete them all. I knew Young's widow, Fern, personally from a county arts organization to which we both belonged. Unfortunately, this amazing and philanthropic lady was too busy overseeing the medical mission in Africa to be able to finish her husband's field of religious dreams.

The Youngs were responsible for one other major change to the landscape near Bluff Road, however. A large rise on their land, known as Young Hill, was the site of a gigantic Christmas star lit every year for the month of December so that it could be seen for miles. Not far from Young Hill, on Lowland Road, was an active family farm where then-teenaged Judy Wallerman lived. Around 1970, Judy enjoyed looking at the star with binoculars at night. The massive decoration turned the hilltop into a brilliant mix of light and shadow, especially when the ground was covered with snow. One night, she thought that she spotted movement in one of the shadows. Following the large shape with her binoculars, she was amazed when it popped out into the light and appeared to be a large man completely covered with shaggy fur!

"It seemed to be focused on something," said Judy. "It didn't stand fully upright, and it had a lumbering gait. It was slightly stooped but definitely on two legs." Judy saw it several other times but only when the star was lit. Moreover, she discovered four or five other people who had also seen it. "It was rumored he lived in the hills," she said. "I didn't go hiking in those woods at night. During the daytime and when you were brave enough, you'd go and look but we never saw tracks. But then we never wanted to stay around there long enough."

A creek on the farm's "back forty" flowed from nearby Blue Spring Lake, so there was a water source nearby along with thickly forested areas. Wallerman says the farm is still inhabited as a farm, although the original buildings were torn down and have since been replaced by a new house.

A friend of Judy's, Rochelle Klemp, also lived in the area and was another Bluff Monster eyewitness. "Judy and I were best friends," Klemp told me in a phone interview. She remembers seeing the creature running on the lighted hill, too. "We were out driving around, and I saw something moving around up there. It seemed sort of human. I know exactly where we were, on Highway H in front of the star. We looked up and there it was."

But it was not human, said Klemp. "It was bulky, almost more like a shadow," she said. "It seemed human because it was upright, but size-wise, it was taller than an average human."

Klemp eventually managed to almost forget about what she had seen, until about twenty years later when she was applying for a job as a nurse at Elkhorn's Lakeland Hospital, which is near Bray Road. "This was during the time when people were talking about the were-wolf by Bray Road," she said, "and a lot of the nurses said they had seen it when they would step outside to smoke at night. I thought it was strange they actually told me about it when I was applying for the job as a sort of heads up, that they had this thing going on out there."

There was some difference in appearance between the Bluff Monster and the Beast, however. Wallerman drew a sketch of how she remembered the creature, and it does not look like a Manwolf. It's a rather classic witness drawing of Bigfoot, but with long claws that she remembered seeing flash against the snow. The claws don't really match the usual Bigfoot descriptions, but they are something very often described in Beast of Bray Road sightings, as is the shaggy, dark fur. Wallerman was unable to contact her other friends who had seen it, and I had the name of one other alleged witness but was unsuccessful in reaching him.

A Seventies Wolfman

Another sighting from the early seventies happened considerably farther north, near Glidden in Ashland County. Tony Woiak, a historian and paranormal researcher based in Washburn, heard about it from his own parents, Larry and Helen Woiak, who were on a Sunday drive on Highway 13. "She and my dad were driving along when they saw a wolf-faced man walking in the woods, just off the road," said Woiak. "They said it was taller than a human and hairy." Interestingly, they also described the creature as

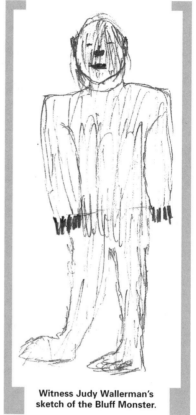

Witness Judy Wallerman's sketch of the Bluff Monster.

"moon-faced," meaning that while wolflike, its face was wider than that of a normal wolf. His parents, now deceased, were rather unnerved by the experience and didn't like to talk about it much, said Woiak.

The sighting is interesting because while it occurred in the northern reaches of Wisconsin, normally Bigfoot stomping grounds, and while the creature's height and upright gait do match Bigfoot sightings, that description of the wolflike face starts us thinking about Manwolves again. Could something located 350 miles or so north of Walworth County be related in any way to the more southward Manimal? It's worth keeping in mind, I think, especially since we also have sightings of "Dogmen" this far north in Michigan (see Chapter 7 in *The Beast of Bray Road*) and in other states. There is also the 1941 Muscoda sighting, which is far out of geographical range but at an early point in time.

Still, up to this point, almost all the sightings are either somewhat ambiguous in nature or sound more like a Bigfoot. Recapping some other examples from the first book, the St. Coletta creature spotted some thirty years earlier in Jefferson, about fifteen miles to the northwest of the Bluff Monster area, featured a head that combined characteristics of both ape and dog. The Dennis F. sighting in 1964, west of Delavan and about twenty miles south of Bluff Road, was emphatically described as a Bigfoot and "not a werewolf." I have interview transcripts and videotapes of this witness telling his story, which was actually featured in a book about Bigfoot sightings. The Bluff Monster has nothing doglike about it. And the 1959 possible Bearwolf sighting is just too far from wolf or ape to put it squarely in either camp.

I think, therefore, it would be a little rash to declare that these were all sightings of "The Beast of Bray Road," as if we were talking about one particular entity. Instead, I suggest that for now they should be viewed as pieces of this entire puzzle. For one thing, just knowing that there was a preexisting heritage of sightings of furry man-beasts and unidentifiable-yet-terrifying creatures in this general area for decades lends historic precedence to the later Manwolf sightings. Of course, it must be admitted that if area residents did whisper legends about seeing "something" in the woods for all those years, just hearing the stories may have primed later generations to see something that they would otherwise not have imagined.

Or, as some Bigfoot enthusiasts have been opining all along, does this mean that the entire Bray Road flap is simply a case of mistaken identity, with these apelike sightings confirming that it's been Sasquatch on a southern vacation spree all along? Time to look at some more sightings, then, and see what all this foreshadowing may have presaged.

CHAPTER FIVE

THE 80s:
LONGER GLIMPSES

"It is a universal condition of mankind to want to know."
— Hernan Cortes in
J.H. Elliott, Spain and its World, 1500–1700

Dynamic Duo

Rick Renzulli held his '78 Caravan Suburban steady to take the curve he knew was coming up on County Highway ML just west of Kenosha. He braved the early morning darkness every weekday about this time, near 5:00 AM, on his way to his job as a concrete finisher. It was October 1984, and the cornfields lay newly shorn of their stalks, stubbled and desolate in the waning moonlight.

"There's a little cemetery on the curve," he told me in a later interview, "and this was just before it. I had just gone through the intersection with Green Bay Road, so I was only going fifteen miles an hour when it ran right in front of my truck."

Readers can probably guess by now what "it" was.

I met Renzulli when I was invited to speak at the Kenosha Public Library about *The Beast of Bray Road*. The city's newspaper had run a story about my book the previous week, featuring a large reproduction of my "indigenous dogman" drawing, and when Renzulli saw it, he was incredulous. "The article was the first time I'd ever known that somebody else had seen it," he said. He attended the signing and afterward, came forward to tell me his story. As it turned out, Renzulli's tale was something of a breakthrough in Beast sighting lore.

The highway he traveled on his way to work that morning passed through a wooded area with a creek winding around it and a tiny cemetery on one side. (Upon later examination of the area with friend and fellow investigator Richard Hendricks, we also discovered a rather

41

eerie, seemingly abandoned doghouse [for a very large dog] in the middle of the woods near the very spot where Renzulli had his run-in. There were broken pieces of pottery, shards of an old toilet—evidence that perhaps a house had once stood here.) With its sparse population and no benefit of streetlights, this stretch of country road would have felt like one spooky place in the autumn darkness, with or without a questionable creature popping out of the bushes.

But there it was, emerging and then running across the road on all fours like a streak, said Renzulli, who was twenty-seven at the time. "It had to be seven to nine feet long. Its head was as high as the hood of my truck," he said.

Renzulli slowed even more to avoid hitting whatever it was. "My first thought," he said, "was that this thing is not natural. I didn't think of a werewolf. I thought of evil."

But Renzulli immediately had to refocus his frenzied first thoughts. "Within seconds of the first one clearing my headlights, the second one came through! It was about three-fifths as big, just as fast, and then they were both gone. I don't scare easily," he added, "but that was wild. I didn't tell anyone but my wife; it was a shock."

Even in his state of surprise and despite the briefness of the encounter, the animals showed up well enough in his headlights that Renzulli felt he had a good look at them. "That look this thing had seemed mean and angry," he said. "My headlights caught its eye but it shined up well. It was bigger than a wolf. I used to have a St. Bernard, and this was three to four times its size."

The fur on the animal's back seemed longer and thicker than on the rest of its body, noted Renzulli, almost as if it had a mane. He was unable to see a tail on either animal. They also had unusually long snouts, he recalled, longer than that of a dog.

"It was like something out of a movie," he said. "The first thing I did was take my elbow and lock my driver's side door."

Renzulli, a burly, dark-haired man with a gravelly voice, remembers that he was heading northeast. Both creatures ran across the road at an angle, he said, so that he had a clear view of them for a little longer than he would have if they had run straight across. "Another few seconds and I would have hit it," he added.

His wife was reluctant to believe him. "She kept trying to explain it as a wolf," he said. Now a widower, Renzulli said he had talked to his wife about it many times, trying to figure out for himself what it was he saw. "Your picture brought back my memories right away," he said. "I clear as hell saw it. When I saw your picture, I thought, God dang, that looks like what I saw. It was definitely something I've never seen before and never seen since. I've never sighted anything else or made a claim to anything else."

Renzulli has never had paranormal experiences, seen a ghost or a UFO, he said. But he did see these two creatures. And that was the key point of my excitement over Renzulli's sighting: he saw *two* creatures. That was the first time anyone had ever reported seeing more than one. I had often speculated that if the Beast of Bray Road were some type of natural animal, there would have to be others to create a breeding population, however small. The size difference between these two could have indicated that one was a female or perhaps a younger offspring.

I also found it interesting that from the brief glimpse Renzulli had of the creature's eye, he interpreted its expression as "mean and angry." That's not the usual way people describe wild animals. They might be described as calm or ferocious, but normally we don't ascribe human emotions to wild creatures we encounter. A coyote surprised on a roadside will just look blank. Sneak up on a bear and it will look you over and most likely (you hope) move calmly away. A deer or cat crossing the road will appear intent on its goal of reaching the other side. But angry or mean? To me, that interpretation possibly suggests a particular emotion emanating from the creature, to be expected only in situations such as encountering a bear protecting its young or a cougar that is about to eat you. It's simply not the usual assumption a person would make about an animal in a split-second sighting. But I've heard it on more than one occasion about the Manwolf.

As for territory, this part of Kenosha County is about fifty miles east of Bray Road. That's well within a large carnivore's roaming capability, especially if its breeding population must expand continually in order not to crowd itself too much for good hunting. It must be said that this sighting has all the earmarks of a flesh-and-blood, natural animal of some type. Renzulli did not see the animals morph, materialize, or levitate. They merely ran like the dickens and glared.

However, it should also be pointed out that there was a cemetery in the very near vicinity. Not all cemeteries are haunted, and I've been unable to discover any unusual headstones or legends in this particular cemetery. But it's a cemetery, and such places are known to be preferred sites for two groups of people: teenage drinkers and those wishing to perform certain magical rites.

These running quadrupeds also had attributes that seem to set them apart from normal Wisconsin fauna. They were super-sized, more like large humans in weight. And they looked angry, according to the witness. So I think that an argument could be made for placing Renzulli's sighting in the realm of the extraordinary, as well. But watch for mention of this dark duo later on when we come across some similar creatures in other places. The next story's creature, however, leaves no doubt as to which camp it's in.

Mineral Point, Where the Werewolves and Vampires Run

In Eastern Europe and Russia, the Slavic peoples traditionally see werewolves and vampires as essentially two sides of the same ancient coin. It's believed that a werewolf will turn into a vampire, for instance, if grisly precautions aren't taken with its burial. Slavic werewolves also retain a more human-looking face, the better to show off their Dracula-style fangs. It's brilliantly efficient, really, the way they are able to combine the cannibalism of the werewolf and the blood feasting of the woodland vamp into one scary package. And although the following blend isn't quite the same, one werewolf sighting that was reported to me also had a sort of vampiric connection.

The picturesque former mining town of Mineral Point in southern Iowa County, about thirty miles west of Madison, has been famous for some time for its "vampire," a tall, thin, pale man in a black trench coat spotted by policeman Jon Pepper near the city's Graceland

Cemetery in April 1981. According to Chad Lewis and Terry Fisk in *Wisconsin Road Guide to Haunted Locations,* Pepper chased the supposed bloodsucker but was unable to catch it due to its supernatural fence-climbing abilities. Lewis and Fisk add that the incident was widely believed by townspeople to be a practical joke played by Pepper, who also liked to run around town in a gorilla suit. Still, the report brought widespread publicity to the town, and the Vampire of Mineral Point became an instant folk story.

In April 2004, a woman named Kim (last name withheld on request) wrote me after finding my Web site and said she also knew of a werewolf sighting in Mineral Point. It happened in 1987, she said, about six years after the Pepper/vampire incident. But unlike that purported sighting, where only a known practical joker claimed to have seen the creature, Kim wrote that between fifteen and twenty people saw this reputed werewolf. She didn't hint at the gathering's purpose.

"The way the story goes," she wrote, "is that it was on a spring day, during the middle of the afternoon, sunny and everything, which is a time you don't expect a werewolf. But it was the day before the full moon, I believe.

"A bunch of people, maybe fifteen or twenty, saw a werewolf running as it was changing, and then it went into a building and fell and clutched a railing and then changed back into a human in front of everybody. There were a bunch of people that talked about it in the eighties."

Unfortunately, there was no word as to whom the werewolf turned out to be. Presumably, everyone in such a small town would have known and been able to identify such a bold person. As for the small crowd of people, Kim did name names. One person who talked about it the most, she said, "sounded really scared like he believed it and a lot of people teased him so I don't think he was making up something for no gain. I think he did believe his story."

I was able to track down this man and talk to him, but unfortunately he claimed to have no memory of the incident. Another person Kim named turned out to be deceased, so the investigation ended there, with only her second-hand report to go on. Still, the story has a certain charm. This was a very melodramatic werewolf, I'll give it that. Talk about chewing the scenery. Sprinting through the town, panting desperately for cover from the hot spring sun, it stumbles and sinks its claws into a railing to save itself. It turns to face the gawkers, its yellow eyes squinting balefully at them. Unable to contain its wolfish form any longer, the fanged muzzle shrinks back into a human proboscis and the heavy fur recedes until at last, a naked human being cowers in the shadows of the mysterious building. The crowd goes wild.

I'm reluctant to buy it, especially in light of the town's previous history of pranksterism. Jon Pepper had left town by that point, so it probably wasn't him shedding an ape suit, but Lewis and Fisk noted that Pepper had a friend who also liked to play gorilla, and as far as I know, the friend never left town. Replay the imagery, this time with a sweating man trying to pull off a furry costume as he runs—he gets one foot caught in the fur pant leg, trips, grabs the railing, the costume falls the rest of the way down and there he stands in his tighty-whities. The crowd laughs their derrieres off.

And even if that's not how it actually went down, this story simply smacks of exaggerated rural legend with so many people supposedly having seen a werewolf transformation and nobody ever reporting it until seventeen years later. If someone who was there and saw it now contacts me, perhaps I might change my mind. But it's a pity, because this story would have made a fabulous case of witnessed "morphing" if it only could have been authenticated by even one witness. As is, it just sounds too much like something out of a scene from the movie *Teen Wolf.*

And yet, strange things happen around Mineral Point. Jay Rath, in his book, *The W-Files,* notes that an unidentified light was seen around the Mineral Point area on January 5, 1986, well within the vampire/werewolf time line. Several area residents and a local sheriff separately saw a very strange, bright light that first appeared to be motionless and then took off at a high rate of speed, soundlessly. A historic inn called the Walker House, site of a pioneer-day hanging, is widely reputed to be haunted. And a former policeman says that he chased a vampire out of a cemetery one fine spring evening. If there ever was a town where a dashing werewolf might molt in public, Mineral Point seems a very likely candidate.

The Danger of Smoking That
Your Doctor Never Told You About

Denise Benson of Helenville was also a teenager when she saw what she is now sure was the Beast. "It was back in '82 when I was in high school," Benson told me in a phone interview. "We lived a couple of miles outside of Dousman on Highway 18."

Dousman sits almost due north of Bray Road, in Waukesha County, about a thirty-minute drive away. It's just north of the Kettle Moraine State Forest Southern Unit, laid out along the Bark River and surrounded by tiny lakes. Highway 18 runs east and west past Utica Lake, crosses the Bark River, and then continues just north of Dutchman Lake, making it highly typical werewolf-sighting territory.

Benson had a secret habit at the time, she said: a nicotine addiction that she didn't want her parents to find out about. "I had sneaked outside to smoke some cigarettes," said Benson, "and I had my ten-year-old brother with me by this big, huge old barn and silo. There was a stone platform between the barn and silo, so we could sit there and look out at the cornfield."

The time was just after dusk, Benson estimated, "and it was in the fall so the corn was six feet tall at least...over our heads. It was dark, there was not a full moon. So we were sitting there and getting ready to go back in. We were looking to the west and about one hundred to two hundred yards out, we saw a glowing red dot, almost like a cigarette end moving parallel to us."

Fascinated, Benson and her brother watched the little red dot continue toward them until it was directly in front of them in the cornfield, above the cornstalks. And then, Benson said, a sense of horror dawned on them as a second red glow came into view, and they realized that the red lights were the eyes of some creature turning its head to look directly at them. And of course, two eyes with a frontal view implies the face of a predator, not a cow or horse which have eyes on the sides of their heads.

"They were glowing red eyes, like LED lights, at least a foot over the corn," said Benson. There were no yard lights to reflect from the creature's eyes, and the house was over a half acre away. The highway was desolate at the time.

"As it came toward us, it seemed to get bigger, so it was coming closer. I could not make out any form. The only thing we could tell is, it was above the corn. We never told our parents because they would have found out I was smoking.

"Eight years later I was at school in Platteville and my brother and parents came to visit and we finally told them the story. To my surprise, my dad said his friend who lived on a deserted road near Rome had seen something, too, and he was a hunter with a big coonhound. One night he was at home and his dog started barking. He looked out the window from his door and saw two glowing red eyes. He went for his gun, but when he came back it was gone. He could not find tracks later, but his dog would not go outside." Benson places that sighting in the same time frame as hers.

Rome is a small community with a large nature area around a body of water called Rome Pond. It's about ten miles west of Dousman, but in Jefferson County and is best known as the supposed location of the TV show "Picket Fences." Other sightings have been reported in this very rural area surrounded by agricultural fields and woods. One person told me that a woman who worked at an area convenience store often told of two teenagers who saw a Manwolf standing and watching some deer in a nearby field, though I wasn't able to confirm this.

But Benson says that she and her brother Karl, now a married father of two and a preschool teacher, have never forgotten that eerie sight. Whatever they saw, it had to stand seven feet tall for its eyes to be seen above the corn. And worst of all, they knew that whatever it was, it saw them, too.

Of course, neither Benson nor the hunter (whose name I have on file) could describe the creature that belonged to those eyes, but we can draw a few conclusions. As I noted before, it was some sort of predator, whether canine, feline, apelike, human, or raptor. We can probably rule out a bird from the slow, even motion and the constant position above the corn. It would have to be bipedal to be moving so easily through the cornstalks with its eyes visible above. That would sound like a very tall human except for the fact that humans, even albinos, do not have glowing red eyes. This leaves us with some type of bipedal canid, felid, or Bigfoot-type creature, and we can't rule out a Lizard Man, either (more about him later). Since there haven't been any sightings of bipedal felines to my knowledge, even though we've had plenty of cougar and black panther sightings on all fours, I'm going to eliminate that category, too. Lizard Man is also unlikely, being quite rare and since so far, I have no confirmed sightings in this area.

That leaves us with our same two local yokels, the Bigfoot-like Bluff Monster and the Manwolf. Dousman and Rome are both about fifteen miles north/northwest of known Bluff Monster territory, so the Bigfoot may be the best fit. Still, this is also known Manwolf territory. I'll call it a draw. The red eyes may be a clue, but they've been noted on both the Manwolf and Bluff Monster, although the Manwolf's are usually described as yellow. (Lizard Man has been seen with both red and yellow eyes, too.) At any rate, it's an intriguing pair of sightings.

Cruising: American Wolffiti

Another teenage sighting from the early eighties was forwarded to me from Richard Hendricks' *Weird Wisconsin* site. The estimated year, '83 or '84. The place, Twin Lakes, just east of Walworth County and over the line into Kenosha County.

Twin Lakes, as you might imagine from the name, is another well-watered community built around the shores of Lake Elizabeth and Lake Marie. Folk crooner John Prine sings of meeting his ex-wife at a barbecue on the shores of Lake Marie. I once did some long-term substitute teaching at Lakewood Elementary School, sandwiched between the lakeshore and cornfields, so I know the place a bit. It's a quiet little town, made livelier in the summer when seasonal homes are opened and the lakes fill up with watercraft and fishermen.

Pete Peterson grew up in Twin Lakes, and it was the summer after his high school graduation, having just purchased his first car, when he had his encounter with the Beast. In his own words:

As with all teenage boys, I loved nothing more than to drive my car around. It was a newly restored 1971 Mach 1 Ford Mustang and I drove everywhere, all the time, all hours, day and night. Now, I should state that when I saw what I've come to know now as the Walworth County werewolf, I didn't at that time know anything about it. It was only after I had related what I saw to my father, that he saw an article in the Kenosha newspaper or some newspaper about the werewolf.

It was late at night maybe, well round midnight or 1:00 AM in the morning and I was out cruising on my way to Lake Geneva. Now, I'd always taken back roads and I believe I was coming down Powers Lake Road but I can't be sure, but it was one of the back roads between Twin Lakes and Pell Lake Drive. There's a real swampy area, just before you get to Pell Lake Drive, and it was there I saw the beast. He did not try to harm me or do anything to me. He just came out of the swamp on the right side of the road and crossed over to the left side and back into the swamp. He did, however, make eye contact with me.

I had never seen anything quite like him, and quite frankly I'll never forget him. He was extremely tall, but honestly having not gotten out of my car, it was difficult to say just how tall he was. But he was a lot taller than most men I've ever seen. I could clearly see his face and his ears and his very long fingers. His face was very caninelike, and he walked hunched over slightly, and had very long arms and extremely long fingers. He had very long ratty, stringy hair. I could not smell him, for I had the windows closed and the air-conditioning on. I can still remember him looking back at me as he strolled off into the low fog that covered the swamp. I must admit that my encounter with him was not as exciting as others have been, and it's quite a ways from where he's normally seen, but that's where I saw him.

When I talked with Peterson later, he added, "I know some people may think I'm nuts, but I saw what I saw!" He was one of the few witnesses who did not profess any fear of the creature. "It made no aggression toward me," he said. In fact, he recalled that the creature "looked at me just as a deer does when they cross the road, and as he crossed the road to the swamp on the other side, he did keep looking over his shoulder at me as he disappeared into the fog."

Peterson also added, "I was amazed at how tall it was…it was at least seven and a half to eight feet tall. Long ears just like a German shepherd, which is what his face more or less resembled, only with very long hair. I could not say for sure what color it was, but in the moonlight you know how the tips of hair looks like it's glowing, it appeared to be grayish. I did not see a tail as such; like I said, it had very long hair. It could very well have had one and I could not have told. I thought at first that it was a sick bear because it was so skinny, but it walked upright like a man. I think about it sometimes, but it does not haunt my thoughts or anything like that. I can see him still today as I did when I first saw him. I feel that there are lots of mysteries in this world that we (humans) don't have answers to. Maybe some day we'll find out what a werewolf really is."

No problem putting this one in the Manwolf category!

Pawprint in a Moon Boot

In the eighties, the sightings began to heat up around Bray Road. Farmer Joy Smage doesn't remember the exact year, but the month was November, sometime in the second half of that decade, when she was out disking a snowy back field on her family's Bray Road land. "I remember because I saw some strange animal prints I had never seen before in the mud," she said.

Smage didn't take a photo or cast of them. She was out in the field without a camera and had somehow forgotten her plaster of Paris kit that morning, but she was wearing ladies' size-nine "moon boots" and was able to place her entire foot inside one of the prints. And since she *was* disking that field, it's certain that the prints didn't survive for later examination. So what made them? Nothing the farm woman had ever seen, although she described them as animal-like rather than human. But from what several other people witnessed nearby, we can make at least an educated guess that perhaps it was a six- to seven-foot-tall Manwolf.

In Broad Daylight

It isn't often that I want to whack a Beast of Bray Road witness upside the head, but I had to admit I was exasperated enough with my friend Marv Kirschnik to tell him that was exactly what I wanted to do to him. Kirschnik, who was mentioned in my first book for his Marinette County brush with something very tall and yellow-eyed, had just admitted to me—at my first book signing for *The Beast of Bray Road*, no less—that he had also experienced something far more specific and close to home but had been afraid to tell me about it before. The sighting in Marinette County seemed less threatening, he felt, because it was both harder to pin down and much farther away. Therefore, he didn't mind sharing that one. But now that the book was out, he said, he felt he could tell me the other story.

That was when I had to resist the urge to mar his nicely combed hairdo. Of course, he couldn't have imagined at the time that I'd be writing a second book. (If this were an e-mail, I'd be adding a smiley-faced emoticon at the end of that sentence.)

Kirschnik was tooling down Highway 11 in his white cargo van in September 1981, he said, not far from the intersection with Bray Road, when something caught his eye in the field off to his right. "It was a nice September day, about 3:30 PM in the afternoon," he said. "For some reason, I looked off to the right where there was a broken tree and saw this big thing behind the tree. It put its 'hands' on the tree and stood up and stood there watching me. I pulled over in my

Marv Kirschnik

cargo van and looked out the passenger window at it for about a minute. It was about six feet tall, had dark eyes, a doglike face, and humanlike body features. I finally got scared and left because I didn't know what the heck it was. It watched me drive away. I didn't tell anyone for two weeks and then I told my wife and she laughed at me." (Kirschnik and his wife are no longer married.)

A thoughtful artist and outdoorsman who stands over six feet tall himself, Kirschnik was so shaken by the experience that he drew a pencil sketch of the creature after he got home. He obligingly left the book-signing to go home and fetch the drawing, which was faded

Tracing of Marv Kirschnik's drawing of the Manwolf.

with age. The paper was turning yellow and brittle; this was not something he had whipped up the day before.

But simply drawing the creature was not enough to shake it from Kirschnik's mind. A skilled creator of marionettes, wood carver, and craftsman, he began churning out werewolf likenesses in various forms and selling them in a small bead shop called Mrs. Beadz (now closed) in downtown Williams Bay. His favorite was probably the large werewolf puppet named "Willy B.," but browsers could pick over hand-cast pewter werewolf charms, concrete werewolf garden stones, and elaborate, painted werewolf dioramas with moving parts such as the "Elvis Werewolf Blue Hawaii" scene. Kirschnik even made himself a pair of faux fur knickers with a tail to wear when he feels like cross-species dressing. It's a way to have some fun and vent his long-lasting trauma at the same time, he says.

His sighting, though, was more than just traumatic; it was surprising in two ways. First, this was not typical sighting territory. Highway 11 is a very busy road, serving as the main connection between the cities of Elkhorn and Burlington. A bustling construction company stands near the intersection. But the fact that Kirschnik saw the Manwolf in the middle of the afternoon, in broad daylight, is even more unusual. Most of the other sightings have taken place at dusk, night, or the wee, dark hours of the morning such as in Renzulli's case. But Kirschnik's sighting happened a few years before Renzulli's, and a good six to eight years before most of the other Bray Road sightings. Nobody was talking werewolves, Manwolves, or anything of the sort at the time, at least in this part of the country. No wonder Kirschnik felt like the Lone Ranger in seeing something so strange.

Treed by a Werewolf

Another sighting occurred on that same stretch of Highway 11 a few years later. The neighbor of a young girl who lived on a farm on that highway not too far from Bray Road told me this story. The girl, a young teen at the time and whose name is being kept confidential, liked to take refuge from her siblings by sitting and reading in a comfortable tree behind the barn. She was perched on her favorite limb one day when she saw something come out of the woods and walk toward her. It appeared to be some kind of large dog, except it was walking on its hind legs. The girl caught her breath as the creature stopped, sniffed, and then looked directly at her in the tree and came closer. She scrambled to get higher in the branches as the creature began jumping, trying to claw its way up. Luckily for the girl, the creature did not seem to have climbing skills.

Eventually, she said, it gave up and headed back to the woods. She stayed up there for an hour to make sure that it wasn't hiding and lying in wait for her, then finally summoned enough courage to drop back down to the ground and hightail it into the farmhouse. When she breathlessly explained to her family what had happened, they laughed. The girl never told anyone else outside the family, but she did show her neighbor the claw marks the animal had etched into the tree. And when the news stories came out a few years later about the Beast, the girl knew that she had had her own sneak preview.

Dining on Deer?

The creature was seen again at the other end of Bray Road in October 1986. Diane Koenig, a fifty-nine-year-old factory worker from Elkhorn, was returning home one evening from visiting her daughter in Burlington when she decided to turn off Highway 11 and cut over toward Elkhorn on Bray Road. It was a clear night, she remembers, not foggy or raining, and she had somehow escaped hearing about the Beast that was purported to hang out there, so she was watching for deer, not monsters. She had all four doors on her old station wagon unlocked, her window rolled down a few inches and the radio blaring her favorite country music station.

She had almost reached the end of Bray Road, where a sharp turn leads onto Highway NN, when she saw something in the open field to her right. She had no trouble recalling her surprise nine years later. "My headlights hit it," she said, "and it was just sitting there. It looked like it was sitting or stooping. At first, I thought it was a person sitting with a deer, then my headlights hit the face and it looked like a wolf. The little hairs on the back of my neck all stood up."

The creature just stared at her, said Koenig. "It was a grayish color, with ears like a wolf. I thought it was holding a deer; I saw the white legs criss-crossed over its chest, like deer legs standing up. It had mean, mean eyes and a big long nose or muzzle. It was shaggy. The hair was darker around its face. Those eyes followed me as I went past it. It was just too big for a wolf. And it wasn't a deer. I had never heard of the Beast when I saw it, but later I met Doris Gipson (her encounter is told in my first book) at ECM Motors where we both worked, and she told me about when she saw the same thing on Bray Road."

Koenig said that she is sure it wasn't a wolf or coyote. "If I saw a coyote, I'd just say, 'oh wow,' I wouldn't get a creepy feeling. But I didn't say, 'oh wow.' I don't know what I saw but it was creepy. It scared the hell out of me."

Koenig told me about her sighting when she attended a book signing in Elkhorn. Her son still makes fun of her for it, she said, but she doesn't care.

This does seem to be a classic sighting, even though Koenig wasn't able to observe the creature walking. The upright position perceived as "sitting or stooping," is one clue, as is the giant size and the aggressive glare. "It was like he was saying, keep on driving, lady," said Koenig. She couldn't remember the particular color of its eyes. At the time, she thought of turning around and going back, she said, but then she remembered that her doors were all unlocked and they weren't automatic. "So I just kept heading for home."

Palmyra Peeper

Jefferson County garnered its share of the eighties action, too. Tom, a Palmyra man who asked me to withhold his last name, was driving north at about 10:00 PM in 1986 or '87 on Highway H about halfway between LaGrange and Palmyra, very near Bluff Road and right in the Kettle Moraine State Forest, when he thought he saw a grizzly bear. It had to be a grizzly, he reasoned, because it was too tall and the wrong color and kind of fur for a black bear. Never mind that grizzlies do not exist in this part of the country. Then Tom, a printer who was 49 on that cool, clear October evening, realized that it wasn't any sort of a bear at all.

"It was peeking out from behind a telephone pole," he said. "It was on my right in a field. It stood about five and a half to six feet tall and was a light gray, dirty color. It stood upright. Its legs were like a furry dog's. It wasn't real long hair, like a short-haired terrier. I couldn't see the eyes or the details of the head. But it was like seeing a ghost—it shocked me that much. You don't expect to see something like that."

Interestingly, Tom also recalls that someone he knew who lived on Highway H often called him to report seeing UFOs on that road during that same time period. "He saw the light-type," said Tom. Of course, as anyone who studies UFO reports knows, the "light-type" more often than not turn out to be either stars or airplanes of some kind. Still, someone believed that UFOs were hovering on Highway H at the same time Tom saw this creature and others were seeing the Bluff Monster.

Since he said that the legs were like a dog's, I will put this one in the Manwolf category even though he couldn't confirm the ears and the color seems a bit off. Most people describe Manwolves (Bigfoot, too, for that matter) as dark and shaggy, not light gray and short-haired. But perhaps this was a senior Manwolf. If they do turn out to be living creatures, some of them would certainly show signs of age.

Tom had kept his story mostly to himself for all these years, sharing it with only a few friends, one of whom told me about it. Talking with Tom on the phone, it was obvious that the incident was still very fresh in his mind.

Hunting the Hunters on Bray Road

Dennis Hasting, owner of Hasting's Carpet and Flooring in Paddock Lake, is an avid coon hunter, right down to the accompanying blue tick coonhound. In 1989, he and a friend managed to secure permission to hunt on what he considered a "coon-hunter's paradise" on a Highway 11 farm that backed up to some woods on a country lane called Bray Road, near Elkhorn. Hasting's wife told me a little about what happened to him on that land, and I later interviewed him in person at the Starbucks in Lake Geneva.

One night in November 1989, he and the friend decided to make the half-hour trip from his home in Lily Lake to try out the new hunting land. "We pulled into the farmhouse and knocked on the door," said Hasting, a trim man with graying hair, "and told them we were there to hunt. The lady said fine, maybe you can chase away whatever is scaring our horses. Every night about 3:00 or 4:00 AM, they are crying and whinnying."

Hasting and his companion didn't worry too much, figuring that it was probably coyotes upsetting the horses. They headed back into the field, trudging for what he estimated was a half mile, until no houses or buildings were visible from where they stood. "Just hedgerows and cornfields," said Hasting. "Within a half an hour we had a coon treed and shot it. There was lots of noise with the coon squalling, us yelling, the dog barking. We would have attracted anything. Then we went into a cornfield and let the dog loose again. It caught another trail."

"That Ain't No Buck in Rut..."

Hasting and his friend stood waiting for the dog in that cornfield, when suddenly they heard a noise from the woods, in the opposite direction of the way the dog had run. "Something was walking," said Hasting, "snapping twigs and rustling leaves. It sounded like a person walking. My buddy said, 'Maybe it's a buck in rut.' As soon as he said that, it let out this roar. I said, 'That ain't no buck in rut.'"

At that point, it began pacing and making a growling, slathering noise. Hasting was able to reproduce that sound. He said that he'd been doing it for friends and family ever since he first heard it. His imitation of the growl was blood curdling, and it was the very same sound I would later hear over the phone from a man in another state who never heard of Dennis Hasting. It varied in pitch and intensity, almost like a cappuccino maker, and was very distinctive, like that of no other creature I've heard. He later put both the growl and the roar on audiotape for me. I have to admit that I can't imagine what I would do if I heard those sounds near a dark woods at night.

"All of a sudden," said Hasting, "the dog came back toward the patch of woods and the thing stopped. The dog walked back into the woods within thirty yards of the thing, and there was still no noise. The dog came out again and went in the other direction, still on the trail of his coon. Once he was gone, we heard sounds of something coming down a tree and hitting the ground. Then it started pacing again and making that growling sound. We finally got the dog and literally backed out of the woods with a flashlight for about an eighth of a mile. It was a coon-hunter's paradise, but I never went back there."

I should make it clear that Hasting was not a novice woodsman when this happened. He estimated that he was in the woods hunting raccoons around one hundred nights out of the year, usually between the hours of midnight and one in the morning. "But I've never been that scared in the woods anywhere," he said. "That night, there was no doubt to me it was on two legs, not four, from the size of the sticks it was breaking. Right when it jumped down from the tree, the sound made it evident it was something heavy. That night I thought maybe it was a bear, but there were no bears here then and bears don't jump out of trees. This thing jumped from a considerable height."

Hasting added that not long after his experience, he was talking to another coon hunter who told him that he was deer hunting on Highway 11, "shining" deer at night (driving around trying to catch them in his headlights), when he saw a pair of eyes in the middle of the field. The man drove toward the eyes in his truck, thinking that they must belong to a deer, but he was wrong. He told Hasting that to his surprise, "it was a hairy thing standing on two legs. Then it dropped to all fours and ran off." The man said that it frightened him so much, he never shined deer again.

Hasting says that he isn't sure the creature wasn't something beyond the natural world. "I'm a Christian. I know there is a spiritual realm," he said. "And that night when I was out there, I was thinking, *thank God* I'm a Christian."

It's hard to categorize Hasting's sighting, of course. Since it did happen near Bray Road at the time so many others out there were seeing Manwolves, it's tempting to classify it as that, especially since the creature the other hunter saw near that area dropped to all fours to make its escape. Bigfoot has never been seen to do that, to my knowledge.

However, whatever this creature was, it was able to quickly and silently scale a tree, then drop back down rather than descending by climbing. If you remember the story of the girl caught in the tree by a Manwolf (also on a Highway 11 farm), it appeared that the creature couldn't climb, unless it didn't really want to and was just trying to scare her, as usually seems the case with these beasts.

I would imagine that a Bigfoot could climb a tree and also jump down from one. Neither Bigfoot nor Manwolf seems inclined to show itself unnecessarily to people, so the fact that it remained hidden from sight doesn't tell us anything. However, the fact that the growling sound Hasting made exactly matched the sound someone else produced on the phone for me (which was heard while looking at the creature) is a strong argument for the Manwolf. People who hear Bigfoot vocalizations report a wide range of sounds resembling grunts, hoots, and screams. But growls and roars, such as the creature in the woods made, sound much more canid than apelike to me. These conclusions are very speculative and subjective, however, and doubtless others may beg to differ.

I'll probably leave this one in the Undetermined Big Furry slot. But there is a strange twist to Hasting's story. A few months later, he told his sister, a college student at the time, about his experience. She gasped and confessed that she had also had an encounter with a Big Furry that same month. She was also stalked, but not in some lonely woods. Hasting's sister had the run of her life just a block from downtown Lake Geneva.

Terror on Motel Strip

I interviewed Hasting's sister, who prefers that I just call her C., by phone right there in Starbucks, only a few blocks from where the incident happened. She now lives in Chicago and is married to a prominent medical professional. The odd thing was that someone she had known from the past had written to me the year before, saying that a friend of hers, C., had a strange experience in Lake Geneva, but she no longer knew where C. lived and was unable to find her. She tried several mutual friends to no avail, and I had put C.'s name in the dead-end file. And now here she was, being dialed up by her brother before my very eyes, agreeing to tell her story.

"I was a sophomore in college," she said, "in the fall of 1989, and I had come home early from the semester and was staying with a girl-friend in her apartment near the YMCA in Lake Geneva. Behind the Y was a small dirt road that led to the apartments."

The girls were up late that night and about 1:00 AM decided that they wanted something to eat. The only thing open at that time of night was a White Hen Pantry on the other side of downtown, across the street from the library. Lake Geneva's library is on the shore of Geneva Lake, and the downtown area is only a block from the shore. The whole area was once covered in burial mounds, with an impressive water spirit mound covering part of the downtown and lakeside park area. Just past downtown to the east, after a major traffic intersection, Wells Street winds up a hill and becomes what is known locally as "Motel Strip," for the long line of older motels that cater to the town's hordes of summer tourists. At the base of the hill, closest to downtown, stands a Kentucky Fried Chicken restaurant, then two other fast-food establishments, and then the YMCA parking lot and building. There is still a small road behind the YMCA, and on one side of it is a tiny wetlands area and woods. Not far away is yet another group of apartment buildings fronted by a strip of woodlands that runs almost parallel with Wells Street.

Between Memorial Day and Labor Day, Lake Geneva is jammed with cars and tourists, but at 1:00 AM in November, the downtown area is as dark and quiet as a ghost town, a few street lights providing the only signs of life. C. and her girlfriend had a fairly good walk ahead of them, down the hill, past the intersection by the KFC, then several blocks to the White Hen.

"We got out to the dirt road and then Motel Strip," said C., "and then headed toward the Kentucky Fried Chicken. I heard heavy breathing, not human. It sounded like a strange animal noise." She demonstrated for me over the phone, and it sounded rather like a growling asthmatic and quite like the sound her brother made, although she could have been influenced over the years by hearing him tell his story. "It got louder as we kept walking, but no one was around…. Nothing was open that time of the morning. My friend heard it, too, and we said on the count of three, let's turn around and see." Bravely, the girls did just that.

At first, said C., her impression was that they were looking at "a creepy homeless person in a fur coat, a fur coat with a hood." It was walking on two feet, she said, and its arms were held in front of it, "facing forward."

> It was hunched over and seemed to be propelling itself forward by its very long arms, but they were not touching the ground. The head was apelike; I didn't notice a muzzle. And it continued to follow behind us. I said, 'We gotta run.' So we ran, and the thing was running down the middle of the road towards us. It sounded angry or distressed, so we started screaming. It followed us for fifty to one hundred feet. I was running so hard, I felt like my chest was going to burst. I turned and looked at it again when we got under the streetlight and saw that it was not a human in a fur coat.
>
> As it was running, it looked like a tall person hunched over. The hair on its legs reminded me of dreadlocks, long and matted. It was more muscular than a human, and it seemed like it was not easy for it to run on two legs. Its hands were paws. The thighs looked well developed. It almost seemed like it wanted to hunch forward and go on all fours, but it didn't. This thing appeared unsteady, and its gait was off, but it moved quickly, not lumbering.
>
> I saw enough of its face as it got closer; the head looked almost humanlike, but it was covered in hair. It appeared to have pointy ears on the side of its head, higher on the head than a human's. It was about six feet tall.

Suddenly, said C., just before they got to the Kentucky Fried Chicken, the thing took a ninety-degree turn and ran "in leaps" toward a thicket. "It ran straight into that and never put its hands up," she said. "It tore right through it. A human would be hurt."

C. and her friend kept going and made it to the White Hen. "We waited before we went back," she said. "We waited a good hour." Luckily, it was nowhere in sight when the girls returned to the apartment. "Sometimes, I wonder if we freaked it out as much as it freaked us out," she said.

This sighting amazed me. In 1989, most if not all of the sightings were rural. This one occurred right in the middle of the county's busiest town. The creature was evidently sneaking

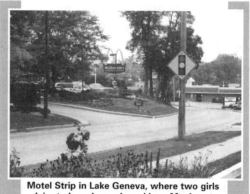

Motel Strip in Lake Geneva, where two girls claim to have been chased by a Manbeast.

around near human habitations and was bold enough to chase two women down the middle of a major street. Was it because they were women and the creature was looking for love? There are plenty of anecdotes from Native American tribes regarding the attraction of Bigfoot to human females. The women were not acting aggressively or being threatening in any way. Indeed, they would not have been aware of the creature had it not decided to stalk them. And even then, they may not have noticed, had it not been a slobbering mouth-breather.

But what was it? The beast sounds like the right size for a Manwolf; the shaggy dark fur is consistent, as is the muscular build and well-developed thigh area. Arms that "face forward" are also something that sound like canid anatomy. The idea of it propelling itself by swinging the arms sounds very apelike, however, even if it was not knuckle-dragging. So does C.'s impression that it "wanted" to get down on all fours to run.

Then we have the puzzle of the head to contend with. She didn't notice a muzzle, but if she was facing the creature head-on every time she looked back, and its head was held up toward her, the muzzle length may not have been apparent. Pointed ears set higher than a human's also sounds doglike...and very un-Bigfootlike.

Another enigma is her description of the "hands," which she described as "paws." Monkeys and apes have very handlike appendages, and Bigfoot's are always described that way, too. I don't put quite as much weight on her statement that it seemed to be running flat-footed, because she told me she couldn't see how the legs were shaped below the knee, and others like Doris Gipson in my first book have described the running creature's heavy footfalls hitting the pavement like a man's. That makes sense, since the two legs were bearing all its weight. The odd gait is also consistent with many other Manwolf observations.

Throwing in the grating, heavy-breathing sound the creature made as it followed the young women, I'm inclined to call this one a Manwolf. It's not 100 percent there, but these descriptions were from glimpses caught by two very frightened young women running for their lives, under shadowy streetlights. C. told me that she has totally lost contact with the friend who shared her experience, and she was too frightened to tell anyone else about it until her brother related his memorable coon hunt. She later shared it with a few others, including the woman who had first tipped me off about her story. I'm just glad that Dennis Hasting's wife came to that book signing, or neither of these sightings would ever have been made public.

It is interesting that there seems to be a gap of about two years between the 1983-1984 Twin Lakes sighting and the subsequent cluster on Bray Road, starting with Koenig's in 1986. It may just be that the creature(s) managed to stay out of sight, or that no one who saw anything during those years has dared to come forward. Or was it that the creature was somewhere else, on a cyclical feeding tour, during those years?

Whatever the reason, when you compare the seventies with the eighties, the sightings seem to begin to intensify both in number and in the apparent "solidity" of the creatures seen during the latter decade. Could something or someone have been getting better, gathering strength, at manifesting these beings? Or were the creatures simply growing bolder as a natural species forced out of hiding by encroaching development?

Either way, it appears that something was happening—a preparation or, perhaps, a crescendo drum roll to herald the sightings boom of the nineties that would finally transport the stories out of the woodsy legends and into the hungry eye of the national media.

CHAPTER SIX

INTO THE 90s: MONSTERS AMOK

"At no time and in no place, will nature ever ask your permission."

— Fyodor Dostoevsky,
Notes from the Underground

The Bulge in the Sightings Chart: Why Bray Road?

Although Lori Endrizzi and others saw Manwolves in the 80s or earlier, no one except a few trusted family members knew about their experiences until the December 29, 1991, issue of *The Week*, a Walworth County newspaper, came out with my first article on the Beast of Bray Road. This event heralded a burst of sightings that is still the largest known cluster of these appearances.

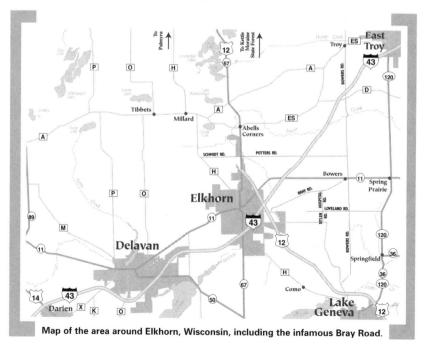

Map of the area around Elkhorn, Wisconsin, including the infamous Bray Road.

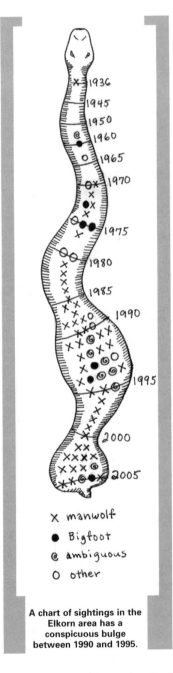

X manwolf
● Bigfoot
@ ambiguous
O other

A chart of sightings in the Elkorn area has a conspicuous bulge between 1990 and 1995.

If you can envision a graph of all known Beast sightings with 1936 at the top and 2005 marking the bottom (see chart), the biggest sighting years will bulge like an undigested meal in a sated python. The python's biggest repast, then, balloons near its bottom in the space designating 1990 to 1996. Why did the major feast occur in that time frame? Did all the hoopla that followed the first publication encourage more witnesses to come forward? Was there truly a hike in creature activity in those years, or were there simply more people aware of the phenomenon and looking for it? It's very hard to say, but I think it's safe to assume the sighting spike was due to all of the above. For some reason, the Beast did seem to be frequenting the Bray Road area east of Elkhorn at that time, and once word was out, people weren't as afraid to report what they had seen.

At first blush, Bray Road seems a very unlikely sightings area. Almost every other locale boasts marshy areas, rivers, streams, lakes or ponds, with close access to dense stands of woods or tall cornfields. (Three city sightings in Madison and Milwaukee are notable exceptions, but these incidents did not occur with the other clusters.)

Bray Road is about three miles long and well-populated with farms and single-family residences. In fact, a new subdivision of upscale homes has been added in the past several years. Most of the road, however, winds between agricultural acres backed by sparse stands of woods that separate the fields. The cornfields do provide excellent cover for large animals from August through mid-fall, but the rest of the time, it's hard to see the attraction this short highway might hold for a competent, free-ranging Unbelievable.

Bray is not a lonely, deserted road, either. Anything wanting to cross it regularly would need to be adept at dodging traffic. And at first glance, Bray does not fulfill the usual requirement of proximity to a marsh, lake or river. However, if a big, thirsty critter were to follow the ditches of Bray Road and keep heading northeast after Bray joins Highway 11, it would quickly run into a watershed area for Honey Creek within a mile or so (see map). And the road originates less than a mile away from Elkhorn "Lake," a man-made body of water near the community's industrial park just south of town in Babe Mann Park. A few small creeks and irrigation ditches wind through some of the Bray Road properties, with several visible from the road. There are, therefore, more places for a beast to slake its thirst here than a casual drive-through might indicate.

Once the beverage question is settled, we must ask what solid sustenance a carnivore might find in this neighborhood. With all its farms, Bray road could potentially provide a variety of livestock for easy midnight snacking. However, I haven't been able to find evidence that farmers reported missing chickens, piglets or calves in any noticeable numbers during those years. But the road's steady traffic also provides a constant source of squashed possum, raccoon, skunk, and other roadkill, and the creature has been seen time and time again scooping up

Bray Road—an ordinary-looking stretch of rural backroad.

pavement patties. Perhaps the Beast came for the livestock but stayed for the roadkill.

Whatever the combined merits of the place from a monster-eye view, it was on Bray Road at the intersection of what used to be called Sitler Road (now Hospital Road) that Doris Gipson stopped her car to see if she had hit a person and ended up diving back into the front seat and stomping the gas pedal to outrun the "thing" that suddenly came at her from the ditch. (It left its claw marks, which she showed me and the *Inside Edition* TV crew, on the trunk of her car as a memento.) This sighting happened October 31, 1990, and is one of the stories covered in the first book. Other Bray Road sightings discussed there from that time period include Mike Etten's 1990 glimpse of a huge, unknown canid sitting on its haunches, the group of children who encountered the creature on Bowers Road (right next to Bray Road) in 1990, and Sharilyn Smage's Bray Road cornfield sighting in the fall of 1991. There were also a number of other sightings from the 90s covered in that book that occurred at other locations to further bloat my illustrative python. And I'm about to top that snake's meal off with some fresh dessert.

Burlap Man

Angie Beaudoin thought her mind must be playing tricks on her as she drove south on Highway 67 in Waukesha County at about two in the morning in late summer or early fall of 1993. "I was driving my '92 Saturn," she said. "There were no street lights or other cars on the road." When she hit the intersection with County X, she noticed a strange figure heading toward her, coming out of the woods from the west. "It was almost as if he jumped out of the ditch at me but not as far as the road."

She said it was moving on two legs, about six feet tall, and appeared to be dark brown. Her first impression was of a man covered head to toe in burlap. That, of course, didn't make much sense. But that possibility was preferable to what she realized next, which was that the "man" was not covered in burlap at all, but fur. And moreover, it wasn't a man. "It had longer fur, like a dog," she saw when she got closer. It also had a head like a dog, she said. "It had a hairy face, real ratty-looking, and was about seven feet tall, standing straight up. He was on my right, and that area backs up into the Ottawa Campground."

I should mention that the intersection of Highway 67 and X, in the Town of Eagle, is smack in the heart of the Kettle Moraine State Forest, Southern Unit, which I've always maintained is a likely hideout for the Manwolf. It lies just south of a chain of small lakes, and the land to the west of the highway, where Beaudoin saw the creature emerging, is watered by numerous creeks. The area lies just a few miles east of Palmyra, which was covered in the previous book for its many ancient springs and the discovery of the strange, concrete blocks with werewolf faces found buried on the Ugly Horse Ranch. I've also had secondhand reports of the creature being seen several times around a deer ranch in that area.

She added that the creature was muscular, "not fat," but more like a tall man. "He was within a few feet of my car," she said, "and he jumped to the side of my car. I was going sixty miles an hour and I kept on going," she said. "I didn't see where he went."

I met Angie in 2003, while I was a participating artist at the Kettle Moraine Studio Tour, an annual weekend show held at studios located in or near that very scenic area. I was exhibiting my cut-paper collages and prints but also autographing copies of the newly released *Beast of Bray Road*, and she immediately drew a connection between the creature depicted in my book and what she had seen, although she'd been trying to convince herself that it was some sort of man dressed in burlap over the years. I also interviewed her more extensively by phone.

Another interesting facet to Angie's sighting is that a friend of hers who lives nearby on Piper Road told her that as a child, he used to roam the woods within a quarter mile of her sighting and found many strange man-made rock piles or cairns, and oddly arranged wood pieces, as well. He would later recall them when he saw the movie *Blair Witch Project*. There may be absolutely no connection, of course, but it does sound like some sort of ritual sites may have been used in the area at the time, probably fifteen years prior to Angie's sighting.

Road Runner

To a teenager, the entertainment grass is always a deeper shade of emerald in the burg down the road. Bombing from town to town in search of nightlife and the opposite sex (perhaps those terms are synonymous) has been *de rigeur* for Wisconsin youths since the invention of the automobile. Maybe since the horse and buggy. Sometimes, though, a late-night drive through the hinterlands can result in something even more exciting than a rendezvous at the local hamburger joint.

It was in late summer of 1993 or 1994 that Janesville high school students Stacy Doe (not her real name, by request) and several friends decided to drive to Lake Geneva on a lark. They took the usual route for that trip, following Highway 11 to Delavan and then Highway 50 into Lake Geneva. The evening fun finally over, the girls headed back to Janesville, traveling west along Highway 11 just past Delavan. Doe described the road as an "unlit country highway with fields on either side." She remembers the cornfields were high, and that the weather was warm because she and her friends were dressed in shorts. And what happened next is forever burned into her memory.

"My friends were talking and laughing and not looking at the road as I was, since I was driving," Stacy told me in an e-mail she sent after coming across my Web site. "Suddenly from the right side of the road an animal ran across the road in front of the car.

"I couldn't say exactly how far in front of the car, but it was probably in the middle of the range of the headlights. It ran extremely quickly and smoothly, like a shadow going across the road, but it was very long and low. It stretched across nearly the whole lane and was probably two or three feet off the ground at its highest point, running on all fours. It was black with a pointed face and tail.

"It moved quickly enough that it disappeared into the corn on the other side of the road," she continued, "before I thought to apply the brakes. I was very scared and just started saying, 'What was that?' and trying to describe it, but no one else had seen anything and I had no desire to return and check on it."

Stacy described the creature as doglike, yet she immediately knew that this was something else entirely. "I would have immediately dismissed it as a dog if not for the size and speed and smoothness of movement," she added.

Stacy said she managed to put the disquieting experience out of her mind until a few years ago when she stumbled across some references to other sightings and realized the similarities. She was right. There was, in fact, an almost identical sighting along the same stretch of roadway two or three years earlier in November 1991, by a couple who were also just passing through the area. Mr. and Mrs. Robert Bushman of St. Nazianz, saw what they described as something "too large to be a wolf...like no animal we had ever seen," running on all fours across Highway 11 between Delavan and Elkhorn. The Bushmans (their detailed recollection is completely recounted in the first book) also remarked on the animal's "flat out" running posture, very much like what Doe described. They were interviewed about what they saw on the TV show *Inside Edition*.

I think it is interesting that both of these sightings were not only near the same location, but were virtually identical in description. Both witnesses observed a huge creature on four legs, running in a way that seemed unnaturally swift and smooth. It sounds like some sort of natural animal, perhaps an escaped hybrid. Black panthers come to mind, except Stacy noted that what she saw was doglike, and the Bushmans described its fur as shaggy and unkempt...not a description of a panther's smooth coat.

It was also reminiscent of Rick Renzulli's "two-fer" sighting in Kenosha.

As for proximity to other sightings, Bray Road lies just to the east of Elkhorn. The Bushman sighting occurred a few miles west of Elkhorn, and Stacy's less than ten miles west of there. That's an easy range for a large predator, if we are dealing with a flesh-and-blood animal.

There is also the time gap of two to three years to consider. Whatever it was had to be dashing about the Elkhorn/Delavan countryside for quite some time, in well-populated farmland dotted by dense subdivisions. It hardly seems likely that such a startling creature could have gone unnoticed in that period of time.

That is, again, if the creature is actual meat. What else could it be? Well, any of the other supernatural possibilities we've already mentioned could cause a huge, doglike creature to manifest on Highway 11. But the Bushmans' sighting occurred about 10:00 AM in the morning, not a usual "witching hour." Besides, other than what seemed like faster than normal speed, there weren't many reasons to think these creatures were other than natural. Nothing glowing, no mental telepathy. I think these sightings have to score a few points for the side of the actual, hidden animal crowd.

On that same note, a report that is definitely on that cryptozoological side of the fence is a 1993 sighting in Jefferson County, near Hebron. This is not a Manwolf—in fact, I think it's a pretty classic Bigfoot case. But because it's in the general territory and in this time frame, I want to include it. I think it is wise to always take the full scope of what's appearing at any given time into account.

It all came about in broad daylight one strange afternoon when an eight-year-old boy found something besides livestock in the family barn. Andrew Hurd, now twenty-two and a musician in a heavy metal band called "Hebron" after his home town, remembers the incident with complete clarity. But I only found out about it after his neighbor told a friend who in turn contacted me and set up the interview. The incident is not something that anyone in his family has been eager to share.

It was summer, said Andrew, the grass was three to four feet tall in the field. "In the early afternoon, me and my buddy were playing in the backyard, we have an old shut-down farm, and I went into the barn. I heard a noise to my right, and I saw an image get up and move to the left. It was tall, bigger than any man, just a big figure silhouette. It ran east through the barn and out into the north part of the barn on two feet. It ran crouched over and really fast for being crouched. It was just huge.

"I walked in there and I seen it, and I took off fast yelling, 'There's something in the barn,' and just kept going up the driveway." His parents, not knowing whether their son had seen an intruder or some type of wild animal, called the sheriff's department. "When they came, we went in the barn," said Andrew, "and stuff was knocked down. Behind the barn, the grass was knocked down like bedding like deer will do, but we didn't have deer around there. The police just did a report and said they had some other reports like it from Sullivan at the time." Despite the barn's darkness, Andrew did glimpse the creature's face. "It had a really hairy face and head," he said, "and the neck hair was thicker. His nose was more like an ape's than a snout."

He said he did not remember that it had any odor, which is unusual for a close encounter with a Bigfoot. "The barn still scares me," he added.

The family's farm is located on Fromader Road. The immediate terrain is varied, with a large field behind the barn. A few small wooded areas lie nearby, with a treeline along the fields that Andrew says is frequented by coyotes. There is a large forested area about a mile and a half east of the farm, and Fromader Road runs directly south into the Princess Point State Wildlife Area, 1,500 acres of open marsh and woodlands. Hebron also sits just south of Highway 106, a frequent sighting area, and lies only thirteen to fifteen miles northwest of the Bluff Monster's stomping grounds.

Strangely, Andrew and his mother also saw a strange canid near their property after the Bigfoot sighting. "It came out of a field and ran out in front of us and scared us half to death," he said. The creature was running on all fours. "I'm six feet two, and this came up to my waist," he said. "It looked like a wolf. It turned, looked, and took off across the road. It looked like a whitish gray with brown or black on its back. It was not a dog, the legs were extremely long, and the head was gigantic with big, pointy ears. It had a tail, it was about two feet long and bushy. That was not a coyote, maybe like three coyotes put together."

This second creature sounds like a timber wolf to me; the size, coloration, long legs all fit. It did not display unusual behavior or speed, just was a larger size than would be expected for a stray dog. Of course, timber wolves are not supposed to exist in southern Wisconsin according to wildlife officials, but their ranges are known to be expanding southward. It's certainly not impossible. One was killed just over the Illinois border in 2004, according to one Department of Natural

Resources warden I spoke with, and timber wolf prints were recorded on the south shore of Turtle Lake in Walworth County two weeks previous to that incident. I wouldn't include this sighting in the Beast category, therefore, but it's still worth noting that the landscape around the Hurd farm was capable of supporting at least one large predator. And if young Andrew's observations were to be believed, there was a second, quite different species of megafauna also prowling the Hebron countryside: the southern Wisconsin Bigfoot! For some corroboration, read on.

Honey Creek Bridge Jumper

I was still doing book signings for *The Beast of Bray Road* in spring of 2004 and had agreed to appear at the Kenosha Public Library. The *Kenosha News* had printed a terrific article, and with it, a huge image of my "Indigenous Dogman" drawing. This was what had drawn witness Rick Renzulli to tell his tale, and a rural couple, David and Mary Pagliaroni, were also inspired to confide an experience they had had ten years earlier, in 1994 in Honey Creek, on the eastern edge of Wal-

The Honey Creek Bridge Jumper, as sketched by witness David Pagliaroni.

worth County, where Sugar Creek and Honey Creek merge with Honey Lake. A very sweet place, indeed, much of it surrounded by marshland.

The Pagliarionis invited me to visit their lovely, present home in another county and were able to tell me the story of what had happened to them late one night as they drove home after dining out. David, forty-five, was driving. Forty-four-year-old Mary was self-employed, and David did machine repair work for Chrysler Corporation.

"We were coming home from dinner between ten and eleven o'clock in the evening," David wrote. "It was springtime so there was no snow on the ground, we were coming down DD heading north, and coming up on the bridge by Honey Lake to turn left on Potter Road. I slowed down coming down the hill to make a left-hand turn, watching for deer, and as I approached the bridge I saw something reddish coming in from the side of the bridge, so I applied the brakes and got to the front edge, the south end of the bridge. This creature had come out into the middle of my lane and then I realized it wasn't a deer, for sure. So I hit the brakes, had the brake lights on, it froze right in the headlights and just stood there, leaning over and looking at us. The eyes were black; they didn't reflect the headlights because my car was kind of low and we weren't that far away, between twenty and thirty feet."

Mary noted that the fur was a reddish brown.

"It had longish hair," added David,

> ...the hair came down off the head and formed almost a little mini-cape, you could see where the hair all ended. Like an orangutan, the hair kind of goes all into it, this was a little bit shorter by the head so you could see where the head actually was.
>
> It had long arms, the arms were down below the waist, he was leaning over a little, stayed there for a couple of seconds and took two to three steps. When it got to the guardrail on the other side, it jumped over but it put its hand, its right hand...I'm gonna call it a hand because there were fingers and a thumb, it looked like a hand, it wasn't a paw or claw or anything...and put it on the edge of the guardrail and both feet went over to the left, just hurdled and went over the bridge. No tail.
>
> Then we sat there like, what was that? It was too big. It didn't really scare me, there was nothing threatening about it, just looked with a little curiosity like it was thinking 'Ok, he's not going to bother me,' and it took off. It wasn't in any hurry.

Author's interpretation of the Honey Creek Bridge Jumper.

The creature made eye contact with him through the windshield glass, David said.

From his description and the drawing David made at my request, it was obvious this was no Manwolf but a definite Bigfoot. The size, the "capelike" cowl of hair coming down to rest on the shoulders, the apelike face, lack of pointed ears, all look exactly like a typical Sasquatch. Honey Creek is only about twenty-five miles southeast of Hebron, with a nice swath of Kettle Moraine State Forest in between. It's possible this was even the same individual Andy Hurd saw lurking in his family's barn.

Mary noted that their timing was very lucky. "If we'd come even thirty seconds later it wouldn't have been there," she said. "The creek bed is wet, and the drop is a minimum of fifteen to twenty feet. A human couldn't make that. I have photographs of the creek where it jumped off."

Once the animal landed on the creek bottom, it headed west, going upstream in the creek, said David. "We were in the car with the windows closed so didn't notice an odor. The hair on the feet went all the way to the ground and as it went over, I didn't get that good of a look at the bottom of the feet, I was still looking at the main body. When the hand went on the guardrail, that kind of fascinated me because I wouldn't have thought it would jump over the edge and keep going, it was like it had done this before. It lowered itself like you would do if you were jumping a fence and lowered yourself to stabilize yourself. There was something about it I didn't want to go look at."

"What's funny about the experience, is that Dave and I communicate effectively and speak our minds, but we came home that night and never discussed it at all. We didn't even talk about it a day later, a week later, a month later, until we moved away nine years later," Mary said. David said they did mention it briefly right after it happened, "but then we never said another word. I'm a hunter and trapper and was in Vietnam, but I didn't want to go after this animal."

The couple had two sons at home at the time and said they never told them about the creature or brought it up. "But the boys said they always felt there was something out there at night when they would come home," said Mary. "Michael said some nights he would run from the car to the house because he'd have a feeling, other nights nothing. Our pet would have the same thing, sometimes he would go out at night and only make it to the blacktop and turn around."

Around that same time, the house the Pagliaronis lived in seemed to be haunted by the spirit of a former owner, David and Mary told me. That story was featured in *Weird Wisconsin: Your Travel Guide to Wisconsin's Local Legends and Best Kept Secrets*, because they discovered when they moved into the house that every closet contained a hidden rosary, scapular, and bottle of holy water. Strange rappings occurred, and the house was filled with a deep sense of oppression. Neither of them was used to this kind of experience, they said, and not only were they forced to cope with some kind of angry entity sharing their living space, they would often hear eerie howls in the woods beyond the marsh behind their home. Living with both ghosts and a Bigfoot proved too much for their family, and they finally moved.

Lima Center Quadruped: "I don't know what it was; I just know what it wasn't."

Getting back to doglike things, someone spotted another quadruped of possible interest in the nineties, similar in some but not all ways to the wolflike creature Andy Hurd and his mother saw. Less than a year after Hurd's sighting, in January or February 1994, Richard Fanning was snowmobiling about a mile from his Lima Center house in Rock County, about ten miles southwest of Hebron, and had just pulled out of a woodsy area when he caught sight of something he'd never before seen on his land.

"It was big, from the size I saw it had to be at least 150 pounds or better," said Fanning. "It was the closest thing to a wolf I've seen in this area. It was a blackish color, had a lot of hair on it. I know one thing; when it seen me, it was gone. It only had twenty yards to go to get into the woods. I've had big dogs, it wasn't a Labrador, it was more like a wolf. It was not a dog. But honest to God, it was like it seen me and didn't want to be seen. It was something I've never seen before and never seen since. It was too long and low down for a bear. When it broke for the woods it moved with incredible speed. I don't know what it was, I just know what it wasn't."

Again, this happened in the daytime, around two in the afternoon according to Fanning. He described the exact location as a quarter mile west of Shopiere Road, and one half mile north of County Highway A. "It stood out against the snow," Fanning remarked. "It was real dark, big and long. It looked longer than a wolf. It wasn't long-legged, it was low to the ground and longer than a dog would be. It was a matter of seconds. Most animals will stop and judge you, but this thing didn't care what I was, it just didn't want to be seen. It was definitely not a black cougar. The hair I saw on that animal was more bulky and long. There was a fence there or I would have gone down and looked at the tracks. I can distinguish tracks of a dog, coyote or wolf.

"Before that, I'd heard howling at night sometimes that sounded like something between a wolf howl and a loon. Ten years ago in the summer in the neighbors' woods to the east of me one night, I heard this animal. I heard it more than once. When I first heard it, it was almost like a high-pitched scream that turned into a sort of laughing sound. I went out to the side of the hill with a flashlight and it quit making the noise. Then I heard it again and it sounded like it had closed the distance on me. It was an eerie sound, like it could see me and was making the noise toward me to let me know that."

Lima Center is geographically varied. It's an old Scotch-Irish settlement, and I know a little bit about it because my husband's family is from the area, with Godfrey Road named after his great-grandparents. The church, town hall, and a few blocks worth of frame homes lie about seven miles north of County Highway A, between Whitewater and Milton, along a huge, preserved wetland called the Lima Marsh. The marshy Storr's Lake area is situated just to Lima Center's west, creating a well-irrigated tract of land.

Again, it's perfect territory for a Bigfoot or other Unbelievable to pad around in without too much chance of encountering humans, and one can also imagine wolves or large hybrids making a satisfactory living here. The creature Fanning saw sounds much like a wolf (older males can reach 150 pounds) except for the legs. Wolves have comparatively longer legs than dogs; it's one helpful way to distinguish between the two from a distance. Of course, a wolf hybrid could inherit the shorter dog legs of his canine ancestor. It's possible this is what Fanning saw. The "incredible speed," however, does give one pause.

I would eventually learn of another sighting that happened eleven years later in this same territory, a bipedal creature road-walker, but I'll save that for later (Chapter 10). But as is often the case with locations where monsters have been seen, the tiny community of Lima Center cossets a few shocking secrets in its history. Coincidentally, witness Richard Fanning happens to know about two of them firsthand.

Fanning, a lifelong Lima resident, was a young teen living on his family's farm in March of 1950, the year of the Lima Axe Murders. Two elderly, reclusive brothers, nicknamed Long John and Little Pat Fanning, were brutally murdered with an axe by their nephew, Jack Chesney, who was angered that his uncles refused to give him money to buy a car. The brothers were also the uncles of Richard Fanning's father. A bakery truck driver discovered the bodies several days after the killings, still lying where they had fallen. Fanning remembers hearing that the barnyard chickens were pecking at their brains.

Students of unexplained phenomena have often posited that horrendous events like this may leave a malign psychic imprint in the vicinity, one that may still reverberate in the nearby marshy farmlands. Imprints may linger that could manifest as ghosts or strange creatures. Others would argue there is no way to prove these occurrences are related. But at the very least, the congruence of Big Furries and horrific murder make one wonder why little Lima Center should be so unlucky.

The second incident was not so gruesome, thankfully, but not quite so clear cut (no pun intended), either. Fanning told me that sometime in the 1980s, about ten years before his sighting and the strange howlings occurred, he believed that he saw three UFOs in the sky over his farm. "I've got an old VHS tape," he said, "it was around Easter or Good Friday in the southeast sky, when I saw three little lights booking around in the sky. I taped them for ten minutes. Whatever they were, they weren't aircraft."

People have often asked me if I've noted any correlation between Beast sighting areas and UFO reports, and I have to say that this is one of the few times I've been able to do so, however tentatively. There are as many UFO/Bigfoot theories as there are Web sites on the topic. Most theorize that UFOs are bringing strange bipedal creatures to our fields and forests, or that the Furries are alien/human hybrid experiments gone awry, or the creatures are interdimensional beings acting as exploratory agents but didn't get their Earth costumes quite right.

John Keel, in his book, *Guide to Mysterious Beings*, says, "The whole UFO/monster phenomenon is like a nest of Chinese boxes. Open one and you find another inside." Keel, reviewing the motley crew of monster types seen around the world, asks, "Who or what are all these assorted spacemen, monsters, beasts and bogeymen? It does look as if some of them—perhaps all of them—hitch rides aboard flying saucers. If so, do they all come from a single place, or are we being invaded by a hundred different groups from a hundred different unknown places?" Keel also cites the incident in Durango, Colorado, where, in 1960, footprints of both giants and tiny humanoids were found together at the site of a UFO touchdown.

It should be noted that not everyone who subscribes to the UFO/monster connection believes the UFOs are coming from outer space. Many believe they are from "inner space," or hollow places inside the earth, and others think the UFOs and monsters are all from some other dimension.

Again, we'll cover a few of those other theories of incident-connectedness later. But there were a few other bizarre encounters of the nineties that I need to mention in this chapter.

Kettle Canid

Ed Mallonen, a Milwaukee man who has a bachelor's degree from the University of Wisconsin and works in the marketing field, lived in the Whitewater area of Walworth County for several years after he graduated. Mallonen wrote me of an experience he had at this time in his life, which happened in January or February 1994.

It was a Friday evening and already dark out, he said, when he made a trip from his Whitewater apartment to the home of his parents in New Berlin. "I was heading east on Highway 59 about halfway between Eagle and North Prairie," he wrote. "I was coming up a hill which crested with a slow curve."

This location, I must point out, is right on the eastern edge of the Kettle Moraine State Forest, Southern Unit. Numerous small lakes dot the surrounding, wooded environment, with a creek from Blue Spring Lake branching right up to that exact point where Mallonen found himself catching something unusual in his headlights. "Ahead in my brights," he wrote, "I could see the reflection of two yellowish eyes on the passenger side of the road. I slowed a bit, but when the eyes didn't move further from the road, I slowed considerably. There was what appeared to be a very large dog with gray/light brown fur, standing on all fours, watching me approach.

"The best way I could describe it was maybe some sort of over-grown coyote with pointy ears and a barrel chest. I must have slowed to about ten to twenty miles an hour. I got to within twenty to thirty feet of the animal when it spun to its right, away from the road. As it turned, it reared up on its hind legs and ran south into the field!

"As I slowly passed the point where it had been standing, I turned to watch it run on its hind legs with an awkward or odd-looking gait into the field. It wasn't clumsy or anything. It just seemed awkward. I was not going to come to a full stop because the whole thing spooked me a bit. But I was now creeping at five to ten miles an hour until it got out of view. I watched it run upright for a full ten to fifteen seconds. It never stopped or turned around."

This was a very significant sighting, I believe, because it's one of the few incidents where a witness was able to observe what is clearly a Manwolf changing from quadruped to biped while escaping. An earlier example was the late-eighties sighting by Heather Bowey, Russell Gest, and other children on Bowers Road, when they encountered what appeared to be a large dog on all fours which rose up and chased them on its two hind legs. These sightings rule out the theory that this creature is merely some type of natural animal that has been forced to walk upright for some reason because its forelimbs are too injured or deformed to use (Chapter 21). It appears this creature is equally comfortable on two legs or four and occasionally prefers to use two legs in escape mode.

Mallonen's description also makes it clear this was no primate or hominid. What he saw was pure canine. "I don't feel I saw anything remotely human or otherwise unusual in its appearance," he said. "It really just reminded me of a very large dog of mixed breed, very coyote-like in appearance. I wouldn't have thought anything odd about it until it stood up on two legs and ran like that into the field. In fact, when I told others about it at the time I said, 'I saw a coyote run off through a field standing upright on its hind legs.'"

Mallonen says he doesn't think it was a werewolf or supernatural. "At that time I'd heard nothing of the Beast of Bray Road," he added, "but a year or so later as I heard a few of the accounts, the similarity to what I saw was obvious."

Mallonen estimated the creature's height as about thirty inches at the shoulders while on all fours. "My dog weighs 150 pounds and is about two feet at the shoulders," he said, "and this animal was bulkier and taller so I would guess it was in the range of 180–200 pounds." (About the size of a slightly larger-than-average man, similar to most reports.) Mallonen noticed a tail he described as "mid-length," and hairy like a collie's tail. He said it had the same "pronounced snout" as a coyote, along with the "same ears, same bulky chest, shoulders and rear haunches, just huskier."

I sent Mallonen an e-mailed copy of my Indigenous Dogman drawing, and these were his comments comparing his sighting to my drawing:

"The stance, front paws tucked in to the chest, looks very similar. Snout size and shape, ears, tail length are all pretty accurate. The hind legs seemed a bit shorter, especially from the knee to the paw and its torso was more barrel-chested. The shoulders weren't centered at the sides like a man's, but more to the back like a dog's with raised shoulder blades. What I saw looked a bit less "wolflike" and a bit more "doglike." The eyes also look a bit too human. Granted, all I saw of its eyes was a yellow reflection of my headlights, but they were definitely dog's eyes."

I think that's still pretty close, with just minor variations. My drawing, after all, is based on a composite of different witness descriptions. Mallonen's canid still ranks very consistently on the bipedal canid scale. Even the mention of the awkward gait fits well. And it was certainly located in the very heart of Beast territory. But there's one more sighting from this period, two or three years later and about an hour's drive east, heading toward Racine and Lake Michigan. This time, it was two women who couldn't believe their eyes.

All the Beasts were Out...

I was deep into a discussion of *The Poison Widow* with the Racine Page Turners Book Club in late March 2005, when the conversation inevitably turned to werewolves.

The book club members were mostly elementary school teachers, and they were curious about the Bray Road creature as well as Myrtle Schaude, the poison murderer. As we chatted in one of the reading sections of the Barnes & Noble store, everyone comfortably supplied with tea and lattes from the adjacent coffee shop, a fifty-something woman tentatively approached the group and asked the startling question, "Excuse me for barging in, but can anyone here help me protect myself from spirits in my house?"

No one knew quite what to say, so she pushed up her sleeve to reveal her bare forearm. "Look at what they did to me," she announced dramatically. "It's…the mark of the paw!"

Everyone gasped as she displayed an extremely odd scar that ran the length of her forearm, from wrist to elbow. White and obviously healed over, a slim rectangle ran from her inner elbow to near the wrist, where it widened into a pawlike shape with several markings at the end that resembled claws. This, evidently, was why she was interested in hearing about werewolves. The mark was "given" to her by one of the spirits haunting her house, she said, and she had other ones, as well, although she didn't show them.

It was hard to talk with her since we were in the middle of a scheduled meeting, and after a few more comments about "little people" who also inhabited her house, she drifted back to the New Age book section. And then one of the schoolteachers admitted she had had her own encounter with one of those "creatures of the paw," some years ago. "This whole thing has jogged my memory," she told me.

"Heidi, my good friend, was in the car with me when this strange occurrence happened…here is what we remember," said the teacher. "I was glad to know that she remembered this as being a strange occurrence, too…it means I'm not going crazy.

It must have been the summer of 1996 (possibly '97) near the end of June. I was driving Heidi home and we remember this drive so well because we hit a cat and almost a opossum on the way home…I guess all the beasts were out that night.

Anyways, we were on Highway 38 driving west when something ran in front of the car. It was bigger than a fox or wolf but definitely too bulky and hairy to be a deer.

From what I recall, I thought it was on two legs. [She said it was brown in color and "hunched over."]

I don't remember exactly what part of the road we were on, but Heidi thought we were near the church. It was a little bit more woodsy back then, there are more housing developments out there now. It also must have been pretty fast because I was going about 45 miles an hour and it was only about four feet in front of the car. I am amazed I didn't hit it. It ran onto the median and across the road, I couldn't really see where it went and I didn't see it later on my way home.

As is common with witnesses to these creatures, the teacher had managed to blot it from her thoughts for years, since she had no explanation for what occurred. As for the importance of this glimpse compared to the rest of the body of sightings, I rank it fairly high because of the two-legged aspect and the fact that it tends to confirm the Racine/Kenosha area as a well-visited creature habitat. It certainly seems to be the same height and color as most of the other sightings. However, the fact that she was fuzzy on the head shape puts this sighting in that netherworld between Bigfoot and Manwolf.

Given the urban landscape, however, the Manwolf seems a bit more likely. Although Highway 38 is now more developed, even then it was a major corridor between Racine and the southern 'burbs of Milwaukee. It's hard to imagine a Bigfoot, even a smaller species if there is such a thing, navigating such densely populated territory. The Manwolf, perhaps emulating its coyote cousins, doesn't seem to be as bothered by the proximity of civilization, and appears more adept at hiding itself. And if these wolfen forms are indeed something less substantial than fur and bone, their ability to appear and disappear in highly inhabited neighborhoods is even more understandable. Not to mention disturbing.

CHAPTER SEVEN

MISFITS AND THROWBACKS

When I awoke, the dire wolf, six hundred pounds of sin
Was grinning at my window, all I said was "Come on in."
—Robert Hunter of The Grateful Dead, *The Dire Wolf*

A Dire Situation

It was October of 1997, a prime werewolf-spotting month, when Hope Schwartz decided to make the woodsy drive from near Argyle in LaFayette County to Madison to visit her grandmother. And no, she wasn't wearing a red cape or carrying a basket of wine and cake. She had hoped to make the trip before dark, but it was already dusk when she set out from her farmhouse on Biggs Road (which was actually east of Argyle and in Green County).

"It wasn't dark at all but getting gray," she wrote. "There are only two ways to Madison from our farm on Biggs. If you go right, you have to go through Monticello, up through New Glarus and Verona. If you go left (taking county roads A to J to JG to G), you go through lots of quiet countryside and winding roads until you approach the Verona area, but you miss the small town traffic...you're lucky to pass a car at all."

Hope chose what she *thought* would be the quiet way.

"About five miles from my house, I saw something horrifying on the side of the road (my side), eating what appeared to be a small deer/road kill. I was only going about forty miles per hour as the roads are quite curvy. I slowed way, way down in shock of what I was viewing. The thing looked up and looked at me as if to say, 'go ahead and drive up, I dare you,'—it never even budged an inch. I had to drive in the opposite lane to pass it.

"It was not a wolf, bear, or anything else I have ever seen. It didn't look like the cartoon drawing on the *Weird Wisconsin* Web site [referring to my 'kneeling roadkill' sketch]. It was hunched over but not like a man squatting. It was on all fours, but the way it was built, I believe it could have stood on its hind legs. It would probably have been five feet five inches to five feet seven if it stood up. It was quite thin, especially through the ribcage area and had lanky (not spindly) legs and forearms. It was grayish brown, short rough matted-looking fur…not heavily furred, hardly any on the back legs. The most fur it had was around what would be the shoulder area. I saw one picture somewhere a long time ago that made me cringe, as it was a drawing of what I saw."

As I was reading Hope's description, up to this point I couldn't help thinking that it was probably a timber wolf that she was looking at, particularly because it was on all fours. Or perhaps a hungry wolf with a bad case of mange that denuded its hind legs. Then I read the rest of her impressions.

"The head was very round," she continued, "and the ears were smallish and flat, positioned half way where a human's would be and half way where a dog's would be, kind of in the middle of the two. The eyes were round, amber-colored, and very human like (!?!). The muzzle from what I could tell (it was covered in blood) was very short, but my gosh, it was all teeth. Two definite eye teeth/fangs which were large in comparison to the rest of it.

"The darn thing never moved, but glared at me in the most haunting way. I can still see its gaze, and needless to say, came home that night white as a ghost. I went the other way home."

Schwarz is now in her late thirties and teaches school in Florida. She says she will never return to Argyle again.

The name of that town always makes me think of the plaid socks worn by the lead character in the movie *Ferris Bueller's Day Off*. However, I don't know if anyone actually wears Argyle socks in this village set in the rolling hill country about one third of the distance between the Minnesota and Lake Michigan borders. The Pecatonica River splashes right through the village itself, and eight miles northwest lies the 850-acre Yellowstone Lake State Park, which, in turn, is adjacent to a 3,700-acre state wildlife area. Just over the line into Green County, where Hope's sighting occurred, she would have been driving north past such lonely country lanes as Yankee Hollow and Sawmill Roads, with a loop of the Pecatonica just a few miles to the west. Mineral Point, the site of the strange eighties werewolf that appeared and then vanished, is only about twenty miles to the northwest.

Argyle is also mentioned in Jay Rath's *TheW-Files: True Reports of Wisconsin's Unexplained Phenomena.* In the UFO section, no less. The tale is a bit musty, having happened in April of 1964, but its location is significant. A family was driving west from Monticello along County Road C toward Argyle when some strange lights appeared above them. Now, Hope's former farm was located on Biggs Road. Biggs Road is a short lane connecting County Road A and...you guessed it...County Road C. The red lights the family saw overhead were so close they believed it was a plane about to crash down upon them, so they stopped the car and turned off the headlights. They cowered in their vehicle while the "object" bearing the red lights lowered itself to the level of their car and hovered about a hundred yards away. It finally floated on behind them. The family tried to chase it in their car but couldn't catch up, and finally reported it to the Air Force, which investigated and officially listed the lighted object as "unknown," according to Rath.

Another chronicler of Wisconsin strangeness, Dennis Boyer, tells of a haunted schoolhouse just north of Argyle off Highway 78 in *Drift-less Spirits.*

Finally, effigy mounds were recorded along the Pecatonica by Increase Lapham in his *Antiquities of Wisconsin,* about twenty miles south of Argyle but certainly within a reasonable range. Most are of a strange, slim, oblong shape but one has a long, pointed tail, almost like a water spirit without appendages, aimed in the direction of the river.

Water, state-park land, effigy mounds, a haunted schoolhouse, and a major UFO sighting within a twenty-mile radius...the terrain is completely typical for our Big Furry. Hope Schwartz's sighting is not. She describes a short muzzle, for one thing, compared to most people's observations of a long snout. "Her" creature also seems a little smaller and thinner than most others, and the round head with smaller ears "halfway between where a dog's and a human's would be" sounds most unusual. The "humanlike, amber eyes" were what really stopped me, however. While amber is sometimes used to describe a golden hue, which is not far off from the typical report of the yellow-eyed glare, I get a rather different mental image of this creature's head, which almost sounds like certain large dog breeds. The broad head also reminds me, especially with the fangs, of a supposedly extinct animal called the dire wolf.

Dire Wolves in Wisconsin?

As you'll remember, in Chapter 3 we looked at a prehistoric creature called *Amphicyon,* which was more bear than wolf. But another animal, which lived a bit later during the Pleistocene era, or Ice Age, was much more wolf than bear. *Canis Dirus,* or the dire wolf, was found all over the North American continent, and the first skeletal remains were found in Evansville, Indiana…squarely in the Midwest. It was a bit larger than today's timber wolf, with shorter, squattier legs. It also had a broader, rounder skull, and some have guessed from skull reconstructions that its ears were smaller.

Author's sketch of the dire wolf.

Also, remember Hope's remark, "my gosh, it was all teeth"? Here is a quote from the *Natural Worlds* Web site about the dire wolf: "The dire wolf was somewhat more robust than the modern gray wolf (*Canis lupus*). When the skulls of the two species are placed side by side, the difference becomes readily apparent. One of the most noticeable distinctions is in the size of the teeth. Those of the dire wolf are altogether more massive than those of the gray wolf." Like its *Amphicyon* cousin, the dire wolf could probably use those impressive fangs in ways we might fear to think about too deeply.

The animal weighed 110 to 175 pounds, and could grow to be five feet long. It has only been (supposedly) extinct for a few thousand years…a mere drop in the bucket in paleontological terms. It isn't so hard to imagine that some could have survived, given their widespread distribution. I wonder if Hope Schwartz actually spotted a leftover dire wolf? There was nothing otherworldly sounding about what she saw, after all.

And while the dire wolf paradigm won't explain most of the other sightings, since its appearance is so different and because its vertically challenged legs make it hard to imagine it walking upright, keep the jaw-buster in mind as you read the next sighting.

Heads Too Huge for Bodies, Teeth Too Huge for Heads

The next witness happens to be the sister-in-law of Kim Del Rio, whose story about seeing an upright doglike creature as a child in the city of Milwaukee was recounted in *The Beast of Bray Road*. Del Rio's sister-in-law, Marisol, experienced a brush with weird fur in Madison in the early nineties.

Most of the creature witnesses I've interviewed so far have no relation to each other, other than married couples or siblings who happened to both see a creature at the same time. But as so often happens, it was Kim's telling of her own sighting that prompted Marisol to reveal hers. Many times, people "put away" memories that are disturbing or unexplainable, and need only have someone else recount something similar to bring it all flooding back. Or to make them feel they have permission to tell.

It was Christmas in 2003, said Kim, and she was spending a pleasant day with her husband's family after exchanging presents. For some reason, she began telling Marisol about the upright canid she had seen as a young girl in her Milwaukee neighborhood. But before she could finish, Marisol was excitedly interrupting her, saying she had seen the same thing in Madison in 1993 or 1994.

At the time, said Marisol, she lived on a cul-de-sac about a ten-minute drive southeast from the Square, which is the heart of downtown Madison. That places her in a very well-populated area.

As Marisol watched television late one night, at about 11:00 PM, she was startled to hear something banging and moving her garbage cans outside. When she went to look out the window, there were what she described as "two enormous animals" sniffing and poking at the cans, which had been pushed to the curb for pickup the next morning. The cans and animals were directly under a streetlight, so she was able to see them plainly. Marisol described them "as huge, much bigger than any dog she had ever seen before," and "German-shepherd-shaped ears." What startled her the most, said Kim was the animals' heads, which appeared far too big for the rest of their bodies.

"They had a real long muscular body with weirdly small-sized feet, too small-looking," she said. The animals were covered with light gray fur. Their canine teeth were especially impressive, appearing larger than any she had ever seen in any other animal, "too big looking for the mouth."

Marisol also described the snouts as longer than a normal wolf or dog, an estimated eighteen inches long, and "square-ended" with black noses, and the heads as "huge and flat" with pointed ears situated on top of the animals' heads. She puzzled over whether they might be wolves but decided the heads and snouts were not the right shape for a wolf. She stated that she had seen many coyotes and knew that these were not coyotes, either. She also told Kim that they were definitely not wolves, and that their heads were not "doglike" enough for the animals to have been mixed-breed canines. She was able to observe them for about five minutes until an approaching vehicle scared them away.

"So," said Kim, "ruling out dogs, wolves, coyotes, what else is there? This is a very level-headed lady who doesn't drink, do drugs, works a full-time job, has a kid and a happy marriage. Not a nut looking for attention. I believe her one hundred percent."

The description of the animals, the fact that there were two of them and that they were on four legs, not standing, reminds me most vividly of the pair sighted by Rick Renzulli just west of Kenosha. Kenosha is a fair distance from Madison, however, about one hundred miles (with Walworth County smack between them, however). And Renzulli's sighting was a good ten years earlier than Marisol's.

If these were natural animals, it's doubtful Renzulli and Marisol could have seen the same individuals. These unusual beasts almost sound like a different canid species altogether, perhaps not related to the Beast of Bray Road at all. Rottweiler hybrids would be one possibility. And one big difference between the two sightings was that Marisol did not feel these creatures were malign. Of course, that may have been partly because she was able to view them from the safety of her own house.

Leaving this natural world, the pair seen by both Marisol and Renzulli are reminiscent of "hellhounds," large dogs of a supernatural nature found in many cultures, usually charged with guarding the "Underworld," or place where souls went after death. Alby Stone points out, in an article called "Hellhounds, Werewolves and the Germanic Underworld," that one old Scandinavian poem tells of two dogs who guarded an otherworldly place rimmed with fire. One line of the poem reads, "They are strong watchdogs, and they keep watch until the doom of the gods."

Alby speculates that caninelike beings are associated with realms of the dead due to their habits of scavenging corpses. If the reader will recall, Marisol's beasts were caught in the very act of scavenging refuse, and Renzulli's were seen running near a graveyard.

And yet, other than their outrageous appearance and size, neither pair displayed any definitive supernormal qualities. No glowing red eyes, for instance, which are often associated with reports of hellhounds. Other than their long snouts, they sound remarkably like dire wolves. Yet, whatever they were, they still must be tucked into the "super-sized, unidentifiable canine" file and counted among the reported incidents.

There is also some precedent for this type of sighting in our northern counties, beyond bear-wolf territory, up in Spooner in the northwest section of the state. On August 24, 1989, the *Wisconsin State Journal* ran an article that proclaimed, "Mysterious Canines Prowl North Woods." A pack of some type of large, unidentifiable canines, ranging from black to gray in color, had been spotted by farmer Walt Olsen in late May of that year. Olsen took them for wolves, although they didn't act like wolves in that they were not afraid to be seen in the fields as he worked.

Around mid-summer, something started killing and eating sheep at the Spooner Agricultural Research Station. Department of Natural Resources personnel were finally persuaded to set a trap after eight sheep had been discovered partially eaten, having been taken down by their throats. While the agent was still in the trap vicinity, one of the marauding animals came casually striding out of the woods and the agent shot it. The newspaper quoted the superintendent of the research station, Bob Rand, as saying, "It was a tall, powerful animal with big feet and an awful set of teeth on it.… Really long front teeth. You wouldn't expect those teeth on a dog."

True, but you might expect them on a dire wolf.

"It wasn't like any dog I'd ever seen," Rand continued, "and it was big for a coyote. It weighed 266 pounds. They say the biggest coyotes are 40 pounds."

That weight, 266 pounds, is more than huge. The largest timber wolves only go about 150. We are talking prehistoric sizes, weights that compare to the ancient *Amphicyon* or bear-dog. Except…we aren't, really.

A little fact-checking undid the *State Journal* story. I called Bob Rand, who has since retired from the agricultural facility but still remembers the incident very well. The dog weighed sixty-two pounds, he said. "You know how some stories get inflated?" he said in a phone interview. "The further south that one went, the bigger the animal got." He is sure that he shot the true sheep killer, though, because the depredations ceased immediately. Still, authorities weren't sure what the killer was, precisely.

Another story, published years later in the *Spooner Herald*, revealed that even with two specimens to analyze and necropsy, no one was willing to state categorically what the animal was. The first reports alluded to a wolf-dog hybrid, but that label turned out to be politically sensitive. It seems that the program to reintroduce timber wolves into the area was none too popular with local farmers, and the revelation that wolves might be combining with feral dogs to create a new mix of super sheep assassins was considered too risky to the program's reputation. (This also happened in the township of Kennan, Price County, in early 2005 when a number of feral wolf-dog hybrids had to be shot to stop livestock pilferage, as reported in the *Phillips Bee*.) The mix was soon redeclared a coyote/dog mix and then demoted to "hybrid dog." Rand says whatever it was, it was strange. "It was sort of square-jowled," he said. "The fur was about the length of a terrier, and smooth. And it ran in strides, like a wolf, smoothly. Dogs run with a jerkier motion." He had no explanation for the long teeth, either.

At least, with specimens being shot, autopsied, and even preserved as evidence, there is no question whether this creature belonged in the realm of living animals. It was all too real. Whether it fits in the Man-wolf category of sightings is questionable. It was large, but not monstrously so. It was never seen walking upright or behaving in any way other than a wild dog or other canid might act. I'd probably have to give it a thumbs down. Dire wolf? Doubtful, since it was examined by expert biologists. But it's still an incident to take note of, if only for the odd appearance and ferocious behavior of the animal.

But speaking of hard-to-categorize sightings, another really strange, smooth-furred "thing" was encountered a year later near the center of the state, just outside of Oshkosh. Almost as if to defy my meager classification system for counting sightings "in" or "out" of the Beast lore, this one has required me to chuck it into a new folder, the *mini*-unidentifiable canine file....

Half-Pint Trail Mixer

This mysterious sighting, shoved over my e-mail transom, came from a man who prefers to be known simply as Mike. A correctional facility worker from the Oshkosh area, Mike saw *The Beast of Bray Road* and was instantly reminded of a creature he observed between May and June 1990, as a fifteen-year-old bike trail rider.

"Myself and a friend of mine routinely rode our bicycles to Winneconne (a village of about 1,600)," wrote Mike, "from Oshkosh, Wisconsin. In doing so, we took what is known as the "Larsen Trail" from northern Oshkosh and rode straight through to Highway G/116, which we would take to Winneconne."

This State Natural Area is part of the Wiowash State Trail, Winnebago County, and covers 32.7 acres. Bikers pedal over crushed limestone, through old prairie remnants along a former railroad right-of-way, to pass through marshy areas and thickly wooded forest clumps brimming with deer and turkey. The trail also follows a variety of waterways including Lake Butte des Mortes, which, interestingly, is fed by the Fox and Wolf Rivers, probably named for those animals by early settlers to indicate canid dominance of the landscape. But altogether, the whole place comprises a perfect habitat for any number of Unbelievables.

That day, Mike and his friend heard a rustling from a nearby field almost as soon as their bike wheels began to crunch the trailbed. "As I turned," wrote Mike, "I seen a creature. For a split second, I remember thinking it was a raccoon, but I quickly noticed that *the knees on the hind legs were bent inward and it was running on the hind two feet with the front 'arms' held out in front of its body* (emphasis mine).

"The creature was maybe three and a half feet standing, had what I would describe as slicked-back dark hair, a snout like a black Lab, only more narrow, eyes that seemed to glow…and was fast. Man, was it fast. It chased my friend past the trail we normally would take (I stayed back and to the right of this thing) and past one of the only houses on that stretch. As we were passing the house, their dog started barking from the yard and the creature slipped back into the field on the other side of the road. We decided to take old Highway 110 home that night. We were scared as hell, but yet kind of laughing from the adrenaline as we discussed what it was. We ended up leaving it as 'must have been some kind of coon, skunk or something.'"

But that would not be the teens' last encounter with the pygmy wolfman. On July 3 of that year, the boys had decided to attend Winneconne's annual "Sovereign State Festival," derived from the year the little town was literally left off the state map and therefore declared itself to have seceded from the Union. "Taking the same route back as previous," continued Mike, "we again encountered this oddity. Only this time, we were actually on the trail, about a mile in as I remember. This time it came from the brush and bush alongside the trail, ran up maybe twenty feet and back to the same side it came from. It seemed to have grabbed some small dead animal from the middle of the trail before darting back into the brush."

Mike and his friend told their amazing tale to some of their buddies over the years, always to be met with ridicule. Mike remains unfazed. "I assure you, something makes the Larsen Trail its home," he wrote.

I did question Mike further, and he added the following information. The ears, he said, were pointed like a boxer's, only "a bit wider." He also said they were pointed straight up as the creature chased his friend, and laid back when it retreated. He added that the illustration I made of the creature was "so

The Half-Pint Trail Mixer, author's interpretation.

close, it was scary." On reflection, Mike also noted that though it hadn't occurred to him before, he suddenly realized that he never had the urge to take those trails again after his sightings. "I don't think I was intentionally avoiding them," he said, "but looking at it all now, I do find it odd."

Other than the size, many factors do fit the Manwolf profile...the upright running position, great speed, canine snout, pointed ears on top of the head, scavenging of small roadkill, and the teasing chase followed by a fast disappearance into the bush. The "slicked-back hair" is in some contrast to the usual description of wild, unkempt fur, and of course the height, about half the usual reported size, is the biggest bugaboo. There are several possible explanations for that variation, however.

The first, of course, is that this was a juvenile. If we are talking about a natural animal there must be a breeding population, and that means young ones. The playful chase interaction would suggest a younger animal. This might be the most plausible idea.

The second would be that this is a smaller species or genetic variation of the Manwolf, which is also possible since humans and other species can appear in pygmy or dwarf form. It would probably be a favorable adaptation for surviving in populated areas, as a three-and-a-half-foot creature is much less likely to be spotted than one standing twice that height.

Of course, if the creature is a supernatural being, then this is one case where size really doesn't matter. A phantom can appear any height it wishes. And the fact that it showed itself twice to these same two people does lend an eerie air to the stories. We could speculate that some kind of unexpected, etheric connection was established between the boys and this creature that allowed it to somehow "home in" on them when they returned to the area, but then, we could speculate on many things; it could have been mere coincidence. The double sighting does seem to rule out the possibility that they misidentified some other, mundane animal. That's easy to do upon one brief glimpse of something; however, they had not only one good long look, but two.

At any rate, the mental image of this beaver-sized canid hoofing it around the woods and marshes of the Larsen Trail, "arms" held out in front of it like some crazy, dark-furred Speedy Gonzales, is one of the most amusing I've encountered so far, and remains one of my favorites. It's slightly reminiscent of the Clark County hunter I told about in *The Beast of Bray Road* who also encountered what appeared to be a juvenile-sized creature and was too unnerved to shoot. But that sighting was second-hand, and I was never able to confirm it. This one came straight from the horse's, or rather bike-rider's, mouth, and included a second witness as well. It wins hands-down in the pint-sized werewolf category. And I'd bet my bottom silver dollar that other people also saw it but never told anyone or were ridiculed into silence. The question is, does the little fella still pound the Larsen Trail as a half-pint, or has he now grown into a full-size trail mixer?

Before I leave the subject, however, there are just a couple of other possibilities I should mention for origins of unknown creatures of this size. The first one I thought of was "Littlefoot," which, as you might guess, refers to a mini-Bigfoot. A writer known as Valenya who contributes to *FATE Magazine* wrote in the November 2004 issue that the Littlefoot, as seen in Northern California, anyway, "resembles a small, slender Bigfoot, about the size and form of a ten-year-old human child." That sounds a little taller, perhaps, than what Mike saw, and not canid at all. Valenya, who lives in the mountains of Northern California not far from Bluff Creek, where the famous and disputed Patterson video was made, cites a waitress in a nearby town, a long-time resident, as her source.

The striking similarity to Half-pint, however, lies in the Littlefoot's behavior. "Unlike the shy Bigfoot," says Valenya, "the Littlefoot delights in being observed by humans. It likes to tease them into chasing it, thinking they can catch it. Then it leads them into the deepest, thickest woods and gets them totally lost before sneaking away." That description sounds very much like the legendary "Willo-the-wisp," or marsh lights, which also have it in for gullible travelers.

It also sounds exactly like what the half-pint trail mixer was trying to do on its first encounter with the trail riders. In fact, I chose the word "mixer" partly because it seemed the creature was trying to mix things up a bit, messing with the riders and trying to tease them as it zipped around (also partly because of the pun on that nourishing snack, trail mix, I admit). But the creature described by Mike and confirmed by my illustration is decidedly un-Bigfootlike. Perhaps juveniles of both species are playful. Or could it be, flipping to the Twilight Zone again, an example of a trickster spirit?

Native American legends are rife with tricksters, as are almost all bodies of folklore around the world. Tricksters always play exactly that role of "mixing things up," leading humans astray or turning their conceptions of the world about them upside down. They are very often portrayed as canids, and especially, in Native American culture, as coyotes. For instance, the Winnebago or Ho-Chunk trickster, Wakd-junkaga, can appear as a hare, raven, spider, or coyote. It's not hard to see some coyote traits in the Half-pint, although coyotes do not run on their hind legs and are generally a bit larger than this creature. Coyotes also do not, as a rule, chase after humans. Most people find them quite easy to recognize as a species, too.

Finally, the Shoshone of California and Nevada have a tradition of "Water Baby Spirits," which leave tiny footprints and appear as small people, often dressed in tribal gear. In their petroglyph portraits, they look like cartoon ghosts. In Paul Devereaux's *Haunted Land*, they are described as "dream helpers" of the shamans, and to see one is considered good fortune, indeed. But they are humanlike, not part animal. The only thing they would seem to have in common with "Half-pint" is size.

I do think it worth noting that these non-conforming creatures are all found a bit outside the Manwolf's usual turf. It may turn out that they either have mundane explanations, particularly the quadrupeds, or that they are not connected with the Manwolf at all. But since we are veering off-course a little, I'm going to cross the state line to examine a creature that does fit the Manwolf mold in appearance, but brings forth all manner of other associations. And while I wish that I could dictate the terms of these creature sightings so that they would fit more neatly into their assigned cubbyholes, it's apparent the creatures are calling the shots.

CHAPTER EIGHT

THE GREAT LAKES ANUBIS-HEADED SKINWALKER

"Reality is a mass hallucination."
— Howard Bloom, *The Global Brain, Evolution of the
Mass Mind from the Big Bang to the 21st Century*

A Navajo Werewolf in Chicago

Just when I think I've heard every possible version of the big hairy creature sighting, someone will tell me about an experience that makes me stop and wonder all over again how well we really know this planet. The story I'm about to pass on really stands alone in the lore I've collected, so I decided to bless it with its very own chapter. It touches on a different realm than we have discussed so far and occurred in one of the last places anyone would expect such an event.

The strangeness began just over the border from the southeast corner of Wisconsin, following Lake Michigan's shore southward to the Great Lakes Naval Training Center in North Chicago, Illinois. Despite its proximity to Chicago, the base is not in a totally urban area. Part of this military compound is the Great Lakes Naval Hospital, which occupies an enviable location separated from Lake Michigan by only one city block and a few military housing units. Swaths of green, including Illinois State Beach Park, line much of the Michigan shore between the Wisconsin border and the Naval Hospital. The parks and the beaches of both states provide adequate cover for a wily creature of the night to slink around in. And even if this creature possesses the high level of intelligence its actions indicate, it's doubtful that it knows or cares about state boundary lines. As seen earlier, we have sightings documented in Kenosha, and North Chicago is only about twelve miles to the south of that city. Therefore, I'm placing it here rather than blending it in with the other Illinois sightings where it arguably belongs.

Even knowing there have been other sightings in the "flatlands," it was surprising to receive this letter from a former member of the U.S. Navy who came across something quite unexpected while patrolling the Naval Hospital grounds one early autumn night. I will let her tell her own story, noting that the cemetery she refers to is the old Naval Hospital Graveyard.

September of 1994, I was stationed at Naval Hospital Great Lakes in Illinois. Myself and two others, (one was my husband, Jon, then just dating) were assigned to shore patrol, which basically consisted of carrying a flash light and a radio and busting recruits necking in the woods. We used to scare each other on duty by leaving a radio at the cemetery on base, making weird noises, etc. But one night, it was very different.

This has bothered me for some time, and after reading your interview (about other encounters), I have to say, I don't feel nearly as nuts about it now. I was walking the wood path by the lake. Jon, my husband, was on the other side of the breakers. Jim, the other watch, was somewhere near the hospital. I radioed to Jon, goofing around, making smart aleck comments. No response. I figured he was trying to scare me, as we had all been bantering back and forth all night (it was about 3:00 AM).

I walked the path to the other side of the breakers, and Jon was just standing there, staring at the woods. I called to him, no response. He was shaking. My husband is a six-foot-three, strapping Navajo, not much for being fearful of anything. I walked up behind him, and touched him. I shined the light at him. He was staring open-mouthed at the woods.

Now, having been raised in the Jersey Pines, I figured it may have been a little black bear or raccoon he was seeing. I called him a rude word, (as fellow shipmates often do) and shined my Maglite to the woods. I will never forget what I saw. It was tall. How tall, I am not a good judge of, but it was taller than Jon.

It had an odd head. It looked like something from the cartoon *Mummies Alive!* Later I found out the character's name it resembled was Anubis. Like a big man, with a dog-like head. I have tried to rationalize what we saw. It was not a bear, as so many people try to tell me, as I have encountered them many times before. After my shock, I yelled into the radio for Jim to get his ass over here. Jon said, 'Skin-walker, Skinwalker,' about five times. I had never heard of anything like that before, and I was just freaked at what I was seeing.

The 'Thing' didn't seem too upset by us being there. It just stood there, long arms. Couldn't see the hands, big greeny-yellow eyes. It was just weird. We heard Jim coming through the bush, and the thing looked over, puffed up kind of like a cat, and took off, but more upright than on all fours. Jim caught sight of the back end of it.

It took some time to compose Jon, and when we returned to turn the watch over, we logged it in the book. All three of us suffered weeks of harassment over it. After we both ended our enlistment, Jon and I moved to his hometown of Farmington, New Mexico. His grandma enlightened me to what a skinwalker is, even though I am still not sure as to what we saw. Jon has always been adamant though, and swears it was a Skinwalker. Jim, we lost contact with, so I can't say if it still bothers him. As for me, I would just like to know what the hell it was we saw that night, and why the hair on my arms still stands up when I think about it. If this is a similar account to one you may have heard, or if you can provide a rational explanation for what we saw, it would be much appreciated, for this is one event I would really like to explain!!

Thank you for your time,

Emma [last name withheld by request]

The Changing of the Skin

One can hardly imagine what Emma's husband, Jon, must have felt after having been raised on tales of the Navajo Skinwalker in New Mexico, only to come to the Midwest and find himself face-to-face with the object of his childhood fears. You may remember the terrifying Bearwalkers in Chapter 3. Skinwalkers or Skinchangers are a similar phenomenon not only in Native American lore but in ancient European werewolf traditions as well. Of course, one could argue that what the three Naval patrollers saw was some other kind of "real" creature that Jon only *perceived* as a Skinchanger due to his own cultural conditioning, but it certainly fits not only the Native American conception of such an entity, but the standard Manwolf description as well.

It's no wonder that Emma's husband seemed awestruck at the sight of the creature. The *Yenaldlooshi,* Navaho Skinwalkers, embody many fiendish practices in tribal stories. Among these are cannibalism, necrophilia, and using human heads as décor in their communal Skinwalker cave-homes. They are even said to grind infant bones into powder that they use to make their enemies sick, and according to the *Dictionary of Native American Mythology,* also run around naked as the day they were whelped, in total irreverence toward tribal custom. Feared as malevolent witches, the *Yenaldlooshi* are beings that no Navaho in his or her right mind would wish to encounter. In appearance, they are said to look like Coyote, the trickster, and can take the place of a human by throwing a coyote skin over an unwary victim. The usual aim of this ploy is for a *Yenaldlooshi* to land himself in bed with the victim's wife, who innocently believes she is making love with her own husband. Until, the story actually says, she wakes up and smells the coyote urine.

Many outside the tribal tradition of Native Americans assume that the Navajo would not take such a story literally. They often presume wrongly. While there are many layers of meaning to stories such as that of the Skinwalker, it's obvious from Jon's reaction and other anecdotal reports that many do, indeed, believe literal Skinwalkers (shape shifters would be another relevant term) exist and interact within their society. Where most indigenous people's religions are concerned, the lines between the "real world" and the spirit world are not so sharply drawn as they are in mainstream Christianity or modern agnosticism. And yet, contemporary analysts love to put these myth- and ceremony-laden cultural tales into their own, Western-rationalized language.

For instance, in *Werewolves in Western Culture, a Lycanthropy Reader*, the introduction cites an article by Daniel Merkur entitled *The Psychodynamics of the Navajo Coyoteway Ceremonial*. Merkur sees the tribal use of coyote-lycanthropy as a sort of scapegoat on which the people can blame all the horror humanity is wont to enact. It particularly works, in his view, to relieve the supposed guilt of the Navajo over having to hunt and kill animals to eat. The book's commentator adds, "The paradox in lycanthropy is that by projecting into animals what is unacceptable or unfathomable in human conduct, and by assigning human behavioral patterns to animals, human life's darkest moments are exposed. Whether to destruction or repair is difficult to say."

Actually, despite my problem with its rationalization of Native myth, that is a very incisive comment and gropes at the heart of all human–beast transformation stories. No matter what the culture, Native American, African, or Old European, there is something about being able to say, "the animal did it" that can make the rough side of humanity a bit easier to swallow. Perhaps that's one reason were-animals fascinate us.

And yet, Emma, Jon, and Jim were faced not with some psychologist's abstract theory, but with a near-seven-foot, wolf-headed, yellow-eyed, furry biped that appeared to be as "real," or corporeal, as they were in their own human blood-and-tissueness. Two of the three witnesses were not even remotely Navajo. Explain that in terms of "tribal guilt-expiation!"

Which leads us back to the basic question. What was a traditional Navajo entity doing lurking about the wind-swept shores of Lake Michigan? It would seem a bit out of place geographically. But again, the term "Skinwalker" and similar appellations are not unique to the Navajo. The Canadian Cree called such creatures Skinchangers, although wolves, rather than coyotes, were their transformational targets. Ian Woodward, in *The Werewolf Delusion*, also notes that the ancient Romans commonly referred to werewolves as skinchangers, or turncoats, by which they meant a creature that could literally turn its skin or coat from the inside of its body to the outside, in order to change from wolf to man and back. Since we're on this subject, I'm going to digress for a moment to show that this was not an inconsequential assumption in terms of the fates of some human beings.

This Roman legend of the reversible pelt persisted into Medieval Europe and led to the invention of a plethora of ingenuous torture devices designed to discover whether or not a person might have fur on his unfortunate innards and thus be proved a werewolf. If he did, of course, he would be summarily executed for werewolfism—although by the time his guilt (or innocence) was determined, the act of hanging what was left of him would be a mere formality. As Woodward says, "After suspected werewolves had been tortured and tried, always in that order, they were often then quite literally ripped to pieces to expose the wolf hair that was said to be growing on the inside of their skins." The book features an old German print of the devilish instruments used on accused werewolves, which ranged from the sword, stake, and pincers, to elaborate combinations of pulleys, chains, and wheels intended to tear flesh and fracture bone. An incredible amount of human suffering, then, resulted from one small aspect of legend.

The overkill reminds me of the famous line uttered by Biker #4 in the 1985 movie *Pee-wee's Big Adventure* after Pee-wee has accidentally knocked over a row of bikes belonging to a motorcycle gang. "I say we stomp him! Then we tattoo him! Then we hang him! And *then* we kill him!"

Even where the "inside fur" test was not used, the alleged European werewolf was still considered a witch, the same as the Navajo Skinwalker, and therefore liable to any other number of tortures at the hands of sadistic Inquisitors. Often the wolf-change was effected by applying a special salve, and/or performing certain magic rituals and chants. Werewolfism could even be hereditary.

But there are also many Norse and later European traditions that say the change was triggered by wearing a wolfskin or girdle made of wolf fur outside the body, much the same as the Navajo Skinwalker. The remarkable thing is that in both Old and New World Skinwalker traditions, it is usually the hide of the animal that is seen as the transforming agent, and in both places, anthropologists think it was probably inspired by early hunter/shamans actually donning wolfskins or coyote hides to assume the hunting or killing prowess of the animal. The hide, of course, is the most easily removable part of a carcass and, along with the bones, the part that is most preservable. And fur is the most obvious thing we humans lack in comparison to the rest of the mammals. So the idea of a Skinchanger makes sense in many ways basic to the human psyche. If you can change your skin, through witchcraft or by putting on a wolf-fur, you may also change what you are. We get that. But can a human really turn into a Manwolf for all the world to see?

Breathless Anubis

The point of all this is that although Jon saw the creature as the Skin-walker of his New Mexican heritage, that concept was not necessarily out of place in suburban Chicago because there is universal recognition of the were-animal produced by a change of pelt. But regardless of the name the creature goes by, or what we think of its state of reality, we must deal with the fact that many other people like Jon, Emma, and Jim are continually running into something that conforms to this image in southern Wisconsin, the surrounding region, and other states.

That still leaves the question of whether the creature was a mystical being. Despite Jon's conviction that he was seeing a Skinwalker, something not operating in quite the same dimension as the rest of us, Emma was not so sure it was a spirit being she saw staring back like a shined deer in the beam of her flashlight. Although she later would wonder whether it was perhaps a group hallucination, unlikely as that may be, she was positive she had seen something that was physically present. And she did have a good look at it.

"As far as the fur was concerned," she wrote in answer to my further questions, "it looked sharpish, but I really couldn't say definitely about the color, kind of murky gray yellow, if that makes any sense. At the time it happened, it was so startling that I didn't notice too many details other than the weird eyes and the fact that it was so big and had such a funky head! The only other detail I can offer is that it was very cold out, yet I didn't see 'breath' from it, and that it was solid. I got no impression that it was spiritual," she added. "Jon still sticks with his Skinwalker theory and doesn't like to talk about it much."

It was interesting to me that the first thing Emma thought of was the jackal-headed Egyptian god Anubis. (Of course, I could also say that Emma was preconditioned by her own culture to see the creature as something from a cartoon show she had watched.) It's notable that the *Mummies Alive!* character of Anubis very closely resembles the ancient Egyptian renderings of their god of the underworld. The most prominent features of Anubis are probably his long snout and pointed ears, two of the characteristics most often mentioned in Manwolf sightings.

Anubis is also usually shown as black in color because of its association with wizened or burned human skin and death. Most Egyptian statues and paintings, though, depict either an Anubis that is completely jackal, or one that features a priest's body wearing an Anubis mask while carrying out funeral rites, similar to my illustration.

Also noteworthy may be the fact that Emma observed something that looks exactly like the Egyptian guide to and protector of the Underworld on the grounds of a hospital and cemetery. Anubis is often described as the guardian of cemeteries. The reader may recall that Rick Renzulli's Kenosha sighting involved a cemetery, and we will examine another example of a cemetery sighting later on, in Chapter 10. And there are more threads to this grave topic. The first Beast book discussed David Kulzyck's story of Michigan's "witchie wolves," legendary spirit beings charged with defending old Native American burial grounds near Omer. The fearsome creature seen at St. Coletta in 1936 was digging in an old burial mound at the time. And as we've already noted in the first and second chapters, there may be connections between the Manwolf and the state's mysterious effigy mounds, to be explored later. Also, don't forget the hellhounds discussed in Chapter 7. The creature as burial guardian, then, is a tantalizing thought, and fairly prevalent in the sightings data. Anubis, with all his connotations of the Under-world, might be a very apt comparison, after all.

Emma's observation of the yel-lowish eyes is also consistent with most other incidents. And as for the creature's fur, when she says it was "sharpish," I believe she means it was shaggy, not conforming smoothly to the body but standing away from it in pointed strands. Again, very consis-tent. The one other item that jumped out, though, was that she couldn't see its breath. September evenings can get quite chilly at this latitude, and evidently the humans involved could all see their own exhalations fogging the night air. Either this creature had quieted itself so effectively as to be holding its breath, or…it was not a breathing creature at all.

Anubis, ancient Egyptian god of the Underworld.

But wait, some of my readers who peruse the conspiracy-mill pages on the Web with great regular-ity are probably saying at this point. This is a *government* installation, with a huge hospital building and all kinds of *medical and scientific personnel.* Wouldn't Naval Hospital Great Lakes be the perfect spot for the government's *secret inter-species breeding and cloning program?* Might this creature not be an escapee from the standard *secret under-ground medical experimentation facility?* To which I must answer, with all due respect, to what end would our government be trying to cross-breed wolves and humans? Sure, it would be nice to have a wolf's scent capabilities, but the military has plenty of hounds already on duty sniffing out bombs and drugs. And breeding foot soldiers with the ability to bring down caribou would hardly be on any governmental agenda's A-list. (Just a thought, if you did manage to cross U.S. Marines with German shepherds, would their motto be Semper Fido?)

I'm not even going to get into the genetic incompatibility of the two species. Although, I must admit that in a day and age when scientists can grow a human ear on the back of a laboratory mouse, mismatched genes hardly seem the barrier they once did. Strangely, though, I did come across one other sighting connected to a legend of cross-breeding monkeyshines (see next chapter) but found no evidence that it was anything but urban legend.

In my opinion, since it is not typical for the Manwolf to be sighted near military medical facilities (although admittedly the landscape is not dotted with those), its appearance there was probably coincidence and more related to the hospital's proximity to the green corridor I mentioned at the beginning of this chapter. The gathering body of sightings lore indicates that this is a far ranging, exploratory, scavenging creature that is willing and able to exploit any travel and hunting opportunities it may find. It seems almost absurd to think something ensconced in say, Kenosha, would refuse to set foot over the Illinois border. Having ambled unknowingly from Packers turf to Bears territory, it naturally would end up at one of the few open, green spaces still in the suburban Chicago area.

That haven, by the way, has been saved from condominium and McMansion encroachment only because it happens to be a space owned by one of our armed forces. What goes on, or doesn't, inside any of the military buildings in that space is of little consequence to the creature, I'm sure. Even the cemetery connection may be pure coincidence. As teen partiers everywhere know, cemeteries are conveniently isolated places to hang out in at night. And as we will further confirm in the next chapter, this creature seems to be following the example that coyotes, deer, and even bears have set in recent years as paved areas spread and woodlands diminish—adapt to humanity's idea of landscaping, or perish.

CHAPTER NINE

MILLENNIAL MONSTERS, 2000 AD

"Reality appears at the edge between order and chaos. This edge is blurred, not sharply honed, and no one quite knows where to place such a fuzzy boundary."
—Fred Alan Wolf, *The Spiritual Universe:*
How Quantum Physics Proves the Existence of the Soul

It seems kind of silly and overwrought now when we look back on the year 2000 and remember the hysterical predictions that all Hell and Armageddon would break loose when the official New Year's date changed. If you remember, computers and other machines that used microchips were to be clogged suddenly in utter cyber-confusion, and then the world would go blooey at the stroke of midnight. Jail doors would spring open and loose hordes of criminals upon us, elevators would jam on the fiftieth floor, all of our lights and power would wink out, and Chaos personified would roam our streets, devouring children and puppies in the unholy darkness.

Almost none of that happened, of course, but 2000 did mark another upsurge in sightings. And while the specter of Chaos may have been shooed from our mental landscape, Manwolves apparently still felt free to saunter.

Urban, but Not Legend

Brookfield, Wisconsin, is a fast-growing suburb of Milwaukee with one of the busiest stretches of highway in the state. Where Moorland Road ramps on and off the east–west freeway, I-94, with traffic headed to the big nearby mall, downtown Milwaukee, or the vast stretch of retail businesses packed around the intersection with Blue Mound Road, any two- or four-legged creature with a lick of sense would fear to tread. I've always maintained that the Beast has more brains than to be seen someplace like that; it's normally been sighted only in areas where there is some kind of cover handy...cornfields, woods, or just a deep, old-fashioned ditch.

But just off I-94 West in Brookfield is exactly where three young women did see the creature in late December 2000. The only cover that existed in the area at that time was the shield of darkness, and evidently that was enough to make the creature feel safe.

Tiffany S. (last name withheld on request), a nineteen-year-old UW-Milwaukee student majoring in elementary education, was returning from a trip to Milwaukee with her fifteen-year-old sister Erin, who attended New Berlin West High School, and their twelve-year-old cousin, Maddy, a student at Holy Apostles School in New Berlin. They all remember that there was snow on the ground and it was near Christmas, between 8:00 and 9:00 PM. The three had been on a mission to the Wisconsin Humane Society to look for a new puppy for Maddy, but hadn't found a suitable animal and were returning home dogless. Imagine their joy and surprise when, as they exited the expressway on the circular ramp leading to Moorland Road, Maddy exclaimed that she had just seen a stray dog sitting in the snow-covered grass in the middle of the ramp.

"We are all animal lovers and we couldn't just leave the dog alone," explained Tiffany. "What if it was someone's pet? Needless to say, we pulled over about a block away and walked to the area where she saw the dog."

Since it was so close to Christmas, there was still a lot of traffic at that hour, said Tiffany, and there was also construction work being done on the ramp. "So we were not afraid to go get the dog," she said, "even though it was dark out. We walked up to the grassy area and visually scanned the area, searching for the dog. We didn't see anything and started teasing my cousin. Then we called out for the dog and started moving forward a bit, thinking he may move at the sound of our voices, or come to us. All of a sudden, something jumped up from out of the grass and sprinted super fast away from us in the direction of the expressway."

Tiffany estimated the creature was about thirty feet away. "I do remember it was hairy, ran on its hind legs, and was pretty tall," she said. "Also, I'll never forget the weird way it ran. I've never seen anything run on its hind legs like that before. It took huge, leaping skips away from us, not like anything I've ever seen before and not something any human could do.

"In a split second, we all knew it was not a dog. We looked at each other in disbelief at what we had just seen, started screaming, and ran back to my car. The whole way home, and to this day, we still tease my cousin about the 'dog' she saw and how we could've gotten killed trying to rescue it. It was the weirdest thing I've ever seen in my life and I still have trouble believing it."

My own first thought about the probable identity of the creature was that it may have been a kangaroo, considering the "leaping skips" Tiffany described. The nearby 'burb of Waukesha became famous for a kangaroo "flap" in 1978 when a number of people, including a school bus driver, spotted kangaroos hopping around area highways (more in Chapter 21). And more recently, in January 2005, the western side of the state had been aflutter over a 'roo that had the run of Iowa County. Although such "phantom" kangaroos are almost never caught, this 150-pounder was actually captured near Dodgeville and now resides in the Vilas Park Zoo in Madison. Its origin is still a mystery.

I had received Tiffany's report in an e-mail, so I wrote back and asked about that possibility, along with questions about other details of the sighting.

"It couldn't be a kangaroo," replied Tiffany, "because it didn't look like a kangaroo or move like a kangaroo or any other animal I'd ever seen or read about before, and I was a zoology major when I started college. While it took big skips, the motion resembled running with its legs moving separately, not together, rather than hopping." Also, she estimated the creature's height at between six and seven feet.

Tiffany added a more complete description of the animal after consulting with her sister and cousin. Maddy, the first to spot it, had the best look at its head, and maintained it was definitely doglike. "She said when she first saw it, it was on all fours," said Tiffany. "It looked like a dog to her because of its head shape and hairy body." But the girls soon realized this "stray" was nothing like the forlorn pets they had just visited at the shelter. Said Tiffany:

> The fur was around three or four inches long, and black or dark brown. It didn't have a tail. We couldn't see its eyes, claws, or teeth because we only saw it from the back. I'd say proportionately its body was like a human's body with arms of relatively 'normal' length compared to the rest of its body. It didn't have a thin frame, but it wasn't super-bulky like a Bigfoot, either. It was muscular, especially the legs and back. I'd say it was between 200 and 250 pounds.
>
> It's hard to describe it as any other animal I've ever seen. I'd say it was like a tailless dog or an ape because it was hairy, but its body resembled more of a human shape. Also, its body was upright like a human and moved unlike anything I'd ever seen before. When we first saw it, it jumped up like a spring and 'ran' away from us in a straight line towards the bushes on the side of the expressway. Its movement was very springy and agile, but also controlled and powerful. With each step, its body came about five feet off the ground and it covered a distance of ten to fifteen feet. That might sound like it moved similarly to astronauts walking on the moon, but it was very different from that because it moved much faster and it hit the ground with more impact. It moved quickly and gracefully (like a gazelle), clearing one hundred feet in a few seconds, all on its hind legs.
>
> Describing it sounds crazy and it was. It was really weird. What it looked like and how it moved are what amazed us the most. After we saw it we were all like, 'What was that?' It was like nothing we'd ever seen before. It's kind of hard to describe it in detail because it was so weird that there isn't much to compare it to. Also, some time has passed, and when you see something like that, you're not trying to remember it.

It's hard to blame Tiffany, Erin, and Maddy for not wanting to keep such a memory alive in their minds. But they did provide a wealth of interesting information about what they saw. And what they say seems to point away from a Bigfoot. The dog-shaped head is the key identifier. And Tiffany noted that it didn't have the size or bulk typically associated with the "ape-man." (It's fortunate for cryptozoologists that in this day and age, almost everyone is familiar enough with the described characteristics of Bigfoot that they know what it does and does not look like!)

On the other hand, the fact that none of the girls observed a tail while the creature's back was in plain view is also significant. Bigfoot is never seen with a tail. Tails are not usually observed with the Manwolf, either, but do occasionally unfurl as you'll see later on in this chapter.

The bounding leaps are probably the weirdest and most surprising feature of this sighting. In two other incidents where the witnesses described giant leaps and bounds, however, the appearance of both the creatures involved was more consistent with that of Bigfoot. In one, the 1964 Delavan incident in which the creature was observed to leap a fence without breaking stride, the witness was positive that what he saw was a Bigfoot and definitely not wolflike. In the other, the 1994 Pagliaroni sighting of a creature nimbly swinging both legs over a bridge fence and dropping fifteen to twenty feet to a creek bed below, the witness sketch appeared to be a classic Bigfoot.

Going back to Maddy's first glimpse, it has to be admitted that perhaps a crouching, hairy Bigfoot seen in the dark from a moving car could resemble a dog on all fours in a young girl's mind, especially a young girl looking for a dog at that moment. This leaves us with a rather ambiguous, though still amazing, sighting.

But Bigfoot or Wolfman, why would the creature be at that spot and where would it be headed? Driving through the area, it all looks much too industrialized to attract any kind of wildlife. But a close look at a map reveals Westmoor Country Club's sizable golf course, bordering the ramps and freeway interchange directly to the east, which would be virtually deserted in December. Directly to the west of the interchange is the Brookfield Hills Golf Course, which is bordered with a meandering branch of the Fox (Pishtaka in pioneer times) River. That gives us the usual water source. Following the stream westward, Ruby Park is directly connected to Brookfield Hills. The stream winds on through some forested residential areas and then heads south into a relatively open area of New Berlin, where there are also some large ponds. This would take the creature far enough south to skirt the city of Waukesha, still heading west, and make it to the Vernon State Wildlife Area in Waukesha County. From there it's only about seven or eight miles to the friendly shelter of the Kettle Moraine State Forest, Southern Unit, the apparent epicenter of the Beast's wanderings in southeastern Wisconsin.

I would also point out that if the path of the Fox is followed westward toward Pewaukee Lake only eight or nine miles, we find a cluster of water panther and turtle effigy mounds that were described by surveyor Increase Lapham in his *Antiquities of Wisconsin*. More of these were located in Waukesha, only five miles directly west of the sighting area, which again lends that aura of Native American mysticism to the landscape.

So as hard as it seemed at first to imagine this creature wandering into Brookfield's freeway ramp system, it seems that there is a viable corridor with a water source present, the usual ingredients for a Beast walk. And other creatures use the same pathway. Deer make it to this area from the woods all the time; I've personally seen dead ones lying by that freeway. The creature Tiffany saw could have been stalking a suburb-savvy whitetail for its dinner and just ended up a little farther from home than it intended. Or maybe it just hadn't finished its Christmas shopping and was on its way to Brookfield Square Mall. Whatever the reason, this sighting demonstrates that even the busiest highway is no obstacle for a determined hairy biped.

North of Madtown

About the same time, in late fall of 2003, a woman saw something canine with an apelike twist just north of Madison near the border with Columbia County on Highway DM. Sheryl Cunzenheim, who lives in Arlington, was returning home from a party sale in Waunakee about 9:00 PM with her mother as a passenger, when a creature ran across the road in front of her car. It was running on its back legs, "sort of hunched over," but also using its knuckles on the pavement, "sort of like an ape." She estimated it would have been about six feet tall if standing fully upright and said it was "doglike" and covered in black and brown fur. She slammed on the brakes to avoid hitting the creature, and it continued running across the road and into the field.

Cunzenheim's husband e-mailed me after his wife came home and told him her story, badly shaken by what she had seen. "My wife is not one to make up stories," he wrote, "and I am not sure she knew what a werewolf was before that night." He later bought her *The Beast of Bray Road*, and she identified my Indigenous Dogman sketch as best representing what she saw.

This sighting occurred about half a year before the strange morphing incident on Madison's Isthmus that I told about in the first chapter, and about thirteen miles due north of the Isthmus. It's interesting that both of these sightings seemed to have characteristics of the dog and ape, but since Cunzenheim stated the creature was doglike and that it ran mainly on its hind legs and on its toes like a dog rather than flat-footed, I'm going to place it in the Manwolf category.

Many witnesses report that "hunched over" stance, but this is probably the only instance I have of a Manwolf running with its knuckles hitting the ground. Gorillas and chimps are knuckle-draggers, but Cunzenheim was sure it was not a primate or monkey. "It reminded me of a later creature on one of those evolution charts," she said in a phone interview. She also ruled out Bigfoot because the creature wasn't thick and muscular enough, and because she noted a bushy tail. "This had shoulder blades like a thin dog," she added. And yet it was much larger than a wolf, panther, or even a big dog, she said. "I grew up in that area," said Cunzenheim, "and I never saw anything like that before. There's so many unexplained things out there."

Her mother declined to be interviewed.

DM is a fairly short stretch of road that runs east and west in a rural area, about eight or nine miles southeast of Lake Wisconsin and the Wisconsin River. It is crossed by several small creeks and lies about a mile and a half south of Schoenburg Marsh, and less than a mile south of a wild goose sanctuary. Tender vittles right at hand! In addition, the Yahara River snakes up from the Cherokee Marsh State Wildlife Area on Madison's north side, with the Milwaukee St. Paul Pacific railway corridor creating a convenient walkway right up the Yahara floodplain. It's all there: water, food, and a creature highway. I have a feeling there are many other sightings yet to be reported from that area north of Madtown.

Wolfen Home Invasion

Earlier that year, in May, someone had another urban experience with a wolflike creature that is more disturbing and fantastic than the Brookfield sighting. This one, however, occurred in Eau Claire, well north of the usual sightings area, and happened not on a busy freeway but in someone's home!

Paranormal investigator and speaker Chad Lewis forwarded this account to me. Be warned, we are headed out of the world of nature and grunting sprinters, and back to the liminal universe of curious perceptions.

A young man wrote Chad that this happened after he moved in with his friend, Sabrina. The couple was evidently involved with some type of New Age spiritual activities, since the man wrote that Sabrina "performed energy work on me." Often this involves some kind of action that will open or release various energy centers, usually called chakras, believed to be located in different sections of the body. He did not mention why he felt he needed the energy work performed, although he did say that she had previously "cleansed" his apartment for him. I doubt he was talking about the kind of cleansing that involves detergents. He meant she was ridding it of unwanted energies and spiritual forces, which sometimes indicates that something scary has been going down.

"But on the day in question," he wrote, "I woke in the early afternoon (2:30 PM) and just finished using the rest room. My room that I was renting from her was on the east side of the house facing

Cameron Street. As I left the bathroom, I noticed a creature that stood about six feet, five inches and about three hundred pounds. It had a large, jet black muscular body. Its skin was oily, similar to sweat, shiny all over, yet wasn't [caused by] sweat droplets. There was not fur at all on this creature. The hands were huge; I would say a little smaller than a large frying pan and had long, jagged claws.

"However, the face disturbed me most. It looked just like a were-wolf; I mean a face that could have been a wolf's head without the ears. The lips were snarled back exposing the teeth and gums, like an angry wolf sensing an unwelcome presence."

The man said he stood in the bathroom in shock, the creature only a few feet away from him. "That's why I remember it so well," he said. "I thought I was going to die." Strangely, it took the creature a few moments to notice the man standing there staring at him, but then it focused its "yellow, wolflike eyes" on him. The man's mind raced...should he grab for the baseball bat standing about three feet away, or take two steps backward into the bathroom and try to slam the door? As he pondered, the creature turned its head toward another room. The man took the chance to glance at his baseball bat and was considering making a lunge when the creature simply vanished. Of course, he added, the creature had been slightly transparent in the first place. The man said he "rationalized" the experience as a hallucination, and I think many people would agree with that assessment, including me. I hesitated to even include it in the book, but finally decided it was worth at least a quick look for a couple of reasons.

The main reason, of course, is that he described it as looking like a werewolf, the *raison d'etre* for this book. It differs from most other sightings, however, in that there is no chance this could be a flesh-and-blood animal. It even stands out from the "materializing" wolves in the Edgerton and Bearwolf incidents, because those occurrences had more than one witness each, making a diagnosis of hallucination much less likely. And even the first sighting described in this book, the Madison Morpher, occurred outdoors, witnessed by a person who did not claim to be normally interested in paranormal matters.

And yet this Eau Claire story shares some characteristics of other sightings. The glaring yellow eyes, the taller-than-an-average-man height, the wolfen face, heavy musculature, and even the way the creature disappeared at the first opportunity, in this case the man's quick glance at his baseball bat.

Whether this was some sort of hallucination, a visitation from a spirit world, or perhaps even a "pop-in" from some other dimension, it begs the question of why the image took the form of a werewolf? If the subconscious mind is going to play tricks on its owner by some random process not subject to the conscious mind, why not display a giant pizza, or a braying donkey, or a mime performing the invisible box trick? Any one of these projected three-dimensionally in front of a person would be startling, to say the least.

Or it could be that the young man in question has simply read too many comic books, and had unwittingly spooned the basis of this vision into his own head. But considering all the other sightings people keep having of this particular wolfen form, an inquiring person must begin to wonder whether something more general is at work. Perhaps the Manwolf betrays some innate fear in us, a warning coded into our subconscious by early survival requirements when we were more often prey than hunter. I'm not the first person to think of this.

British writer Stuart Ferrol wrote the following in an article for the January 2005 issue of *Fortean Times*, regarding a 1904 mystery animal of Northumberland, England, dubbed the Hexham Wolf. It was seen often roaming the countryside, it allegedly killed many sheep, yet it left no discernible evidence behind to prove it existed:

"It's interesting to ask just how much environment may play a part in the production of phenomena," he wrote. "Perhaps our surroundings sometimes trigger flashbacks in the collective unconscious, or, more mundanely, give rise to fascinations quite appropriate for a community nurtured in the woodlands of prehistory.

"It does appear that a likely, and usual, suspect is our own unconscious, whether in the creation of these thought form embodiments of our savage origins, or in the building of an acceptable framework by which we classify these sightings, *even if the original identities of such apparitions can never be deciphered"* (italics mine).

The Hexham wolf's original identity was certainly never deciphered. It reminds me of another observation, by Colin Bennett for the March 2005 issue of *Phenomena Magazine* in an article about the existence (or non-existence) of Bigfoot. Commenting on the various books documenting Bigfoot sightings, Bennett wrote, "...the various animal forms reported are bewilderingly incomplete. There is no food swathe, no evidence of fights, illness, urine, fur or feces. There is no mass of DNA from saliva, sweat, or wounds, and there are no corpses or evidence of lairs or nests. Yet the Bigfoot variants are seen."

As was the phantom-like Hexham wolf, and as is our contemporary Manwolf, and all the other Beast-type variants. While the English community finally did locate and kill a wolf that seemed to end the livestock predations, the local paper reported that it was not the same brutish creature that people had been encountering. That incongruity started the legend. There is a full account of this incident in Charles Fort's compendium of strangeness titled *Lo!* Fort also noted that, in that area at the same time as the purported wolf sightings, there were many other strange manifestations including a fevered religious revival, houses haunted by rapping noises, and even spontaneous human combustion.

But here is the strangest link between American phantom wolf manifestations and the Hexham stories. In the early 70s, two stone heads that were passed off as ancient Celtic artifacts were dug out of a cottage garden less than a mile from the former stomping grounds of the Hexham wolf. It was said that wherever those stones then resided, people would be visited by a thrashing, violent entity that appeared to be half man, half wolf, exactly what the Eau Claire visitation looked like. And while the young Eau Claire man hadn't dug stones out of his garden, readers of the first book will remember that there are concrete blocks I called "wolfenstones" with faces of werewolves and devils occasionally dug up around the Palmyra area, which is adjacent to the Kettle Moraine forest, home turf of the Bray Road Beast.

How to explain all this? I have to shrug and admit that I can't. But whenever someone like our Eau Claire friend meets up with a personal

Unbelievable outside his bathroom door, the least we can do is scratch about for similar tales in the hope that comparing the two will shed some light. What we *can* safely conclude here is that at least some of the time, when people see Manwolves they may not be viewing actual muscle and corpuscle. But then, this man knew that. And with the exception of the Edgerton teenagers, no other eyewitnesses have included semi-transparency in their description.

Blame it on the energy work.

CHAPTER TEN

UP TO THE MINUTE

"That devils have visited this earth: foreign devils, human-like beings, with pointed beards; good singers, one shoe ill-fitting—but with sulphurous exhalations, at any rate."
— Charles Fort, *Book of the Damned*

The Nuclear Family

Bored teenagers and urban legends go together like Boris Karloff and creepy old castles. In the summer of 2003, then, it was hardly surprising that fifteen-year-old Katie Zahn and three of her friends decided to explore a few of them by driving out to the little...and I do mean little...Village of Avon in the southwest corner of Rock County, almost on the Illinois border. Early settlers dammed the Sugar River and put up a gristmill, which has long been demolished and the dam site returned to public land. The tiny town once had hopes of being a large city, but lost its bid for a bigger population when the railroad changed routes before laying tracks through the town.

More interesting than the town itself, however, is the Avon Bottoms Wildlife Area, a 168-acre tract that follows the Sugar River's floodplain. The sandy soil supports a low-lying hardwood forest, a diverse mix of maple, oak, green ash, shagbark hickory, bur oak, elm, basswood, and others. The damp woods are thick with plants like poison ivy, wild cucumber, and river grape. The marshy natural area is heaven for birds and frogs. Avon may have failed as human habitation, but other species have succeeded admirably.

To Janesville teens, Avon was known as the site of a haunted bridge and a field where monsters could sometimes be glimpsed. As Katie and her friends found out, there may have been more than a kernel of truth to one of those legends. And what the four teens discovered has startling implications for the true nature of the bipedal wolf-creature. It started with a typical urban legend.

"There was a myth," said Katie, "that a trail went through a field, and there was a group of scientists breeding animals but something went wrong, they were too powerful and killed the scientists."

Rampaging mutants notwithstanding, Katie's two male friends thought it sounded like a good place to shoot their BB guns, which, they argued, might also come in handy for protection should any monsters turn up. The teens also had a Rottweiler with them that they planned to sell to some potential buyers from that area who were supposed to meet them at the field. It was a multi-purpose expedition.

The teens arrived at the site sometime between noon and 1:00 PM, and the two boys had taken off across the field, said Katie, while she and the other girl stayed closer to the car to wait for the dog buyers to arrive. The day was pleasantly balmy, very sunny, with not a cloud in the sky. Katie remembers that she wore Capri slacks that day.

The girls were standing near a large graveled area near a tree. They had been there before without incident, and knew there was a stream nearby, behind the tree line at the far edge of the field. As they meandered around waiting, they noticed a huge paw print in a patch of mud, with claw marks at the ends of each toe.

"It was bigger than my hand, about seven or eight inches," said Katie. The claw marks, of course, meant that the print was probably from a dog or wolflike animal, since members of the cat family walk with claws retracted until they are just ready to pounce on something. The girls had just finished examining the print when they heard what Katie described as "a big howling." It seemed to be coming from the field, and she and her friend wondered whether a dog was hurt somewhere.

The girls walked into the field for about twenty feet, said Katie, looking for the supposedly wounded canine, when they heard it again. About that same time, they saw the two boys running back down the trail toward them, looking frightened. "Run!" they yelled at the girls.

"We turned around," said Katie, "and it was there, about one hundred feet away. The guys were about ten feet in front of it, it was chasing them but not that fast, it kind of curved over when it was running, it ran kind of wobbly on two feet. It had a lot of fur on it, the arms were straighter than the legs. It had a tail, we could see it, it was kind of bushy. The shoulders were really big. It made no noise as it ran. I couldn't see its eyes; they were small. The boys were shooting it as we got in the car, and it was standing there. It was six to seven feet high, probably closer to seven because it was taller than Jason and he's six feet tall."

As terrified as the teens had been, perhaps they were in a state of denial; at any rate, they decided to forget about meeting the people who were interested in the Rottweiler and to drive to where the fabled haunted bridge was located. "After we left the field, we went to this bridge we'd heard stories about," said Katie. "The story of the bridge was that there was a dance club and bar nearby. There was a girl who went there with her girlfriends and they got drunk, and these guys asked the girl if she wanted to come home with them but they took her to the bridge and raped her. Her claw marks are still in the cement under the bridge. When we went over the bridge, all of our cell phone service stopped."

Questioned as to why they weren't all too frightened to stay in the area, Katie confessed that once they were all safe in the car, they decided that the creature they had seen was "cool," and were actually hoping to catch another glimpse of it. The teens pulled over to one side of the bridge and got out of the car. "We were walking around and I noticed this old cardboard box with four gorillas on it," said Katie. (The coincidence and symbolism here seem almost too much, but then we are dealing with an event of the highest strangeness.)

> We kept walking toward the stream and then suddenly we saw these creatures by it. They were bent over and getting drinks with their hands, not lapping like a dog but drinking like a human would in a kneeling position. They were right at the edge of the bridge at the water. They were just like the other one we saw, pretty much the same size but a little smaller and less muscular. We hid behind the trees and looked over at them. They jumped up then and started walking across the stream toward us. They were on two legs.

Their faces were thin, with a long nose, pointy ears
that went straight up. They had thinner necks, like a
human. They were walking straighter than the first one.
They had broad shoulders, tails, and their legs were bigger
on top and smaller at the ankle but they had really big feet,
which were longer than a dog paw, like oval. We were fifteen to twenty feet away.

They had long claws on more humanlike hands, and
their teeth were like a dog's teeth but real long. They were
like half-human, half-dog. Their hips were like a human's
with longer legs than a dog would be. They were like
human, but covered with fur and with a dog head. The first
one we saw had seemed a lot more angry.

Their fur was long, it hung from the body straight and
was thin enough to move with the breeze, like ours. I am
positive they were not people in animal suits.

We all got really warm. I don't know if it was adrena-
lin but we were all sweating instantly. They just got across
the stream and then stopped, and that was when we got
back in the car. I don't think they wanted to hurt us, they
just wanted us to leave. They didn't act mean or anything.
We didn't look in their eyes, though, as soon as they looked
up at us, we ran.

This sighting, if true, is staggering for many reasons. The key
phrase of that last sentence being, of course, "if true." Teens are notorious for embroidering their tales of thrill-seeking adventures. But having interviewed both Katie and her father at length several times, I have
to say that I believe she was telling her story truthfully. Now seventeen, she still remembers the incident very clearly. Her father, whom
I met at a book signing in Janesville, was the one who told me that his
daughter might have seen something like the creature in my book. She
had come home that day of the incident, he said, and told him the
entire story, still in shock at what she had seen. She even drew maps
of where the teens had been. He kept the maps, although they weren't

clear enough to help him find the same spot later, and often puzzled over the incident himself.

Before the book signing was over, he phoned Katie and asked whether she would be willing to come and tell me her story. She finally agreed, and we were able to stay past the signing time and chat on the sofa in Janesville's Book World. I thought that Katie was very well-spoken and quietly self-confident. She never hesitated while telling the story, and when I would stop to ask for detailed explanations her answers were never in conflict with things she had already said.

Moreover, her father insisted her story was exactly the same as she had told it to him the day it happened. Also in her favor is the fact that she agreed to let her real name be used. As often happens in youthful relationships, she is no longer in contact with the three friends who shared the sighting, but she did say they did not like to talk about the events of that day. I've often found that to be true in cases of shared sightings; there is usually at least one person so uneasy with the implications of having seen an unidentifiable creature that he or she prefers not to acknowledge the reality of the experience by discussing it.

And finally, my gut instinct as a former newspaper reporter who interviewed several people a week on various topics for ten years was that Katie was being truthful.

That leaves us with the fact that what sounds like a family of Manwolves was seen by four witnesses. Four witnesses, four Manwolves. Three of the creatures were of a smaller size, implying they were either females or perhaps older juveniles. And they were seen in broad daylight, which is not the time of day figments of magic normally prance in the fields of Wisconsin. All of this argues very strongly for the flesh-and-blood, cryptozoological theory of the beast's origin. These creatures do sound quite exactly like whatever was seen on Bray Road and other highways and byways around Wisconsin and other states, Sasquatch-type sightings excluded.

The amount of detail in the description of the creatures is also unparalleled. Katie and her friends had long looks at these beings, and were able to see them in clear sunlight, out in the open, in a variety of positions and postures. Looking at my *Beast of Bray Road* illustrations (she was not familiar with that book before her father bought one at the signing), she picked out my illustration of the "indigenous dogman" as most similar to what she saw, especially the head and ears. The arms of the creatures she saw were straighter, she noted, and the tail was longer and bushier, but otherwise it was an accurate depiction.

I found it a very interesting observation that the creatures used their "hands" to hold water. We've seen this behavior before, with food, and while it does look strange and is not typical behavior with canines, it's not impossible. The action of cupping one's hand is called "convergence" by biologists and is achieved by flexing what in humans would be called the knuckle joints. According to Richard E.F. Leakey in *Human Ancestors; Readings from Scientific American*, convergence is a skill many mammals are able to master. "Two convergent paws equal one prehensile hand; many mammals hold food in two convergent paws to eat."

Also consistent with the other sightings is that Katie described the first creature as "curved over" while it was running, just as so many others have noted a hunched posture. That is a detail she would not have been able to know about, and very unlikely to make up.

There are several ways to interpret this sighting.

Possibility 1: We have a breeding population of a physical animal that at least occasionally roams in small groups, perhaps family packs. Origin, unknown.

Possibility 2: We have semi-supernatural creatures that occasionally band together and are fully capable of appearing in strong sunlight to multiple witnesses, leaving footprints and drinking water.

Possibility 3: Four teenagers shared a mass hallucination of a very specific creature that behaved in ways consistent with dozens of other sightings that do not have characteristics of hallucinations.

I suspect most people would like to choose Door Number Three, because the least scary thing is likely to come out from behind it. But shared hallucinations are not common, especially those that tally so well with the observations of other people. The teens did have an expectation of seeing some sort of mutant, but, as I asked with the Eau

Claire sighting, why would they all hallucinate an apparent wolf/human hybrid and not some sort of Frankenstein's monster, or a hybrid of a human and our usual lab subject, a pig? This was not a late-night drinking party, the four were sober and conducting other business with the dog and the BB guns. And it's doubtful Katie would have recounted the whole story to her father when she returned home that afternoon if she had thought it was all in their heads.

I guess, disturbingly, we are left with Doors One and Two.

Honey Creek Giant Dog

Back to the eastern side of the state, to the same area the Pagliaronis spotted their bridge-jumping Bigfoot, we have an intriguing sighting of what this time is definitely canid. Chuck Hampton of Honey Creek sent me an e-mail in September 2004 about a sighting he had in January of that year. Hampton is often up early as he needs to travel to Mukwonago three times a week for kidney dialysis, and it was on one of these mornings, as he walked out to start up his car at 5:30 AM, that he received a shock.

Chuck wrote,

> I had heard about the Bray Road thing before, but really didn't know what to make of it until one day last January. In the winter I normally start the car and let it run for a few minutes to warm it up before I take off. Well, on one Saturday morning I went out to start the car. We have a driveway that is fifty to seventy-five yards long. At the end of the driveway we had left out the garbage cans overnight. When I got to the car door I looked down to the end of the driveway because I saw something move.
>
> Initially I thought it was a deer. I had hit a deer just prior to that and seeing one at the end of my driveway kind of ticked me off. When I yelled at it, it stopped rummaging around in the garbage can and looked at me. That's when I realized it wasn't a deer!
>
> It was the same height as a deer but it had a short neck and pointed ears like a dog or wolf. Its hind legs looked

131

shorter than its front ones and I didn't notice any kind of a tail. When it heard me, it just kind of trotted away into the woods without making any kind of sound. The closest thing to a canine I know that looks anything like the thing I saw would be an Irish wolfhound, but they have floppy ears and a long skinny tail. It was pretty creepy looking.

A woman I know has also claimed to have seen the same animal, but when she seen it, it was running around with some other smaller animal. This leads me to believe there may be more than one of these things running around up here. I don't think they're dangerous or anything, and I don't really think they are some kind of werewolf. But I have seen it and I think it is some really strange combination of dog/wolf/whatever. Regardless the thing is REAL.

Hampton noted that it was still dark outside at the time, but the front yard and driveway were illuminated by a front porch light.

The first thing I noticed was the size of the animal. It stood from three to four foot at the back, the next thing I noticed was the color, it was tan to a light brown in color. These two factors accounted for my initially thinking it was a deer. When I yelled at it, it turned in a counter-clockwise direction, (it initially had its head in my garbage) and that's when I realized it wasn't a deer. Its legs were thicker than a deer's with shaggy hair, and its head was definitely canine.

I am enclosing a picture I Photoshopped of an Irish wolfhound's body with a shepherd's head. This would be a close representation of the animal I saw.

I'm still convinced there are probably several of these animals and they are some kind of mixed-breed strays. There is plenty of wildlife in the area to support a pack of strays. However, I am a 'dog' person and I have to admit this is the strangest looking animal I've ever seen wandering around. I'm glad the thing wasn't aggressive when I ran into it. I'm sure it could have had me for breakfast!

This was an interesting sighting, but the beast Hampton saw was on four feet, and sounds more like some kind of feral hybrid than a Manwolf or anything spooky. Irish wolfhounds can indeed grow very large, as can mastiffs and some other breeds of dogs. If mated with a wolf or German shepherd, a very strange-looking mix would result. This animal really didn't display any other Manwolf characteristics, so I think I will agree with him that it was probably some kind of natural, hybrid dog. But I was glad to include the story as a point of comparison to the stranger, more convincing and much more frightening Manwolf and small Bigfoot sightings. Besides, it is also reminiscent of the dire wolf model.

I've had other, similar reports at various times that I haven't included, but this one was of interest partly due to its proximity to the Bigfoot sighting. It shows, at the very least, that more than one type of large furry creature is running around the Honey Creek area.

New Year's Eve Party Crasher

It was about four in the morning on January 1, 2005, and UW-Whitewater student Erik Binnie was the designated, and therefore sober, driver as he and two buddies made their way home from a party. The trio were traveling on Highway N about eight miles south of the intersection with 106, near the Bark River and many adjacent marshes, and Binnie was just pulling back onto the road after stopping to allow one of his friends to relieve himself outside the car.

Suddenly an animal appeared in Binnie's headlights on the road in front of him. "At first I thought it was a deer," he said, "and I was scanning the horizon for other deer. Then I realized it had a wolflike head and body, but was the size and height of a doe. The head had an elongated muzzle, and the ears were pointed and on top of its head. It was dark black with some gray, and had really bright, glowing yellow eyes."

His two friends were not so inebriated that they missed the creature's appearance, and he said they all made various exclamations of surprise. None of the three could identify the animal. All agreed it was much too large to be a dog or wolf, and yet it had wolfen features.

Binnie described the creature again as "extremely tall," and said it was "sauntering" toward his vehicle at first, then broke into a run, "going really fast." He added, "it didn't look like it cared about me." The creature was soon out of sight and the young men continued on.

Even though this was a quadruped, the "elongated muzzle" and yellow eyes, coupled with the size and dark fur, make this sighting more suspicious than some of the other four-footed sightings. For Binnie and his friends, it was quite weird enough just as it was.

The Jack-in-the-Box Manwolf of Sharon

A little over a year after Katie's strange encounter, in 2004, another Manwolf incident occurred near the state border with Illinois, this time farther east in southernmost Walworth County. Renee Fritz and her husband Carl had moved the previous April to the small community of Sharon from Chicago, and had never heard of *The Beast of Bray Road*. Carl first e-mailed me about his wife's sighting and said, "She didn't tell me about it for a few days because she wanted to forget the incident. When she told me about it, she was literally crying from fright!" When Renee finally did confide in her husband, he mentioned it at work and someone told him about the Bray Road beast, and he was able to contact me.

I interviewed Renee only a couple of weeks after that. The Fritzs have a young daughter (and recently added another child to the family), and Carl works in the construction business. Their recently purchased home was tidy and comfortable, and we sat in their living room, the couple's young daughter playing nearby, as Renee told me of her encounter. Again, Renee was moved to tears and grew very anxious reliving her tale. It was a unique and unsettling story. When I showed her a drawing of the Michigan Dogman, the prizewinner at the Traverse City radio station, she literally jumped from fright, saying that was very like what she saw.

Renee had to leave for her job as a medical secretary at about 5:00 AM, and in the first week of October it was still dark out at that time. The date was either October 4 or 5, and the sighting happened about 5:20 AM.

There were so few other cars as Renee drove east on Stateline Road that she had turned her brights on as she approached a small bridge over a stream. As Renee came closer to the bridge, out of the corner of her eye she caught a movement in the ditch on the passenger side of her car and turned to look, instinctively pulling a little closer to the metal railing to have a better look at what had attracted her attention. Her car was only about four feet away from it, she estimated, when she realized that she was staring into the face of a surprised-looking, large, wolfish creature. She made total eye contact for a few horrifying moments in which the monster's features and, incredibly, what seemed to be its thoughts were indelibly stamped in her mind!

"He must have been kneeling," said Renee. "The bridge railing was about three feet high. It was something I'd never seen before, something I didn't think was an animal, not really of this world. It was black, furry, with spiky hair around its face. It had a white patch on the top of its head, big bulging eyes. Its teeth were white, long, narrow, and seemed very sharp. Its ears blended with the hair but were spiky and came to a peak. . .there was a point to them. The hands were down. I saw the head, neck, shoulders, and part of the chest. It had just popped up out of the ditch like it was sitting up straight, it gave me the "teeth," then it popped back down, like it was in the kneeling position. This was like a human being where you see the head, neck, and shoulders. The head was almost similar in size to a human's, the neck and shoulders were smaller.

"I could see the muscular part of the shoulders," she continued, "the bones in the neck. At first I told myself it wasn't of this world, it was like nothing I'd ever seen before. It wasn't a wolf, it wasn't a dog."

The menacing, fanged "grin" was the feature that Renee noticed most. It reminded her, she said, of a Tiki love god in the movie, *Trilogy of Terror*. "The mouth wasn't long across the face," she said. "It was more 'opened up.' It either vibrated or shook its head. It was like, 'I'll scare her so she'll never talk about it.'" Renee was so frightened that she instantly threw her hands up as if to guard herself and then slid a few inches under the steering wheel, but quickly regained her composure and took control of the car before she went off the road. By that time she was past the bridge and the creature was gone. She continued shakily on her way to work.

Renee was left with the strange conviction that the creature was telling her not to talk to anyone about her experience, or it would somehow "get her." "It seemed like it had the capability of knowing where I was or if I was talking about it," she said. "So I didn't tell my husband it took me two days. I believe it wasn't just an animal, I feel truly it was evil. I drive by the same place every day and wait for it to show up again."

Renee drew a jittery sketch of the face, but displeased with her results, asked her more artistic husband Carl to make a clearer version based on her impression and instructions. Neither is an exact replica of what she saw, of course. They are both rather cartoonish, and the creature in the ditch was anything but funny.

Unlike many of the witnesses, this was not Renee's first strange experience in life. "Of course, it would happen to me," she said. "I

Renee Fritz's sketch of the creature she saw.

Renee Fritz's husband Carl's interpretation of what she saw.

always have things happen to me. I had precognitive dreams as a child, a few ghost experiences, and some premonitions that came true." She did not feel this creature was an apparition or hallucination of any kind, however, and its only supernatural aspect was that it seemed to be able to impress thoughts and feelings upon her.

Visiting the bridge site later, I was able to confirm that the ground behind the metal railing slopes away at an angle that would have meant the creature had to be either on its knees or standing up on very short legs in order for the face and shoulders to show over the railing from a motorist's point of view. The bridge is in a very rural area, surrounded by fields, about three miles east of the Sharon town limits. It's easy to imagine something large being able to get around this area mostly unseen. And again we have the water connection.

There is also a marsh nearby. The aptly named Swamp Angel Road, which runs north from Stateline a little farther east, is known among local residents for mysterious dancing lights of the type often seen in marshes. Most people believe the lights are from gas caused by vegetation slowly rotting in the damp environment. Others ascribe supernatural origins to them as we discussed in an earlier chapter and

Devil's Lane.

call them willo-the-wisps or devil lights, trickster spirits that lead travelers deep into the muckiest bogs until they are hopelessly lost. They are often connected with other anomalous phenomena, such as UFO, Bigfoot, and black panther sightings. And now, perhaps, with Manwolves.

By the way, anyone consulting a map will notice the village of Bigfoot near the state border, not far from Sharon. The community, as well as Sharon's high school, were named not for the eight-foot hominid but for a Potawatomi chieftain named Maunk-Suck, which translates to Big Foot. The chief had left very large tracks at one time, perhaps from snowshoes, and the name stuck. Interestingly, Bigfoot High School is located on Devil's Lane. Again, not as lurid as it sounds. I did some digging and learned from a local historian that the street used to divide two farm fields. Both farmers had to donate some land for a lane between the two, and their phrase at having to give up a strip of valuable topsoil was, "the devil take the hindmost." Still, it sounds funny. And some believe names do have more significance than we generally understand (see Chapter17).

Big Foot mascot.

Lima Marsh Monster

People often ask whether any one characteristic is common to all witnesses. I can't say that I have found any that applies across the board, but I have noticed there is one thing many have in common: Most have reason to be out late at night, often because they work a job with odd hours. That was the case on March 9, 2005, when a twenty-two-year-old UW-Whitewater history major on her way home from a late-night theater job caught an unexpected creature feature. She was so upset by it that she immediately went to her computer, found me, and wrote to ask what it could have been.

She asked me to keep her name confidential, so I'll call her Amy. She works at a movie complex in Janesville and was on her way back to campus in Whitewater, headed east on State Highway 59. We visited the small community of Lima Center and the adjacent Lima Marsh between Milton and Whitewater earlier with the 1994 Richard Fanning sighting of a huge, wolfish quadruped (Chapter 6). Farms along the north side of Highway 59 in the Lima area back up to the marsh, with a railroad track separating their fields from the grassy bog. Amy said she had spent many childhood summers with her grandparents in that neighborhood, and with her frequent commute to work, she was very familiar with this stretch of road.

That familiarity was all the more reason for her surprise at what she saw that night. It was about 1:45 AM, when she said she spotted something that "spooked" her. "Off the right shoulder of the road (in a rain ditch) I caught two glowing

Isolated and wet, Lima Marsh is perfect Manwolf territory.

yellow eyes in my headlights," she wrote. "Immediately, I thought I saw a deer. I flashed on my brights and slowed the vehicle down. The moment I flashed my brights this animal started to run across the

Swamp Angel Road, near the state line in Walworth County.

road. What struck me immediately was that this animal was *upright*—it was striding fast, like a human would but it wasn't running. It was NOT human, it was NOT a deer. Somehow, it disappeared on me. I didn't see it completely cross the road.

"I have 20/15 vision," she continued. "I was not sleepy, I know what I saw. It wasn't human, it wasn't anything I've ever seen before. It was a creature with glowing yellow eyes that walked/strided upright. As of right now, I am desperate for explanations. I am too spooked to sleep."

The actual point of the creature's crossing, she said, was past Vickerman Road but not too close to County Road KK. (She later figured it as .7 or .8 miles past Vickerman.) The creature was on the right or south side of the road. Amy didn't have a clear memory of its head or ears, she said, but its fur was brown, somewhere between a deer and a chocolate lab's color. She said it was more fuzzy than shaggy, and estimated its height at between five-feet eight inches and six feet tall.

"My impression of the animal was that I had spooked it more than it spooked me," she said. "It was more interested in getting away from me than anything else. The detail that sticks with me was its yellow, glowing eyes and its stride. It literally strode, almost floated across the road. It was not traveling at a great speed. It had meaty legs from hip to foot (not like a deer). Its legs appeared longer than the torso. I think it had armlike appendages, but I never focused on them. I was mostly struck by the humanlike legs. I believe he ran straight across the road. This would make him headed toward the Lima Marsh, I believe."

Other than its smaller size, the Lima Marsh Monster could go in the Bigfoot category. The humanlike legs and the fuzzy rather than shaggy fur, plus the long strides, all sound like Bigfoot, albeit Bigfoot Junior. The Bluff Monster, though, is also described as smaller than a typical Bigfoot. But since Amy did not get a clear look at the head shape, it's impossible to judge for sure. The glowing eyes and relatively short height, however, are more indicative of a Manwolf. They've been seen striding quickly, too.

It was definitely an upright furry biped, or BHM (Big Hairy Monster), that much seems safe to say.

Kenosha's Red-Eye Special

Early March 2005 was an active month for sightings. About an hour's drive almost due east from the Lima Marsh, a Racine teen saw something so frightening she couldn't bring herself to say anything to the people who were with her at the time. She doesn't want her name divulged, so I'll call her Ann. It was very close to Ann's sixteenth birthday, and she had been on a car-shopping expedition that day with her father, brother, and a friend. She was unable to give me an exact location, but it was between Racine and Kenosha, two cities located on Lake Michigan with a swath of urban sprawl nearly connecting them.

During the drive home, the car they were driving developed a troublesome rattle, and Ann's father pulled over to open the hood and see whether he could determine the cause. Ann and her friend got out of the car, too, but soon became bored with her father and brother's "car talk."

"I happened to be looking into the woods by the bank to the side," wrote Ann in her e-mail to me. "I heard a rustling and I was like, 'what the heck...?' and then I looked more intensely and saw what looked like red eyes appear in the trees. The red eyes went from one place, then up, slowly, like something was rising up.

> I saw what looked like a pit bull, but real hairy, and mean! I think I saw it stand, like a dog would beg on its hind legs. I know you're gonna think I'm crazy, but I swear it knew I saw it and knew I was scared, almost like it was happy I was scared! That freaked me out even more. I just said 'ohmigod' real quiet and got into the car. I didn't even say anything to Michelle or my dad or brother. They didn't even know I saw anything. I almost felt like it would have

attacked us but I was too scared to say anything. Then when I looked back out the window when I got in the car, I saw these 'eyes' and what little part of the body dash away, back into the woods.

It seems mild, but it was REAL scary!! I still can't forget what I saw and if it wasn't for the red eyes, I'd not have been THAT scared.

I'm taught not to believe in supernatural creatures that aren't of the devil, so I don't like to talk about it. But [another friend] said you could explain some beast sightings other people had? Make me feel better maybe. I don't know, though, that was really freaky. Well, there it is. Thanks for hearing me out and I hope you don't think I'm some nut job. I know what I saw!

Ann was referred to me by a mutual acquaintance who attends the same conservative Christian church as Ann's family. Ann never did tell her parents about what she saw, as far as I know, because she felt they would disapprove of the fact that she saw something they considered Satanic. Monster books and movies were not regular fare in this household, so Ann would not be as culturally pre-conditioned to see monsters as many teens today. The mutual friend she confided in, however, is known for "cleaning" unwanted entities from homes, so Ann felt she could spill her troubling experience to someone who would understand. She was right. Our friend, familiar with my book, immediately understood and explained as best she could, then had Ann contact me. I'm very glad she did.

My best guess as to the location after talking to our mutual friend is that it occurred somewhere around State Highway 32 and County Road A. Anywhere around that spot would put it in the vicinity of Petrifying Springs Park and the Pike River, which flows eastward and then parallel to the Lake Michigan coastline. The park contains a golf course and recreational trails and other facilities, but in early March in Wisconsin it would still be relatively cold, possibly partially snow-covered, and unused.

One thing that fascinates me about this sighting is that like the Sharon roadside incident, the witness almost simultaneously felt a sort of psychic intimidation emanating from the creature upon seeing it. With the description of the face like a pit bull, the furry body, and the bipedal stance, I definitely have to add this one to the Manwolf category. And I wonder if any other members of that little expedition also saw it but, like Ann, were too afraid to say anything? Seeing something that looks like a demon is not a comfortable experience for anyone, let alone someone who believes that anything answering the description of a Manwolf is certainly "of the devil." I wonder how many other sightings remain unreported for this reason.

Pioneer Cemetery Guardian

An even more recent sighting happened on Friday, September 16, 2005. A young man's mother wrote me that her son witnessed a Big Furry that day just east of Pell Lake, near the Wisconsin/Illinois border in southern Walworth County. Her son, Matt Wakely, twenty-one, was returning home to Lake Geneva, heading north on White Pigeon Road at about two in the afternoon. The road is crossed by Nippersink Creek and lies only a few miles southeast of the east end of Geneva Lake. While this part of the county has fallen prey to rapid development in the past few years, there are still plenty of open fields, large tracts of acreage planted in corn, and wooded areas.

An old cemetery lies on that road, and as Wakely passed it, said his mother, "he looked back at the cemetery in the trees and said he saw a large something that had shaggy fur all over its body and he was standing there staring out at the road."

I talked to Wakely on the phone a few days later, and he gave more details. "It was a warm day," he remembered, "but I was chilly in my T-shirt, so when I saw it right away it seemed weird that someone had their shirt off. I wasn't expecting to see anything there, I was coming home, kind of in a rush. It was a bright, sunny day, and I looked through the trees as I turned the corner (from County Highway B onto White Pigeon) and then I saw something other than a tree, watching me as I went by."

Wakely instinctively scanned the roadsides and cemetery drive for either a car or bicycle but saw no vehicle of any type. There was a log laid across the cemetery entrance, and the creature was standing behind this log, he said.

At first having assumed it was merely a dark-skinned person standing there, he next realized that the creature was covered with fur the color of "milk chocolate." The creature was standing with one leg raised up as if it were resting one foot on a rock or something similar. "It looked like a human arm and hip," said Wakely. "It had one hand on its hip, but the other one hung to its mid-thigh. He had no fat on him and was not real muscular, he was adult male size, maybe a little taller than average, I'd say about 200 pounds.

"It had a real hairy back and real hairy chest. I didn't see pants on it. The leg was hairy but not as hairy as the chest and back. His head was real round, his hair was messed up, sticking out from his head in all directions. He resembled more of a human but had a big face like a caveman, a really round face. The face was darker colored, it could have been covered with fur or just dark colored. Do you know that Geico commercial with the caveman? It looked just like that. I couldn't see its foot."

Eerily, the creature turned and looked back at Wakely passing by in his truck. "He watched me the entire way by," said Wakely. "I got kind of freaked by that. He turned his head, and his nose was flattened and wider, not sticking out. I didn't want to go back, not knowing if he might charge the car or something."

Wakely then continued heading for home, but was so startled by the incident that he called his mother on his cell phone immediately and told her he thought he had just seen a caveman. His mother went back out to the cemetery soon after he arrived home (Wakely was due at work, so he couldn't), but saw no trace of the creature. "He isn't one to fool with me about things like this, so I believe him," she told me.

I was struck by the statement that the creature was standing and staring at the road when observed. That aspect sounded a lot like Marv Kirschnik's sighting in the 1980s near Bray Road, which also happened in broad daylight. In both instances, the creature stood its ground and waited until the vehicle passed, rather than diving for cover. It seems to contradict the usual statement of most witnesses that the creature somehow appeared upset or angry at being seen by a human. However, Kirschnik's creature was definitely canid…this creature sounds definitely hominoid. In fact, it sounds to me almost exactly like one of the classifications in Coleman and Huyghe's *The Field Guide to Bigfoot, Yeti, and Other Mystery Primates Worldwide,* the "Erectus Hominid." According to the description, these creatures are about six feet tall with "slight barreling of the chest." While they are mostly covered with body hair, the head hair is longer. Male hominids are often noted to sport a "semierect penis," says the *Field Guide,* something Wakely didn't notice. It does have an "upturned" nose, says the *Guide,* and is often mistaken for a Neandertal, which sounds very much like Wakely's description of a "caveman." The biggest problem with this classification is that, according to Coleman and Huyghe, the Erectus Hominid is only found in Pakistan, China, Southeast Asia, and Australia. However, if the White Pigeon Road watcher is an Erectus Hominid, it would not be the first to be seen in Wisconsin or several other Midwestern states.

Coleman and Huyghe believe the famed "Minnesota Ice Man," a hairy, manlike creature about six feet tall with a wide, "pugged" nose that was supposedly shot in 1960 near Aurora, Minnesota, was an Erectus Hominid. The creature was preserved in a block of ice and exhibited at shopping malls around the Midwest, where it came to the attention of researchers Bernard Heuvelmans, Mark Hall, and Loren Coleman. Hall, according to Coleman's book, *Bigfoot!,* considered the creature an example of an extinct hominid named *Homo Erectus,* and both he and Heuvelmans suspected the animal was shot in some part of Asia and then shipped to this country. However, some cryptozoologists believe the "finder," Frank Hansen, who said he was hunting with four other people, all military officers, when he shot the creature right here in the States.

So while the Ice Man creature was definitely "seen" in the Midwest after death during its many exhibits, perhaps it has also been seen alive, but not recognized for what it was. It would explain the Bluff Monster, the Rome "Bigfoot," and perhaps even the Honey Creek creature, all of which are smaller than the typical Bigfoot. It is certainly easier to believe that we have two creatures, the Manwolf and Erectus Hominid, running around Wisconsin and possibly other nearby states, rather than three…Manwolf, Erectus Hominid, and Bigfoot! An unholy trio, indeed.

I visited the sighting area the week after it happened and examined the ground carefully for prints or other evidence, but didn't find any. It had rained between the day of the sighting and my visit, and the black dirt road was pliant enough that I could make a print with my sneaker if I pushed my foot down hard enough. If the creature had been back, it probably would have made some kind of marks. We'd had a drought before that rain, however, so it's doubtful any tracks could have been made on the day the creature was seen. I also unsuccessfully looked for droppings, and carried a tri-field meter that did not register any jumps in electric, magnetic, or radio/microwave readings as I walked around the old gravestones. The cemetery, known as the Old Bloomfield Pioneer Cemetery, is inactive and one of the oldest in the county. Some of the headstones are broken, either from age or vandalism, and it is surrounded by cornfields to the north, east, and across White Pigeon Road to the west. To the south is a wooded area bounded by County Highway B, and just to the southeast is a big silo complex belonging to a farm across the road on B. The silo area was busy that day, since it was harvest time, but I imagine it is not a hubbub of activity most of the year.

This sighting was only about ten miles east of the Sharon State-line Road bridge.

It's interesting that one of the other 2005 sightings, the four creatures seen in Avon Bottoms, was also near the Illinois border. Perhaps Illinois may soon find itself with a Manwolf invasion, if it hasn't already (keep reading).

Werewolf Fur and Footprints

Lack of physical evidence is the bane of most cryptozoological investigations. Things are no different in hunting the Manwolf. I'm still waiting for a good plaster cast of a footprint, although several people have seen tracks and, as you'll learn in the chapter on the Georgia swamp creature, at least one person has drawn a carefully observed diagram. It looks like a giant dog print. And I've heard from several witnesses that they actually recovered a shred of hair clinging to the auto bumper after a car/beast encounter, but they had lost it or not thought enough about it to even throw it into a plastic bag for preservation. Hair, of course, is the next best proof to the creature itself, because it can be analyzed for DNA if even a few follicles are included.

Well, we now have a giant chunk of matted fur from what may have been a Manwolf. It's been tentatively identified by a Wisconsin State Department of Natural Resources Wildlife Specialist as canid, probably some type of "wolf-hybrid." Which is exactly what one might expect to hear about hair from a Manwolf. At this writing, I'm still looking for a lab to do further analysis, although the best that can be hoped for is that it will be pronounced "unknown," since I'm willing to bet the farm that no lab in the world has a sample of werewolf fur on hand as a control specimen for positive identification.

The "sighting" itself is not as quantifiable, however. And it isn't exactly a sighting. But it happened in the summer of 2005 when a Williams Bay man e-mailed me that his wife, Mary Philippsen, had a disturbing experience and that I should contact her.

It was a pleasant Tuesday afternoon near the end of April when I found myself teetering on an outdoor barstool with a barbecue spatula in my hand, attempting to shovel an eight-inch-wide mass of unidentifiable feces from a moss-covered roof into a big plastic Baggie. Mary Philippsen, the woman whose husband called me, stood nearby, gingerly holding the Baggie and watching the disgusting pile plop into it. Peering closer, she noted, "It's got hair and bone in it, and birdseed." We could also see an intact turkey claw poking out.

A braver woman than I am, Philippsen then actually took a whiff of the fairly fresh-looking droppings, and almost retched. Which, in turn, nearly made me lose my lunch and almost fall off the barstool. But we did manage to capture the unknown, giant pile of scat. It was all in the interest of determining what it was that ran across her cottage roof one night the previous week, thumping from one end to another "like a human would run." Philippsen did in fact believe that a man was pounding across the roof of her single-story cottage as she cowered in her living room with her two little dogs fastened like shivering stick-tights in her lap.

In horror, Philippsen listened as the "thing" then crashed partially through her roof at one point, its "foot" making contact with the rafters just above the ceiling board, and finally dropped down onto her freshly mulched flower bed on the side of the house and disappeared. "I was scared to death, I didn't move for five minutes," said Philippsen. She called her husband, who was out at the time, and said, "I think there was a man running across the roof of our house."

In the morning, she stepped outside and saw the tracks. "At first, I was angry about my flower beds," said Philippsen. She began raking over the tracks closest to the door, then realized what they might be and called the Williams Bay police to her north side cottage. The officer was already grinning as he got out of the car, she said, and making cracks about "Bigfoot." Still thinking a human had been on her roof, she asked the officer whether they had been pursuing anyone, perhaps an errant teenager, the night before. He said they had not. After looking at the eight to ten imprints, he told her that he thought a deer had jumped on her roof, then down onto the flower bed.

Obviously, courses in wildlife are not required for police officers these days. Assuming that a deer would find any need to jump up on the roof of an isolated cottage on the outskirts of the small village of Williams Bay, it still would have made a much different sound than that of a running human. Also, if it had broken through the roof and its hoof had penetrated several feet inside while at a dead run, it's hard to imagine that it wouldn't have broken its leg or made a much larger commotion trying to extricate itself. And equally obvious is the fact that the six-inch-wide tracks were not made by little deer hooves. At that size, they are bigger than either wolf or cougar tracks. They were not long and flat-footed like bear tracks. However, it must be remembered that the tracks were made in bark mulch, which is far from an ideal medium for accurate impressions.

The Philippsen house in Williams Bay.

The footprint Mary Philippsen found in her flower bed.

So what did run across the Philippsens' roof? My guess at the time was, believe it or not, a cougar. The cottage is small, with a mildly sloped, thatched roof about seven feet from the ground at its eaves. There are trees next to it. A cougar could easily jump to it either from the nearby deck or a tree. It would have to be a smallish cougar, however, because the trees are not large enough to support a big animal like a full-grown cougar or bear without breaking some branches, and the trees appeared intact. It also fit in a behavioral sense, since cougars like to jump on prey from a tree limb or other high vantage point. And interestingly, another Williams Bay resident living near the Philippsens had reported seeing a cougar to local police just the week before, according to the officer who visited the Philippsen site. And it was the officer, scanning the cottage roof for other signs of animal trespass, who discovered the large pile of strange scat about a yard from the edge of the roof. Neither he nor Philippsen felt inclined to take a sample at the time.

That was how I came to be scooping spatulas of mammal doo from the Philippsens' cottage roof that day. When Mary Philippsen told me what had happened, the fact that it sounded like a man running across her roof sounded too suspiciously like a Manwolf to pass up the chance for some possible concrete evidence.

This would not be the first Williams Bay appearance of the creature. In *The Beast of Bray Road*, I told the story of Bay resident Jessica Anderson who saw the creature snarling at her ground-level window as she lay in bed with her newborn child in 1998. That residence lies about a mile south of the Philippsens', closer to Geneva Lake and near the spooky Conference Point. Williams Bay lies between two major lakes, Geneva and Como, and is hugged on its northern side by a large wetlands area, Kishwauketoe (Clear Water) Nature Preserve. This tract covers 231 acres and is the largest and least-disturbed wetland area on the lake. The Manwolf's tendency to appear near water and especially marshes has already been well noted.

I also took plaster casts of what remained of the pawprints after six or seven days and a couple of rains. I must say the casts look inconclusive. As I've already said, mulch is not an ideal medium for imprinting fine detail, and would tend to enhance "spreading" of the print measurements. But the casts do confirm the general size of about six inches across. An average cougar print is three and a half to four inches; gray wolf prints will run up to four and a half inches, maybe five inches for an adult male. The imprecision of the mulch could easily account for the difference. They are certainly bigger than a dog, coyote, housecat, or even a deer would make. Near the time of this incident, a bear cub had been spotted and captured in suburban Milwaukee, about an hour's drive to the northeast. Mary wondered then if a bear might be the culprit. But again, the prints do not look like bear prints, and that is quite a range for a cub to make within a day or so.

And Mary was certain that whatever ran across her roof weighed at least 150 pounds or more. We figured it would have to weigh that much, if the unknown runner was indeed the creator of the giant pile of scat. However, after consulting books on animal tracking, Rock County's Department of Natural Resources wildlife specialist Doug Fendry, and I came to the disappointing conclusion that the doo-doo was from raccoons. And it didn't take a 150-pound Rocky to make the pile, either, the expert explained. "They like to make latrines and go in the same spot," said Fendry. I offered to make him a present of the odoriferous Baggie, turkey claw and all, but he politely declined. The scat was thus ruled irrelevant.

The cougar theory was looking better and better. I asked Fendry why wildlife experts are so reluctant to admit that wild cougars could be moving back into Wisconsin. "It's not that at all," he said. "We don't say it's impossible. We know some people have them as pets. Recently a state trooper stopped someone who had two cougar kittens in their car. It's just that we want definite proof."

The plaster pawprint casts, alas, were far from definite. Although one newspaper story first printed in the *Janesville Gazette* and regrettably spread by the *Associated Press* inexplicably reported that I had sent the prints into the Department of Natural Resources for analysis, that was not true. The castings were far too blobby to bother a specialist over them. The case, especially without an actual sighting to go on, seemed doomed for the eternal mystery pile.

However, a month or so later, Philippsen called and told me she had found the same footprints in the same flowerbed again. The next day, her sister visiting from Florida discovered a large, matted hunk of fur on Philippsen's lawn, between two large trees. The women knew it had been deposited very recently because the lawn had been mowed just two days previously, and the fur would have been shredded had it been there earlier. She brought it to my house to show me.

The piece resembles a humongous "mat" like those dogs or wolves will chew out from under their top layer of fur in spring. It was, indeed, the molting season for timber wolves at the time. The chunk is dark brown on one side, and dark brown with gray "topping" on the other.

It measures about six inches long and three inches wide, and close to an inch thick in the center. Not quite big enough to turn into a werewolf fur stole, but quite large for a single mat. No skin was attached, and there was no visible blood, so it did not appear to be torn from an animal in a fight. Examination with a magnifying glass revealed small worms and seeds, and the entire piece was permeated with remains of grass and plants. It was evident it had been discarded by something that had been living in the wild, and was probably scraped off using one of the two trees as a convenient scratching post.

I wondered if it might be goat or longhorn sheep hair, since around that time, Walworth County was abuzz over an out-of-place, shaggy-haired bighorn sheep, native to Colorado, running amok in the countryside and even downtown Elkhorn. The sheep was, in fact, finally hit by a car on State Highway 67 only a few miles north of Philippsen's house about the time the fur was discovered. I showed it to someone who raises goats and dogs, however, and she gave me a definite no on the goat/sheep thesis, saying it looked more like some kind of dog fur…although she couldn't say what breed it might possibly be.

I consulted another DNR Warden, Craig Kopacek, who said that to the best of his knowledge, it was either from a large wolf, or probably, due to the color and hair length, a wolf/dog hybrid of some sort. Which, of course, is precisely what the Manwolf appears to be, except for its bipedal stance, large stature, muscular torso, and humanlike use of its forelimbs. The main portion of the fur specimen remains in Philippsen's possession, although she did cut off a small piece for me to show people (we had to use heavy-duty kitchen shears to make a dent in the inch-thick mat).

One other wrinkle in the Williams Bay location turned up only a few weeks before this manuscript was due. I learned that a Williams Bay man had taken a photo of what appears to be a very large wolf print in the Kishwauketoe preserve, found on the trail along the creek about fifty feet from the Highway 67 trailhead, in the spring of 2003. The soil was moist and loamy, although covered with a fine grass, and the prints were very visible. Their depth indicated that something very heavy, probably walking on two feet, made them. They change direction within the space of about a yard.

Michael Nettesheim, who took the photos, placed his size-thirteen gym shoe next to one of the prints. It was just as wide and about half as long as his shoe, as can be seen from the photo. His shoes measured four and one quarter inches across the ball of the foot, and exactly twelve inches long. That makes the print roughly four and a half by six inches, just about the same size as the plaster casts I took from Mary Philippsen's flower bed.

The footprint Mike Nettesheim photographed was nearly half as long as his size thirteen shoe.

They also match the forward part of the print diagrams made by a Georgia witness. True, they were made two years before Philippsen's roof incident, but they were found perhaps only a quarter of a mile from Philippsen's home, in a great area of natural cover.

Philippsen has since moved to another state, as a strangely high number of Manwolf witnesses seem wont to do, and her cottage has new owners who have already replaced the green roof. But Philippsen became so convinced that her midnight visitor was

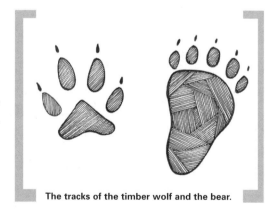

The tracks of the timber wolf and the bear.

actually a Beast visitation that she convinced a Florida production company, the Misplaced Comedy Group, to film a documentary on the Beast of Bray Road. Her sister (who found the fur) is a member of the troupe. Several members came to Wisconsin in September 2005 and interviewed me along with a smattering of witnesses. And another documentary producer has expressed interest in creating a program for the The Learning Channel, with the promise of lab analysis of the fur sample by one of the world's top mammalian experts. If that goes through, we may yet get our confirmation that Kopacek is correct, and this fur is from an unknown canid. It wouldn't be final proof that the bipedal Manwolf exists, of course, but it would certainly fill a large hole in the overall puzzle.

Of course, if the scat pile did have something to do with the incident after all, and the fur should prove to be from a 150-pound, turkey-munching raccoon, we have a new and really nasty problem on our hands in Walworth County.

CHAPTER ELEVEN

GEORGIA WEREWOLVES ON MY MIND

"In the desert
I saw a creature, naked, bestial..."
— Robert Louis Stevenson, *In the Desert*

It was an unusually warm day in June, one of those dog days when even the birds give up and take afternoon naps. Which is exactly what I was doing, the occasional afternoon nap being a perk of writing full-time at home. The phone jangled me out of a fitful dream, and I was surprised to hear a southern drawl on the other end of the line. Blinking my eyes to help clear my brain, I didn't quite catch his name the first time he said it, but when he confided a bit shakily that he wanted to tell me about something he'd seen, my mind shifted into instant auto-focus. I was about to hear one of the best sightings yet, one that would actually leave me frightened by the time I hung up the phone over an hour later. Frightened, and yet grateful something had moved this man to find me and report this.

He had never heard of me or my book, he said, until he was finally driven to the Internet looking for more information about the thing he had seen in early June 2005 in southern Georgia. Part Seminole Indian, he makes his living as a funeral director but is an avid hunter and outdoorsman in his spare time. He asked that his name be withheld for business reasons, so I'll call him Andy. He says he doesn't drink or do drugs; his strongest beverage is coffee. The incident happened on some land he and a group of friends lease for hunting about seventy miles south of Savannah, about twenty miles inland from the coast. Much of the land is covered in waist-high swamp, with roads left by loggers. His Seminole grandfather had told him where there used to be Indian camps on the land Andy and a few companions leased for hunting hogs and other animal denizens of the swamp, and he had been out there looking for arrowheads that day.

"It was just about dark," he said, "so it was between 8:30 and 9:00 PM. I was getting back in my truck getting ready to leave when I saw something down the road in front of me. At first I thought it was a deer, but then I saw it was standing on two legs. I grabbed my rifle when I realized it wasn't a deer, and started toward it. I got within 30 yards when it turned, and as it turned, its head and face came into view. I was in the Marine Corps, served in two wars and been wounded twice, so I know what it is to be scared. But I have never felt fear like that."

Shocked, Andy realized he was looking at something that walked upright, yet had the head and face of a dog or wolf.

Sound familiar?

"It turned completely around," he added, "and stared at me. I was going to shoot it, and when I put the rifle up it leaped off the road and into the swamp. It had a tuft of hair three or four inches long where the tail would be."

Andy had a very good look at it; it was still dusk, and he had turned the foglights up on his truck. "The face was almost like a dog," he said. "It had a long snout, and tall ears that pointed up, similar to a huskie's. The damn hair that ran off the tips of the ears was like a lynx, in tufts. I'd say the ears themselves were about five to six inches long from the base of the skull, and then the tufts added another five or six inches. It had whiskers, thick, big whiskers."

Andy, who in his profession is used to viewing a wide range of body sizes, estimated the creature weighed between 250 and 275 pounds. "It was taller than me," he said, "and I'm over six foot. I'd say it was at least six and a half feet tall. The eyes were yellow, with black pupils, and they glowed."

The teeth were also unusual. "The canine teeth came out from the top lip and stopped where the edge of the jaw ended. They weren't like a saber-tooth tiger, but what I could see was probably one and a half or one and three-quarter inches long. When I first saw it his mouth was partly open."

Andy said the creature was very muscular, "like a body-builder," and its fur grew shaggier as it went up its body from the ground. "At the feet it was not real long, but starting a little above the waist it started getting shaggier, 'til it was a couple of inches long, almost like a man near the head. I could see the chest muscles, they were visible. One other thing I did notice. I always check a hog or coyote to see if it's male before I shoot it. I didn't see any genitals at all, none that were visible."

The color of the animal was what used to be called "brindle," said Andy, who owns seven hunting dogs. That means a combination of brown and black, with some reddish areas mixed in. Andy was also amazed to notice that the legs were shaped like a dog's legs rather than a human's, yet it was able to stand and walk on them. "It didn't run like a human, it ran with its arms down and they stayed down. Its right arm started to raise up and that's when I saw the hand. It was a *hand*, with long fingers, and the claws were three inches long. The closest thing I can think of is an old Ozzy Osbourne poster I used to have where he was dressed like a werewolf with the long fingers and claws."

Andy had a good look at the feet, too, which he said were like a dog's foot, only much bigger. After the creature ran off, he found tracks in the road and copied them into a notebook with a pencil. The track was big enough that his foot, a size eleven, would fit into it, he said. "Where the human's ball of the foot is, this thing had a pad that went across the entire width of the foot. It had four toes, and each one had a point in front of it." Any good tracker knows that point means a claw, and canine prints are recognizable partly because of that very feature. Cougars and other cats will normally

Andy's sketch of the Georgia swamp Manwolf.

SIZE 11 SHOE

**Andy's diagram of the creature's print
next to his own footprint.**

walk with claws retracted, unless they are just getting ready to pounce.

The creature also reeked, he said. "It smelled like shit. Multiply a shaggy, wet dog times ten with a little urine thrown in. It was awful. It will take your breath away. I track hogs partly by smell, and this was not a hog. The thing did stink."

Andy's sighting was also unique because he actually heard the creature make a noise, a low growling sound, when it first knew it had been spotted. More exciting than that, however, is that Andy is one of the very few to have had a chance to see the creature twice. Not that he was exactly looking for it.

About two weeks after his first sighting, the area had a heavy rainstorm, he said. That meant topsoil would be washed away, and arrowheads would be much easier to pick out of the loose soil around the swamplands. He was tempted enough by that to try going back to the hunting land, but this time he took precautions. He brought his cousin and hunting companion, who I'll call "Billy," and three combination bulldog-mastiffs that weighed about seventy-five pounds each. He'd seen the biggest take down a hog of equal weight, he said.

"I had jokingly said to Billy, he might see a wolfman that night. He said, well, what do you mean, and I jokingly told him I had seen one but he didn't believe it. We were about a half mile down the road from where I saw it the first time." Again, it was just getting dark, and Andy and Billy had had a successful day of picking arrowheads and were in the truck, ready to call it a day. Suddenly, Andy was stunned to see the creature again near the edge of the woods, standing on its hind legs and looking straight at him with its yellow, glaring eyes.

"I looked down the road and there it was. I said, 'Billy, dude, that's it. That's the damn werewolf.'"

Andy pulled the back seat up to get his rifle while Billy, after gaping in disbelief, darted around the truck to let the dogs out. "It took me about ten seconds to get the rifle out and ready, and it started walking toward me. Then he started to run, it looked like he was going to charge the truck. That second time when he started to run toward me, that terrified me. I've been out west, seen red wolves, got within fifteen feet of a female desert wolf that had pups, but I've never had an animal run like that at me. This thing charged like it meant to do me some damage. It was trying to get to me."

Right about at that point, said Andy, Billy managed to let the dogs off the back of the truck. When it heard the dogs hit the ground, Andy said, the creature stopped abruptly, leaped about fifteen feet and took off into the brush on all fours. The dogs chased it through the swampland for about half an hour, said Andy, and finally came back to the truck, exhausted.

Seeing the creature has explained a few mysteries, Andy believes. "I have found hogs disemboweled, and a gator that was ripped up and had his tail torn off on this land.

"I was very hesitant to call you, I've never watched horror movies, I'm a redneck from south Georgia; I don't believe in werewolves but I've seen this thing's face. This ain't no cat, this ain't no monkey. It's canine. I'll tell you one thing; I come across the thing again, I'm gonna put a hole in it. I know what it is to be scared, but that night at that moment I was not a grown man, I was a little boy again. I'm not a liar, what I saw was what I saw.

"A few nights ago, my son got scared watching a movie, and I had to tell him there is no such thing as the bogeyman, but I feel like a liar. There really is something out there."

Andy said he heard about the *loup-garou* time and again from his grandparents, and even remembers his grandmother spreading sulphur around the yard to keep the *loup-garou* away. "I never believed it, but now I'm starting to think they knew something," he said. And there were other strange things in the woods that he's heard about all his life. Black panthers, for one. "And there used to be an old woman in the woods people called a swamp witch. I don't know if she was or not," he said. "But this thing was real. It was not a vapor, it was not an apparition, and I was not hallucinating."

Andy says he hasn't been arrowhead hunting since then; he's frankly afraid to go alone and Billy refuses to go back. "He's half Seminole, and like a brother to me, and he won't talk about it," said Andy.

Whoa.

I was ready to hop in my car and drive to Georgia, myself. Until I started thinking about the yellow eyes with black pupils, the inch-and-a-half long fangs, and the 250-pound thing with ears like Anubis that wasn't fearful of charging a man with a rifle. But Andy had contributed a whopping amount of information. And finally, someone had had the presence of mind to at least draw a picture of the tracks. His mention that his foot could fit into them reminded me of the Bray Road prints that the woman could place one of her moon boots in. And the foot structure makes sense.

The hind feet would have to be larger than a dog's in order to be stable enough to walk upright on them…imagine a human trying to teeter around on its toes all the time. Even ballerinas can't do that without special, padded shoes. I'd never had anyone describe the ears as quite that tall, or tufted, but that's a fairly minor variation that could even be an individual quirk.

I thought Andy had two characteristics that made him a very credible witness. As a funeral director, he was trained in physiology and forensics, so that he would be a reliable observer of zoological detail. And as a regular hunter and woodsman, he was familiar with all types of wildlife in the swampy areas he'd lived in all his life.

It should be mentioned that the hogs that he and his friends hunted on that land (which has since reverted to government use) have grown to nuisance level in Georgia. Many of them interbreed with local livestock and reach huge proportions. One giant specimen taken in 2004 in southern Georgia was dubbed "Hogzilla" by the media. It weighed 800 pounds and measured seven and a half feet long, and was discovered to be a combination of wild boar and a Hampshire farm animal. Could Andy's swamp predator have been an errant marsh pig? Hogs do have brown fur and long snouts. They do not, however, have "hands" with claws, tufted tails, or doglike legs. Most importantly, they do not stroll down country roads on their short hind legs. Moreover, in the wild hogs grow large, identifiable tusks if they are males, and a seven-foot-long hog would weigh several times more than the estimated 250 pounds of the creature Andy saw. Besides, Andy has hunted and killed dozens of hogs. He would not be likely to mistake one for any other animal.

I did find a few references to another mythic-sounding possibility altogether, a Seinfeld-esque (the episode where Kramer is obsessed with a short-snouted man he sees in a hospital) hodgepodge of a creature called a Pigman. The notion is not limited to TV sitcoms, believe it or not. Noted Wisconsin historian and folklorist Dennis Boyer tells of one such creature in his *Giants in the Land: Folk Tales and Legends of Wisconsin.*

The creature is called the Sprague Stumper Jumper in Boyer's book, but was described by a woodsman from Necedah, Juneau County, as "half man, half pig." The teller said that while one person had tried to tell him it was an actual human/hog hybrid, a Ho-Chunk woman advised him that it was probably a man who had been cursed by a witch. And the creature did wear tattered clothing. Supposedly, he would live in unattended hunting cabins and liberate certain items he needed from them.

The Pigman or Stumper Jumper, whichever you prefer, was hardly the ferocious predator encountered by Andy, however. It was known for rescuing damsels in distress, and even, it was whispered, for servicing the occasional lonely widow. And it had some supernatural overtones, beyond the idea of the witch's curse, as some said it could turn into other animals, or even become all man or all hog.

Still, as Wisconsin folklore it's a rather flimsy stretch to posit that the Georgia creature could be a man cursed into looking like one of those feral hogs, or vice versa. But Andy did say the area is home to at least one reputed swamp witch. And more interestingly, the *Okefenokee X-Files* site says that there is such a legend as the "South Georgia Pig Man." The description rings slightly familiar: "A large apelike being that walks upright, has abundant hair and a nose similar to a pig."

A "skunk-like" odor has also been noted. The nose "similar to a pig" means that it would have a pronounced snout, though probably not so long or narrow as a wolf's. It also says, however, that the creature has never been aggressive to anyone, and indeed appears skittish of humans, with "sad, expressive eyes." That does not sound like the thing that charged Andy.

The most obvious (though no less mysterious) explanation is the well-known Swamp Ape that has been reported living in southern bogs from Georgia to Florida. Author Jim Miles, in a 2000 book called *Weird Georgia*, discusses many tales of Swamp Apes, which seem similar in most cases to Bigfoot. The creatures are most famous for emitting a rancid, sour, sickening odor much like the rank smell Andy inhaled during his sighting. However, the Swamp Ape is almost uniformly described as possessing an apelike face and a shape like the typical Bigfoot, and averages about eight feet tall. Its prints are normally the giant, sixteen- to twenty-four-inch, flat-footed tracks associated with Bigfoot, too, although some encounter sites have yielded prints with three or four toes and even a few with claws, like Andy's creature.

I would hazard a guess that a doglike print with claws cannot belong to any sort of Bigfoot genus, its Swamp Ape cousin included. This obvious fact would suggest there are at least two types of creatures running around Georgia swamps, just like in Wisconsin. One is an apelike being, seven to eight feet tall and weighing an average of 800 pounds, the approximate weight of the larger feral hogs. The other has doglike legs and feet, although it can walk upright, and a doglike or wolflike head with protruding muzzle and upright ears. Although formidably muscled, it weighs much less than the Bigfoot or feral hog. It can equal the Bigfoot in its ability to stink up a place, though. Of course, as in Wisconsin, some of the Georgia Swamp Ape stories in Miles' book are ambiguous enough to apply to either creature, so that a few of the encounters he classifies as Swamp Apes might actually have been Manwolves.

There is one other large creature inhabiting the Georgia swamps that should be mentioned. Where there are tall brown furries, there are usually long black furries, too, usually labeled panthers or mystery cats. This area of Georgia swamp is no exception; "swamp panthers" are commonly sighted by locals. Although usually perceived as black, animal experts say South Georgia panthers are actually dark brown. Truly black cats, they add, would be black leopards, strictly speaking, which are not indigenous to the area and may have escaped from a circus or wildlife park. Panthers, cougars, or pumas are native to much of North and South America, but are thought to be extinct in Georgia since 1920. Despite official extinction, and whether brown panthers or black leopards, people do swear these felines live in the swamp. It's much like the mountain lion or cougar situation in the upper Midwest.

It's unlikely, however, that any panthers walk upright, even though Louisiana folklore includes legends of Cat People created by Voodoo rites. Remember the 1980s movie set in the sad New Orleans Zoo where giant felines and humans traded places with impunity? Pure fiction, of course, based on very old tales. And probably no more likely than the Pig Man to be true.

But even if the Georgia Wolf Man is not a brown panther or a "hoo-doo" phantom, there is still a strange connection between it and the cats. As I just noted, it seems that in many places where large, unidentified humanoids are found, large anomalous felines go claw in claw. "In the years 1917 and 1970," states a book called *Space Time Transients and Unusual Events*, "hundreds of people in southwestern Illinois reported seeing large catlike and humanoid creatures." But they are both also often associated with strange light phenomena and mysterious energy fields, neither of which were reported by our Georgia witness.

One aspect of the creature, the multi-colored brindle fur, did remind me of the "Marked Hominid" cited in Coleman and Huyghe's *Field Guide*. Marked Hominids, a shorter variant of Bigfoot, are also said to have two-toned fur. However, they are seen in the sub-polar regions and are described as even more humanlike than the classic Sasquatch...not at all canine. Furthermore, the *Guide* says they display visible genitalia, which Andy had taken special care to look for and did not see. In fact, not one eyewitness has ever mentioned seeing a penis on a Manwolf, but then I don't know if any other witnesses were specifically checking for that. It could just be that this creature had extra fur that protected his modesty, or perhaps it was a female. Still, what Andy saw was much too prominently canine and lurking way too far south to be a Marked Hominid if Coleman and Huyghe's guidelines are to be followed.

Whatever the creature's true nature, it had Andy hooked on finding it, and he continued to investigate the section of swamp where he made his sighting. He called me a few weeks later, on July 13, and told me he had returned to the site alone but with several of his dogs. He had set up some cameras with motion sensors, and they'd been flooded with recent heavy rains so he needed to reset them. "I did come across a couple of tracks and took pictures of them," he said. "They went across the road where it's bisque-colored sand in parts. The tracks were a day old, I'd say. I let the dogs loose and they trailed it for two miles. I could hear them and kept driving. Evidently they spooked something; they came across something that scared them to death. One came out just shaking; I've never seen him so scared. I think this thing has got a den between those two points."

The Manwolf wasn't the only big critter in the swamp, however, said Andy. "There's a big boar-hog out there that got away. I said I'd get some guys and get it. I'm going to have the resources of armed men and some hunting dogs." And hopefully, he thought, the crew might flush out the wolfen creature, too.

"Whatever this is, it's bedded down. It's a swampy, wet area covered in cypress. An animal could find a den easily. Years ago when they went in and cut the cypress, they left logs in piles. If this thing has a den, that's where it's at."

Andy was planning his hunt for the next weekend, he said, since the state was taking over the leased property in the first week of August. "They gave us a two-week period to clean out our tree stands," he said. "But I've struggled with the idea of going in with these guys not knowing what's there."

Andy did assemble a posse of seasoned hog-hunters, ostensibly to track down the runaway hog. He finally figured they wouldn't believe him if he did tell them what he was really hoping to find. Billy still refused to go, regardless. But Andy took five armed men and ten dogs, setting it up so that between all of them, every corner of the swamp would be combed. The men did their best, but to Andy's consternation, the creature was nowhere to be seen and neither were any hogs. Andy thinks the creature may have packed a few hefty ham sandwiches and left the area, at least temporarily, after detecting so many dogs loose in its backyard. But Andy is still determined to find out what it is holed up in that piece of swampland, despite his own fear. "I've looked into the mouth of Hell," he declared, "and I didn't like it much."

CHAPTER TWELVE

MICHIGAN MANWOLVES

"Do not follow where the path may lead. Go instead where there is no path and leave a trail."

—Muriel Strode

Werewolf Nation

If Wisconsin and Georgia were the only states reporting furry, bipedal, wolf-headed creatures, it would be easy for the world to sit back on its haunches and howl derisively that this is only a regional phenomenon, not worthy of investigation or further thought. But by now, the attentive reader will have realized this is not, in fact, the case. Upright canids roam freely across our land, and their territory appears unlimited.

This chapter and the following two are filled with incidents gathered over the past two years from various sources, and they range from aberrant wild "wolf" packs to full-out werewolf wannabes. I'm sure there are many more sightings still unreported, particularly in the western states where native societies with traditions of Skinchangers predominate, but at least we now have some idea of possible Manwolf territory (see map). The map, by the way, will always have to be considered a work in progress as more sightings come in. And when all is said, done, and reported, perhaps clusters as large as those in Wisconsin will be found in other states as well. Maybe we will even find that unbeknownst to most of us, a Fifth World nation has always lived right under our pathetically scent-challenged human noses. We might call it the United States of A-Were-rica.

Michigan Dogman

In the first book, I covered the Michigan Dogman, which fits the typical Manwolf description and exhibits the same modus operandi in behavior…the challenging evil-eye stare, leaving nasty scratch marks on

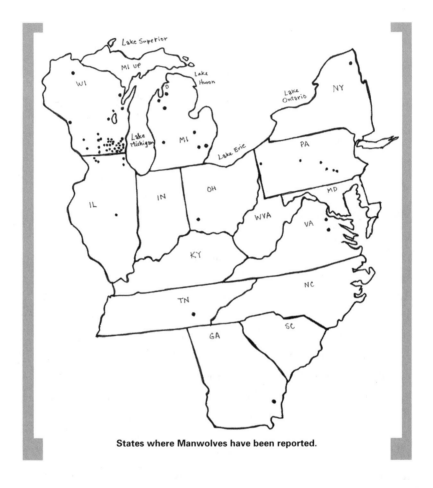

States where Manwolves have been reported.

doors like so much wolfen graffiti, scaring people excrementless, and dashing for the nearest exit upon being sighted. The Dogman prowled mostly around the northwestern part of the Lower Peninsula, and was first made known to the public by Traverse City deejay Steve Cook who wrote an enormously popular song about it called *The Legend*. Whether the lumber camp *loup-garou* still haunts those woods is unknown at this writing; people sometimes take years to come forward and tell their stories, if they ever do so at all. But if it *is* the same Manwolf that is seen in Wisconsin, I'd bet a Medieval wolf hide girdle that people are still encountering the creature but nobody is reporting it, for the usual two reasons: denial that something so strange really exists and fear of ridicule.

Cook's station, WTCM, is still selling CDs of *The Legend,* and is planning a special new edition for 2007. That's because it's the seventh year of every decade when, according to Cook's song, the creature reappears. In reality, however, it seems the Dogman doesn't always wait for its cue. As some Michiganders have found out, it appears when it wants to, unfettered by the boundaries of mere legend.

Acme Woods Dogman

In September 2004, I received an e-mail from Tammy Moss, now of Las Vegas, who was persuaded by a werewolf-savvy employer to contact me with her story of the Michigan Dogman. Tammy estimates it would have happened in the summer of 1989 or '90, about eight miles north of Traverse City in Acme Township. That area boasts an almost embarrassing number of state parks and lakeshore, and, of course, is not far from many of the original Dogman sightings. But I'll let you hear it in Tammy's words:

> I have always thought that the 7th day of the 7th month of the 7th year was a bit farfetched, as I thought the whole Dogman thing was. Well, I was proven correct on the 7 thing but not on the Dogman. I actually saw one. I was following a friend through the woods on an off-road road when I saw something huge and hairy and tall run past the front of his car, which he stopped immediately and then tore again off into the darkness. I stopped and looked around and saw, about seven feet off the ground, yellow eyes glowing in the shadows.
>
> That was all it took to get me to drive away from there like a bat out of hell. When I met up with my friend later that morning, he was very shaky and pale and couldn't really talk. There were many of our group around at the time and I walked toward him, passing his car on the way. Before I got that far, I looked down at his car and there, in the seam between right headlight and front quarter panel, were several very thick, very long, what looked like wolf hairs.

The hairs somehow disappeared, unfortunately, and Tammy was unable to provide any more details on the creature's appearance.

Tammy continued,

> I actually have a theory regarding the Dogman and the Beast of Bray Road since I grew up in northern Michigan and have recently seen your Web site. I think that the Dogman of northern Michigan and the Beast of Bray Road are one and the same...not that there is only one creature, but that they are of the same breed. According to the legend, the Dogman has been around for a couple hundred years in northern Michigan. I have always thought that there were more than one single creature. Now it seems I am right. I really think that the Beast of Bray Road is actually more of the Dogmen that inhabit Michigan. They are either multiplying or Michigan's woods are getting too densely inhabited by humans, or both, and they are now moving to Wisconsin.

Tammy really could be right.

The Creature of Allegan County

Or perhaps Michigan's wolfen clan has merely migrated to other locales. Further south, perhaps. I have found some references to sightings of a "werewolf-looking creature" in Fennville, in Allegan County. Several people are supposed to have spotted a light colored, wolfish creature between four and five feet high east of the city around 54th Street and State Highway M89. That location, by the way, is adjacent to the Allegan State Game Area.

Ironically, Fennville is best known for a restaurant, Crane's Pie Pantry, that features a dead, stuffed dog named "Betty" that sits perched in an antique sleigh as part of a permanent exhibit on the restaurant's porch. And incidentally, Allegan County, according to local lore, is also home to a small, inbred tribe of strange people with oversized noggins called Melonheads. They are supposed to live in cabins and in underground tunnels on the grounds of the historic Felt mansion near

Saugatuck along with a vicious caretaker. Together, they encircle and attack trespassers with sticks.

A county of high strangeness, if nothing else.

Byron Center Shadow Wolf

But while I don't count the Allegan County tales as any part of the sightings record, I did receive a story with werewolfish overtones from Byron Center, just south of Grand Rapids and about twenty-five miles northeast of Fennville. A woman (name withheld) wrote me after my September 3, 2005, appearance on *Coast to Coast AM*, "I have seen the creature you were discussing on the radio tonight as a child, but I remember." She wrote that she saw it often at her grandparents' barn, which was right next door to her house, in the late 1950s. "I even saw it once in our basement," she said. "It was sort of like in another dimension. I remember being *very* afraid and I never told anyone."

She described herself as an "ordinary, 52-year-old lady." Upon questioning, she said she doesn't remember precisely whether it looked like a wolf or a German shepherd. "It was more human, but very large," she wrote. "Of course, I was small, probably under ten. I don't recall it having hair but I don't recall clothes or nakedness either. I remember that it startled me but I also startled it…it was hiding…. It was not expecting a little girl poking around."

She remembers the basement's cement walls, but also made the interesting statement that she has a "distinct feeling" that she blocked out many of the details, noting that when she tried to remember, she "got a feeling of being afraid to see it again."

The woman is highly educated and doesn't know quite what to make of her conflicting thoughts on the subject. "But I know I saw it," she wrote, "and I would know instantly if I saw it again."

This story, of course, has distinctly supernatural overtones. Seeing the creature in her basement is quite unusual, as is feeling that it was somehow "in another dimension." If she had seen it *only* in her basement, I'd be tempted to say this was a screen memory for some unpleasant but more mundane experience, especially since she still has feelings of wanting to block the whole thing out. But with the additional sightings around the barn, which she didn't describe, it becomes more likely that She was actually experiencing something anomalous. Was it a Manwolf? The description is too vague to say. But it's an interesting and frightening tale, and if true, implies that this creature may have more of an interest (and ability to access) our homes and buildings than we would like to think. You'll see an affirmation of that unsettling thought later in this chapter.

Werewolves of Detroit

Michigan has a deep history of Manwolves of the supernatural kind, however. Detroit was first settled by French Canadians, and the *loup-garou* evidently smuggled itself along in someone's great-great-grand-pappy's steamer trunk. "The Werewolves of Detroit" have been documented by several folk historians. Early in that city's history, long before it became known for Motown music and automobiles, Detroit's mix of French and Native American inhabitants contributed to a unique blend of werewolf lore. The following stories are not at all the same as most of our modern-day sightings, of course, which are mainly recountings of witnesses with no legend (and usually no magic) attached, but they offer a historical backdrop that shows these critters have preyed on the minds (and sometimes bodies) of humans here for centuries.

The little island of Belle Isle just outside of the city proper was considered enchanted by both groups, and the story was that a Snake God or Goddess ruled over a coven of witches who sold charms, hexes, and other magical services to the townspeople. One Detroiter, a Jacques Morand, resorted to the powers of the snake witches when he could not persuade the woman he loved to marry him. Hearing that she had entered a nunnery and taken vows there, the despairing man sold his soul to a snake witch in return for the power to become a *loup-garou*. His undoing came about when he tried to snatch his intended from her prayers in the convent, and thus was inconveniently exposed to a particular statue of the Virgin Mary. In a strange twist on the old Greek legend of the snake-headed Goddess Medusa, who turned ordinary mortals into stone upon sight, exposure to the

Virgin Mary statue turned the snake-bewitched werewolf into a harmless chunk of granite.

It's impossible to say whether this tale was based even upon so much as a sighting of a timber wolf at a Catholic convent, although it could have happened at that time and place when wolves had not been exterminated from the Midwest. The following story might also have its origins in tales of one particularly elusive and hardy wolf that settlers and Indians alike found so hard to kill that it assumed legendary status.

In this tale, a werewolf seized a woman from her own wedding dance and dragged her off to the woods. Her bridegroom never stopped hunting the creature that stole his bride and encouraged many others to join his dogged pursuit. The closest anyone came to killing the wily animal was when a neighbor managed to sever its tail with a speeding silver bullet. The tail was recovered by a native tribe and kept by them as a charm. Eventually, the bridegroom was able to corner the creature at the banks of the river, and rather than letting itself be killed or captured, the *loup-garou* flung itself into the water and landed in the jaws of a giant catfish. Supposedly, that knowledge of what might lurk inside river catfish has turned generations of French Canadians against eating that particular species of fish.

The third story is interesting because it again involves witches, only this time the creature is aiding them as their mascot and helper. It seemed a white man had purposely given whiskey to some Native Americans to get them drunk so that he could steal the load of beaver skins they had come to trade. As he was making his way out of the woods, he was beset by witches who grabbed the pelts, while a werewolf who just happened to be in the 'hood jumped on the dishonest trader's back. Luckily, during the fray, a rosary the man carried in his pocket fell out, which caused the werewolf to dive into the earth and the witches to flee. The spring that rose up at that spot where the werewolf disappeared was called Belle Fontaine.

Don't Mess with the Repo Man

By far the most significant sighting to come out of Michigan since the Dogman cluster, however, is a very recent and quite horrifying incident near the small town of Holly, which lies sandwiched between the Seven Lakes State Park to its west and the Holly Recreation Area to the east. The village contains six lakes and nine parks, so there is considerable open or undeveloped land in the area, even though it sits smack between the busy cities of Pontiac and Flint.

A man who heard me on a radio show e-mailed to tell me that his co-worker had seen a Manwolf, and he kindly provided me with the man's phone number. The co-worker, Jeff Cornelius of Saginaw, did not mind telling me his story as long as I didn't give the name of the company he works for. Cornelius is a "repo" man, one who makes a living by retrieving vehicles being repossessed by a lending institution, usually for failure to make payments. People in this line of work generally possess a certain pragmatic toughness, used as they are to encountering all types of uncooperative property owners. Often they run into large guard dogs and other hazards, dangers that come with the territory. As a group, it's probably safe to say that repo men (and women) aren't folks who get rattled easily.

Cornelius remembers the night he did get rattled. "It was the first of June," he told me in a phone interview. "And it was the first full moon of the summer, so I could see things pretty well. It was the third try I had on this guy out on Fish Lake Road." (That road runs north and south, adjacent to the Seven Lakes State Park area.)

The man lived in a remote area surrounded by marsh, said Cornelius. He wasn't home when Cornelius arrived. Cornelius glanced around and didn't see the vehicle he was seeking in the driveway, but he had noticed an outbuilding that appeared to be locked. He drove his truck almost up to it, got out and tried peering into the windows to check for the wanted vehicle.

"Just as I was checking," said Cornelius, "I heard something snap to my left. I looked, and there it was, about twenty-five yards away from me. It looked like it was angry that I saw it, because as soon as I turned my head, it started growling at me. It was a low, scary growl. And as soon as I seen it, it tore ass at me."

"It," or the strange creature that had snapped the twig, was somewhat hunched over, said Cornelius, and stood about five feet five or five feet seven inches in that slightly bent posture. He thinks it probably would have appeared taller had it been standing fully straight. But what shocked him was that the creature was coming at him on its hind legs, its front "legs" far above the ground. "Its front legs were in the air," were Cornelius' exact words. "It had hind legs like a dog's, bent backwards," he said. "It wasn't a dog, wasn't a monkey. I'd say it was more like a cross between a baboon and a hyena. It was coming sideways at me at first, and I could see it had raised hair on its back from below the shoulders up. It had a big head, and straight fur on its face."

Luckily for Cornelius he was only seven feet from his truck, and he managed to leap for it and slam the driver's side door before the creature could reach him. He immediately threw the gears into reverse, backed up a little, and swerved around to try to get the creature in his headlights for a better look at it, and perhaps to scare it off, but by the time he had swung the front of the pickup around, the creature was nowhere to be seen. "It was out of there," he said.

Cornelius felt he had had a very close call. "If I wouldn't have heard the thing, I'm sure it would have been on me in seconds," he said. "I felt it was sneaking up on me. I'm fully convinced it would have eaten me. When it happened, I was shaken up, and that's saying a lot." He left the property on the double, and refused to go back to the place a fourth time. "I took a lot of flak at work when I told them what I saw," he said. But after hearing the story, no one else at that place would go to the Fish Lake property either. "Nobody had balls enough to go out there," declared Cornelius.

He did get a very good look at the creature, even though he estimates the entire incident took only thirty to forty seconds. "The full moon lit everything," said Cornelius.

He said the creature's body appeared "thick, thick all over." When I asked him if he was able to see muscles, he said, "Absolutely. It wasn't some man in a suit. Even if somebody could get a suit like that, how could he make his legs bend backwards like that?"

The creature did not have feet, said Cornelius. "They were paws." The ears were big, pointed, and on top of the head, and he described the creature's fur as not solid black, but a combination of gray and black. "It had shades to it," he noted (perhaps similar to the "brindle" description of the Georgia swamp Manwolf). He estimated the animal's muzzle to be about six to seven inches long and said it reminded him of a baboon's snout, with rounded, "fat" cheeks on either side. The creature was "person-sized," he added, "maybe 160, 170 pounds." Although he was out in the open air with it at close range on a relatively warm night, he did not detect any odor coming from the creature. "The only way I can describe it is like a werewolf," he said.

The reference to the baboon face is something I've heard occasionally before. It's not surprising; their alternate name is "Dog-faced Monkey." Baboons do have a longer snout than most other monkeys. But a baboon's legs do not "bend backwards" the way people usually describe canid legs as doing, and their feet are not pawlike, but long-toed and almost handlike, pressed flat to the ground when walking. The baboon walks on all fours and "runs" by galloping sideways on all fours, as well.

Needless to say, a baboon, designed for much warmer climates, would be very out of place in Michigan. I highly doubt that it was a baboon stalking Cornelius on two legs; it is more likely that the creature's long snout and facial structure simply made Cornelius think of a baboon's face.

I can't help but mention that, like the sightings which reminded people of the Egyptian jackal-headed god of the dead, Anubis, the baboon-headed creature also has an Egyptian parallel. Thoth, god of knowledge, was either portrayed with the head of an ibis or a baboon. Of course, the Egyptians had a whole pantheon of animal-headed deities, including hippos and alligators, so it would be silly to assign too much meaning to this. I simply think it's interesting that these two comparisons keep popping up in our contemporary eyewitness descriptions.

And yet, I keep thinking back to the first incident in this book, the dog/ape shape shifter witnessed by the Madison bookstore clerk. Again, it's very reminiscent of Thoth, the baboon or dog/ape god. Thoth was considered the inventor of both hieroglyphics and magic, in a way that, believe it or not, still impacts many people today. Because

Thoth was also a messenger for the other gods, the Greeks adopted him as a counterpart to Hermes, who fulfilled that role in the Greek pantheon. They called him Hermes Trismegistus, and particularly venerated an ancient manuscript called *The Book of Thoth*, or later, as *The Hermetica*. It contained various magic spells as well as explanations of astronomy and other esoteric subjects, and was used even by the alchemists of the Middle Ages. It still has followers to this day. Some of the spells deal with transformational powers. It seems logical to me that a follower of Thoth might want to use this knowledge, and that the most likely object of the shape-shifting spell would be the venerated dog/ape form. And that would probably look something like a standing baboon or strange dog, or perhaps something that changes from dog to ape, like Preston saw.

I have no idea whether any such thing is really possible, of course, but the connections fall in line too neatly not to point them out, for whatever they are worth. But again, Cornelius didn't say he thought this *was* a baboon, just that its face reminded him of one.

Pressed for other possible comparisons, Cornelius added that he is familiar with what Bigfoot is supposed to look like, "but this ain't no Bigfoot." He says that although he describes himself as a movie connoisseur, he has never read about werewolves, and never had a paranormal experience such as seeing a ghost or a UFO. "I deal with a lot of animals in my work," he said, "and I'm not a stranger to running into a large dog. This was not a dog. It was the creepiest thing I ever saw in my life."

It was also one of the creepiest Manwolf stories I'd ever

The ancient Egyptian god Thoth in his baboon-headed form.

heard in my life. And I do believe that whatever Cornelius saw has enough of the characteristics to put it into that category. But at the time he returned my initial call, I was sitting alone in my house during a power outage, just after dark. I was taking my notes by candlelight, pretty much the perfect setting to hear a terrifying story from someone. And despite the fact that, to my knowledge, the Manwolf has never actually hurt a human being, the way this creature sneaked up on Cornelius and made a furious dash toward him creates a very disturbing picture. Its ferocity is similar to what Andy in Georgia experienced during his sightings, and both men felt sure that their attackers intended to do them bodily harm if possible. It makes me wonder whether there have been other attacks when people were caught and then simply became unsolved, missing-person cases. I also have to ponder the safety of that derelict homeowner, and whether perhaps the reason he wasn't at home...and indeed had stopped making payments...was that he had already whetted a Manwolf's appetite for human flesh.

It's interesting that Michigan has this combination of valid physical sightings and other stories that are clearly embroidered legends, along with at least one rather mystical experience. It may not be coincidental that a creature which appears to select its living range and hunting routes for their closeness to water, should figure so prominently in the lore of a state that is not only surrounded on three sides by Great Lakes, but most generously endowed with inland lakes, marshes, and waterways. It's a connection we will continue to explore.

CHAPTER THIRTEEN
THE PENNSYLVANIA PACK

"He who fights with monsters might take care lest he thereby become a monster. And if you gaze for long into an abyss, the abyss gazes also into you."
—Friedrich Nietzche, *Beyond Good and Evil,*
Aphorism 146

Pennsylvania: Anomalous Menagerie

With a Germanic heritage second to none, Pennsylvania has always enjoyed a lively folktale repertoire including werewolf, or *Woolfmann,* notions brought from the old country where trials of alleged witches and changesters remained vivid in emigrants' minds. As the late Pennsylvania historian Henry W. Shoemaker once pointed out, since no less important a person than state governor William Alexis Stone included a werewolf tale in his autobiography, "there is ample place for the werwolf (sic) in Pennsylvania folklore." Shoemaker also speculated that it would be entirely possible to make up a book of werewolf stories from every county in the state, with some related vampire tales thrown in to boot.

As in Michigan, the Manwolf has a long and rich tradition in Pennsylvania that begins with the earliest inhabitants and continues with some of the strangest contemporary creature sightings anywhere. Does the creature itself evolve, or just the tales? Or perhaps it's something in the water. At any rate, visitors may want to keep a sharp eye on the roadsides the next time they go barreling down the Pennsylvania Turnpike. All those old "hex" signs decorating the barns of the Pennsylvania Dutch were probably not painted for the fun of it.

The Northumberland Werewolf

Robert Schneck, author of a book about strange stories from around the United States, told me the story of a Pennsylvania werewolf encountered near Northumberland by a young shepherdess named May Paul in the mid-1800s. Schneck noted that May Paul was no figment of legend; he had personally spoken to a living descendent of hers.

It seems that young May had an older admirer, a man who would observe her from afar as she worked, never daring to come forward and speak to her. Many of May's neighbors raised sheep, too, and one by one the flocks began to be attacked by some sort of large predator, which was soon identified as a wolf. Strangely, May's flock was the only one left untouched.

The mystery unraveled when a nearby farmer managed to shoot a huge, gray wolf. It was only wounded and managed to escape, but the determined farmer tracked his quarry until he discovered that the bloody trail led to the dead body of May's admirer. The corpse bore a hole in its chest at the same entry point as in the chest of the wolf the farmer had just shot. From then on, the area was called *Die Woolfmann's Grob* (wolfman's grave). According to May's descendent, she remained a faithful guardian of her flock for another quarter century and never suffered one lost sheep. Perhaps her *Woolfmann* admirer was able to extend his protection beyond the grave.

This story, whether taken as fact or Pennsylvania Dutch legend, does bring up an interesting point that figures in the argument over whether Manwolves are indeed werewolves—that is, men changed into wolves. Nowhere in this story is there any mention of the large gray wolf running on its hind legs or kneeling to hold its prey or enacting any of the other strange behaviors that Beast witnesses find so humanlike and eerie. The Northumberland werewolf looks and behaves like a wolf until it is near death, at which time it must revert to human form.

Backtrack to Europe: the Classic Werewolf

This all-wolf to all-human format is consistent with most versions of the werewolf tale from Old Europe. In many European legends, werewolves are nearly indistinguishable from actual wolves in all ways other than their extra size and ferocity, with perhaps an identifying mark here or there. Since Europeans have a much older tradition of were-wolves, perhaps their ideas about what constitutes such a creature ought to be taken a little more seriously than our own Johnny-come-lately Manwolves. Even in this country, early *loup-garous* stuck to the European standards, as seen in the above tales and those such as the Werewolves of Detroit. (Green Bay, Wisconsin, has a similar pattern of early *loup-garou* tales.) But by the late 1700s, werewolves had been going gangbusters from London to Moscow for centuries and were a completely accepted fact of life to most of our European forebears. And while you will find artist portrayals of old European werewolves standing on two legs (medieval woodcut versions of our *National Enquirer*-style sensationalism), in the stories, they are usually repre-sented as quadrupeds.

I'll take just a couple of quick examples from Montague Summers' *The Werewolf in Lore and Legend.* First, this acknowledged authority on the topic states outright, "By the force of his diabolic pact he (the werewolf) was enabled, owing to a ritual of horrid ointments and impious spells, to assume so cunningly the swift shaggy brute that save by his demoniac ferocity and superhuman strength, none could dis-tinguish him from the natural wolf."

One of my favorites among his tales is from Portugal, where a young woman hired herself out as servant to a family with a newborn. The babe was branded with the mark of the *lupis-homens*, and the ser-vant girl, Joana, then convinced his fearful mother to lay him outside at the full moon, his mark covered with the blood of a white pigeon. (Remember that 2005 sighting in Chapter 10 that occurred on *White Pigeon* Road? Hmmm.) The moon would draw the mark up through the blood. Of course, after the babe was set outside, "a huge brown wolf, gaunt and lean," was seen standing over the mangled body of the baby. The wolf was shot, and of course proved to be Joana.

The famous French teen wolf, Jean Grenier, who terrified Gascony in 1603, was said by one witness to appear as "a wild beast with rufu-lous fur, not unlike a huge dog." Also, there is the tale of the Hungar-ian Gypsy fiddler who discovered his wife was a werewolf when he caught her coming home one night as a "huge grey wolf carrying a mangled lamb in its mouth." Although taken aback at first, the musician liked the way his missus brought home the mutton, so he kept quiet until they were both eventually killed by irate villagers.

Interestingly, when the book does mention something that sounds more like a Manwolf, the creatures are acknowledged to be spirits. In the UK's Cumberland region, a newly built house was haunted by a "phantom" described as "nude and grey, something like a man with the head of a wolf—a wolf with white pointed teeth and horrid, light eyes." Sounds very much like a Manwolf. But in a cave nearby was discovered the skull of a wolf and a headless, human skeleton. Their disposal halted the hauntings. Similar figures were also reported in Exmoor, Merionethshire, and at two locations in Wales.

My point, finally, is that *if* (and it's a GIANT "if," I grant you, and not one that I actually subscribe to) for the sake of argument we accept that there is such a thing as a man who changes physically into a wolf, and assuming Old Country Europeans were better able to define its appearance and behavior than modern-day Americans due to the sheer volume of supposed sightings, we have to consider two possibilities. First, if werewolves are almost indistinguishable from the real thing in appearance, the Beast of Bray Road and all its cousins are not werewolves but some type of unknown animal or a different supernatural being, because Manwolves do not look or behave like wild wolves.

Conversely, again following the old European werewolf model, many of the enormous wolflike, four-footed creatures observed by witnesses in this book such as the huge quadrupeds seen by Richard Fanning and by Andrew Hurd and his mother, then, may not be natural animals or Manwolves, but werewolves in their changed state, in which they look almost exactly like other wolves.

That's why I include both types of reports, biped and quadruped. Assuming that we remain open to all possibilities as to the true nature of this creature, even that of the classic werewolf, then animals that trot on all fours are as suspect as those that run on two legs. Manwolves, of course, have been observed locomoting both ways with equal adeptness, and their anomalous nature is self-evident.

But the classic *Woolfmann* is not the only type of incident recorded from Pennsylvania. Just to confuse our slim grasp of furry hominoid anatomy even further, something on the fuzzy side has been whispered to exist in Lancaster County, a setting that may recall M. Night Shyamalan's psycho-horror flick, *The Village*. In that movie, played out in what seems to be the late nineteenth century, members of a small village are terrorized by monstrous creatures that look something like huge, deformed wolves that walk like men and wear crimson cloaks.

The Albatwitches of Lancaster County

In a Lancaster newspaper article passed along to me by researcher Richard D. Hendricks, writer Carla di Fonzo described some true stories of weird creatures in the Pennsylvania woods. They did not wear red cloaks. Skinny, fur-covered humanoids that stood no more than five feet tall, they were said to dwell in woodlands along the Susquehannah perhaps fifty miles or so southeast of Northumberland. (It may be of interest to note that between these two sightings lies Three Mile Island, scene of the infamous partial meltdown of a nuclear reactor in 1979.)

According to local legend, the creatures were called "Albatwitches," meaning apple snitchers, because they were seen picking apples by picnickers in Chickies Rock Park. Legendary or not, di Fonzo found one Pennsylvania resident, Rick Fisher, a paranormal researcher, no less, who had a first-hand experience with something that looked mighty like an Albatwitch. I talked with Fisher by phone and he confirmed the incident, which he has since been able to update for me with other sightings.

Fisher said in di Fonzo's article that he was driving along Route 23 (which runs east and west between Lancaster and Marietta) in February 2002 around 6:00 AM. As he neared an intersection with Pinkerton Road, a few miles from Marietta and the river, he was puzzled to note what at first appeared to be a man dressed all in black walking in the middle of the road ahead of him. As he drew closer to the figure, it became apparent that it wasn't a full-grown person; in fact, it appeared to be almost a "stick" figure strolling along in a human stride.

To his horror, Fisher, who is the director of the Paranormal Society of Pennsylvania and writes an online magazine called *Paranormal Pennsylvania,* suddenly realized it was no man, but a fur-covered creature that stood about five feet tall and weighed no more than seventy pounds.

As his mind struggled to make sense of this unexpected sight, Fisher's training kicked in and he allowed his car to coast quietly up behind the enigmatic being. He turned up his brights, which finally caused the thing to turn and look squarely back at him. Its two bright-yellow eyes glared fiercely at Fisher for a long moment, and then it literally vanished before his eyes. There were no trees or brush for it to dash into; the road was lined by open fields on either side. He told me that it turned its head so quickly, and then was gone so shortly after that, that he had no chance to really see the shape of its head or tell whether it had a muzzle or prominent ears. It did not have a tail, of that he was certain.

"I'm a Bigfoot researcher," he told me. "My first thought was that this must be a skinny one." But, he said, a juvenile Bigfoot would never be that thin. Even a human couldn't be that thin, he added. "It walked like a human, not apelike, although its arms were longer, and it was swinging its arms."

Fisher, obsessed by what he had witnessed, said that he not only couldn't sleep for two days, he wasn't able to bring himself to tell anyone other than his girlfriend about what he had seen. He found himself in the rather strange position of knowing that if he did tell someone, he probably wouldn't be believed because of his position as a researcher of the paranormal. It would just seem too convenient. But he had finally just managed to convince himself that he had dreamed the whole thing, when he met someone else who had seen the same skinny hairdude near Pinkerton Road. At that point, Fisher's rational self had to be denied and the incongruous accepted as reality. This, I've learned, is a process that every witness of unknown creatures must eventually undergo.

He later met a man named Dwight, he said, and happened to mention his Web site while they were casually conversing. Dwight told Fisher that he wanted to tell him something, but was afraid to. With a little encouragement from Fisher, Dwight eventually came out with his story.

He had picked up two of his buddies in his pickup truck one day, Dwight told Fisher, and they were on their way to work, when they spotted a very skinny "thing" walking down the road, covered in hair. It was exactly the same anorexic Furry that Fisher had seen, and the location was just two miles from his sighting and two years earlier! Fisher also later received word of a similar creature spotted in Indiana.

"What is it? I don't know," he said.

Part of his description reminds me of Angie Beaudoin's sighting in Washington County, Wisconsin (Chapter 6), when she at first thought she was seeing a man dressed in dark corduroy. Our society is used to seeing human figures draped in cloth of some kind, and our minds will always leap to help fill in our usual assumptions. But in both of these cases, the "cloth" turned out to be a natural fur coat instead.

The creature's short height and ridiculously meager girth are probably the most interesting facets of Fisher's sighting, however. If its head was either canine or wolflike, we could imagine that this was perhaps a juvenile of the species, maybe a teenager with a foot or two yet to grow. A literal "Teen Wolf." The Pennsylvania Jean Grenier. And the creature's behavior—an intent, yellow-eyed stare followed by a sudden disappearance upon realizing it was sighted—is certainly a classic Manwolf reaction.

Or perhaps we are looking at a pygmy version of the species. There are pygmy humans. Cryptozoologist Loren Coleman argues in his *Field Guide to American Bigfoot* that the Bigfoot comes in a variety of sizes. However, the descriptions of this creature and the Albatwitches as "sticklike" or "skinny" argues against this being a mini-version of the more powerfully built, crest-headed Bigfoot. It does sound rather like the Winneconne "Half-Pint Trail Mixer," although that creature was definitely canid. And in the absence of Fisher's ability to observe leg and head structure, we can't know which category this animal belongs in for sure…canid or anthropoid. The creature does conjure images of something like a large, underfed monkey, such as a chimpanzee. A chimpanzee, however, even fully grown, is not proportioned anything like a human, normally walks at an incline while dragging its knuckles, and its face in the glare of bright headlights would be only too recognizable as a very familiar animal.

I have to say, however, that descriptions of a "walking stick figure" sound like nothing else I've heard of and are likely too severely thin to be a young Manwolf. It may be something entirely different, although exactly what is anybody's guess. Hopefully there will be further sightings and investigations in this area of Pennsylvania that will turn up corroborating reports. In the meantime, what Fisher saw is still, in the final analysis, a bipedal Furry…something that should not exist, but evidently does.

Lancaster County's Goat Man

Lancaster County has other weird beasts, as well, says Fisher. He found a story in a book of Pennsylvania Dutch country legends and lore by Charlie Adams about creatures that sound like some mad doctor's experiment. In 1973, two farmers saw a man-sized wolfish creature grab a chicken. They described it as the "size of a good heifer," gray with a white mane, tigerlike fangs, long claws, and it ran upright on its hindlegs. But here's the good part. On its head were two curved horns like those of a billy goat!

I can understand the color variation. That happens in every species. We've already observed "piebald" Manwolves in Georgia and Michigan. The fangs and claws and chicken-grabbing are all consistent with Manwolf characteristics. But curved horns?

And yet, I recently watched a *History Channel* show, *Weird U.S.*, that featured the famed Mutter Museum in Philadelphia. The place is a warehouse of preserved human medical anomalies with everything from the world-record distended colon to the mummified head of a French woman who had one long, curved horn protruding from her forehead and extending to below her nose. If the French can grow horns, so, perhaps, can a Manwolf.

Still, horns on any sort of canid are hard to imagine. Unless it wasn't a canid. Every now and then you hear of a Goat Man. Remember the story about the Goat Man crossing the road near the witch's cemetery in Wisconsin? But goats aren't carnivorous and they don't have long fangs. Or claws. Whatever the farmers saw sounds more like a true, mythic chimera than anything else. Or the Goat of Mendes, traditional goat-headed ruler of the legendary Witch's Sabbath, which probably descended from age-old goat-worship cults. A particularly notable example was said to exist in Egypt in the time of Plutarch, in the city of Mendes. The goat was often seen as a symbol of the devil in the Middle Ages, as were other horned animals, even, in one case, a dog with horns! According to many sources, in 1617 a Guernsey woman named Isabel Becquet saw the devil in the form of a dog with two large horns. It also had paws that looked like hands, which is something people have occasionally noted about Manwolves.

It's still impossible to say what the creature actually was, but, small comfort that it may be, at least we know the dog/goat man has a few weird predecessors.

Shenango Valley Werewolf

At the risk of acquiring weird creature fatigue, there is still one other Pennsylvania Unbelievable to consider. The creatures in this state, I've noticed, tend to vary widely one from another, constituting what amounts to a veritable freak show of anomalous entities. Consider the following oddity.

R. Jason Van Hoose, an Ohio-based researcher, wrote me about an animal he had been receiving reports on called the "Shenango Valley Werewolf." The Shenango Valley is in the northwest section of the state, about sixty miles south of Lake Erie. It is well-watered by the Pymatuning Reservoir to the north, as well as the snakelike Shenango Lake and numerous rivers and tributaries. A mystically beautiful setting for a bizarrely grotesque creature, whose appearances span the years 1972 through 1998.

"It is four to five feet tall," Van Hoose wrote, "covered with patches of long, black hair, a piglike nose, large round 'fisheyes,' a disturbing mouthful of snaggle teeth, and perhaps the strongest feature of all, its elbow and knee joints bend opposite of a human, somewhat like a dog but not really. It has been described as a mutation between a man and a dog. The face is flat without a snout. It can run on all fours and is also bipedal. Some witnesses stated that it moves very quickly, almost to the point of seeming to appear or vanish into thin air. When it runs on all fours, the elbows jut forward and the hands, which should be angled in to the body, are turned outward. Its hands are similar to humans', with digits, but when running the fingers are clenched, giving the appearance of paws. There is no tail."

Bizarre, indeed! This doesn't sound much like our Manwolf. Lack of a long muzzle is the largest difference, which along with smaller size, places it more in league with its state homeboys, the albatwitches. Perhaps even the South Georgia Pig Man.

The observation of "backwards" knees and elbows also seems more pronounced than the usual observation of doglike limbs in most Manwolf sightings, and the hands that splay to the side when running are downright bizarre. Combined with the goofy overbite and the large, round fish eyes, this is one ugly little sonofa-monster. The facial features differentiate it from the albatwitch, however (I think Rick Fisher would have noticed the googly eyes, even in the dark), as does the lack of emphasis on a skinny frame.

Its territory is not close to that of the Susquehanna creatures, though. The Shenango Valley is right next to the Ohio border. And interestingly, we have an Ohio creature (Chapter 14) who also features much less of a snout. Perhaps it's a local adaptation.

More Pennsylvania Werewolf Folklore

Even more evidence of Pennsylvania's preoccupation with Big Furries can be found in several editions of *New York Folk Lore Quarterly*, a publication first pointed out to me by Robert Schneck. I was able to obtain several volumes of this gem, dated from 1951 and '52, which contain between them three chapters of an ongoing article by Henry W. Shoemaker entitled "The Werwolf (sic) in Pennsylvania."

Shoemaker heard most of the tales as a boy around 1900 in Clinton County, many of them from a former "Indian fighter" named Peter Pentz. The brawny Pentz, who carried a buffalo hide for a sleeping bag, told the young Shoemaker his favorite "werwolf" tale, which he learned from his Aunt Divert Mary DePo, a midwife. On her way home from a delivery one night, she encountered a "werwolf in the shape of an enormous black dog." When she first spied it, the creature was on all fours, but upon seeing Aunt Mary, it rose onto its hind legs and walked toward her upright, grabbing at her with its forepaws.

So far, it sounds exactly like a Manwolf. The timeframe would probably have been the mid-1850s. However, instead of trying to get away, it chased her all the way home. Evidently it wasn't all that fast on two feet. When she finally dashed into her cabin, her husband managed to grab two pewter bullets that had been wrapped in "sacramental wax," almost as if werewolves were expected, and pumped them into the canid. Before his eyes, it transformed into the body of a neighbor he recognized. The man thanked him for ending his torment, and presumably died.

Shoemaker also makes it plain that werewolves were linked to witches, who seemed linked, in turn, to various older women in the neighborhood. People would spy she-wolves lurking around the barn or house, shoot them, and the next day would discover someone's granny or aunt wounded in the same spot as the werewolf, and telling some outrageous whopper about how it happened. The witch-crones also pulled stunts like kidnapping neighborhood horses to ride to their meetings on top of Stone Mountain.

Whole groups of werewolves bedeviled lumberjacks trying to haul sleds filled with logs through Elk Creek Gap in Centre County. Huge wolves would slink down from nearby Hundrick Mountain and either jump on the sleighs or hold them with their paws, making them too heavy for the horses to pull. Even painting the magic "hechs" or hex signs on the sled wheels had no effect on the powerful creatures. The conclusion? The attackers had to be werewolves.

Shoemaker also relates useful information about how to escape from a close encounter with a werewolf; prick it about the face with something sharp so that it bleeds. This will cause it to change form back into a human and end the attack.

There is even a sad story about a young boy who had been born with hair between his fingers and on his feet. As he grew older, the hirsute lad took to hanging out near wolf lairs, and finally vanished into the woods for good at about the age of eight. Shoemaker said, "Quietly all of the family uttered a silent prayer at his complete disappearance." Thus they were spared having to live with a werewolf.

Spook Wolves

The most interesting of Shoemaker's tales may be those of phantom wolves, said to represent the devil, and Spook Wolves, which were wolf spirits that were able to leave wolves that had been killed and stuffed, and go out hunting at night. One of the phantom wolf stories was alluded to in the first paragraph of this chapter, written by Governor Stone in his autobiography. Two of his neighbors, he said, were sitting by the sickbed of a man named Richard Duryea who was rumored to dabble in the magical arts, and was therefore generally considered "evil" by most of the community. Both men saw a black wolf enter the man's room and then leave again. The two neighbors rushed into the sickroom and found the man dead. They concluded that the wolf was actually the devil, come to claim his disciple's soul. A similar story is told of a black wolf frequenting the grave of outlaw Cyrus Etlinger in Centre County in 1894. Again, it was assumed that the wolf was no wolf but Satan himself, looking for the spirit of the outlaw.

The Spook Wolves, on the other hand, were stationary by day and had been mounted by a Czech taxidermist named Jake Zerkow. The stuffed wolves were originally on display at the Philadelphia Centennial, said Shoemaker, but eventually ended up making their nightly forays from a stone house in the Potter County Watershed, a place Shoemaker was personally familiar with. However, the Spook Wolves were not the same as werewolves, he noted, since they were not able to actually kill any prey. Shoemaker also told a story in another issue about a similar creature, the Spook Cougar. This power accorded to animal pelts, stuffed or merely tanned, may be a holdover from the days when wolf hide "girdles" or robes were considered magical enough to turn man into animal. Some traditions die very hard deaths.

In all of these older stories, the creatures' supernatural origins and actions seem to be taken for granted. But in the more modern tales of sightings of the albatwitches and the Shenango Valley creature, otherworldly inferences are lacking almost entirely. The albatwitch seemed to vanish before Fisher's eyes, but it's unknown whether it truly disappeared into thin air or just managed to slink down out of sight and away from his car. Otherwise, it trudges along and acts like some strange, natural animal. So do the Lancaster Goat Man and the Shenango atrocity. Are these the remnants of the once-ferocious shape shifters of settler days? Or are they the same creatures in spirit, only now perceived as warped and deformed by the skewed filters of our modern eyes?

The alternative is that Pennsylvania hosts a whole new, hidden species of emaciated, apple-loving primates. Stick monkeys. Stranger things have happened.

CHAPTER FOURTEEN

ALTERED STATES

"When there are monsters there are miracles."

—Ogden Nash

New York: Werewolves in Champy's Backyard

New York's northern and western regions are not often given enough credit by most Americans for their wildness and abundance of animal habitat. The relatively small part of the state that contains New York City commands the mountain lion's share of press most of the time. But in January 2005, I received an e-mail from a man who wrote that while driving near Plattsburgh in upstate New York in June 2004, with his brother, the two men saw something on the Interstate that was much more frightening than anything they might have encountered in a dark NYC alley.

The area was less than a mile from Lake Champlain (famous for its long-necked sea monster, Champy), near the bridge that connects New York and Vermont, almost on the Canadian border. George Carper and his brother John had spent the day fishing at the lakeshore village of Rouses Point, and were driving home and enjoying the beautiful summer day when George noticed "two huge beasts running alongside the Interstate." It was apparent at first glance that these were not hitchhikers. The runners had no signs, no thumbs sticking out, and were wearing fur suits. Needless to say, they had George's shocked, immediate, and full attention.

Almost instantly after George spotted the pair, however, they swerved, then darted across the highway in front of George's car. He estimated the furry sprinters were less than fifty feet away. "It looked like two huge wolves running on their back two feet," he wrote. And the strange bipeds were running at an amazing speed, he added. "They must have been running nearly 100 miles per hour. I am a dog owner and lover of greyhounds; they run fast but nothing like this animal. It was the most amazing thing I have ever seen!!!!!!!!!!!!!!!!!!!!!!!!!!!!!!!" (exclamation points George's).

He estimated the creatures stood between six and seven feet tall, and both sported very dark fur. Their physiology was not apelike at all; the heads were canid and so were the legs, so this could not have been a mistaken Bigfoot sighting. They were classic Manwolves.

After the two had crossed the highway and vanished into the brush on the other side, George finally regained his powers of speech and gasped to his brother, "What was that?" His brother could only shake his head. "I don't know," he finally answered. George was determined to find an answer, however.

George found me after a co-worker he confided in told him about *The Beast of Bray Road*. I was extremely glad that George had gone to that trouble and reported his experience, partly because he had such a long sighting that he was able to give a description definitive enough to rule out most other possibilities, and partly because this is one of the rare multiple sightings. The other two of those so far, if you'll remember, were Rick Renzulli's Kenosha, Wisconsin, incident when two huge creatures crossed the highway in front of him on all fours, and Katie Zahn's Rock County, Wisconsin, encounter with a total of four Manwolves.

So even if you throw out Renzulli's sighting on grounds that the creatures he saw were not running on two legs at that time, it still leaves us two sightings of more than one bipedal, wolf-headed creature seen at one time by multiple witnesses. The word "pack" comes to mind. So does the word "couple." Whether such togetherness is interpreted as wolfish or humanlike behavior, the knowledge that these things come in duos or even quartets, as I've said before, argues strongly for a breeding population. And with the kind of speed George and others have observed, even a rather small population would not have any trouble at all traversing huge territories in order to scavenge for carcasses and hunt other animals for food. The distance between New York's Adirondacks and Pennsylvania's Appalachians is probably far from insurmountable for a robust Manwolf.

Ohio: Indecisive Creature and a Man Dog

A brief entry on the Web site Cryptozoology.com told of a sighting that was startling to the witness but will sound almost old hat to readers of this book by now. Titled "Strange Humanoid Dog-like Creature," it was posted by an anonymous writer from an unspecified area of Ohio. The person wrote that he or she had been fishing alone in a creek near some woods in 2004, when a sudden growling noise came from behind. The person turned around, and there, only seven or eight feet away, stood "an extremely hairy person hunched over behind a bush." As the fisherman stared, rooted to the spot, the "hairy person" stuck its head through the bush and...glory be...it was no person at all! The shocking visage that presented itself looked like a "mix between a dog's and a human's face," according to the writer.

Evidently, the horror was mutual. Still bent over, the creature ran into some nearby tree cover until it was out of sight. The writer ran, too, fishing equipment thrown to the wind, beating cheeks for home. And yet, while rushing to safety, he encountered the creature again! It stood smack on the path, the only way out of the woods. The writer felt an urgent and understandable need to hide so he jumped into the creek, while the creature, evidently very confused, first ran in a circle and then took a leap into another section of the creek from which it splashed its way up a nearby hill.

The writer lost track of it after that, he said, "on account of me running scared for my life." Sounds like that made two of them. It's rather comforting to know that a creature so frightening to us may become just as unhinged by seeing a human. Did it run home and bark to its cave mate, "Org! I just saw a thing that looked like a cross between us and a skinny pink pig!" At any rate, it was not used to getting so close to a human.

Its face, described as a mixture of dog and human, is something new, though. This is a departure from the usual Manwolf description of totally canine or lupine features, with long muzzles and ferocious teeth. (Although we do have had those pesky Pig Men popping in and out of the sightings.) I wish that the description had been more detailed. Which parts looked human and which like an animal? Did it have an expression? And an always important question: Were the ears pointed and on top of the head or along the sides of the head like an ape or human? Alas, these questions shall have to remain unanswered.

My guess? This was a smaller Bigfoot. Absent other details, we have to assume that the face was probably as furry as the body. The Bigfoot's slightly human facial features, covered with doglike fur, might seem at first glance to be a Human/Fido hybrid. The fact that it was later seen standing on the path, as if teasingly inviting a confrontation or trying to satisfy its own curiosity, also sounds more like Bigfoot than a Manwolf, which is usually much more adept at disappearing once sighted. Ditto its comical, confused response of running in a circle as unsure about whether it should run or stay and get acquainted. It's not as if the creature was chasing its tail (if indeed it had one).

And yet, the witness *did* call it doglike rather than apelike. I do like to trust the gut reactions of witnesses. Are we back to the baboon model and Thoth? Until I am able to talk with this person and ascertain more about the encounter, I'll have to mark it undecided. Which leaves me feeling almost as confused as that Unbelievable seemed to be. I can relate. Sometimes, running in a circle is just the only thing left to do.

Another intriguing Ohio incident turned up on the *Coast to Coast AM* radio show in late August 2005, when a woman called in to say her boyfriend, Scott, had seen a Man Dog. She was trying to relate his sighting to another strange Ohio phenomenon making the rounds of the Internet's paranormal sites about a strange scream recorded near the small town of Liberty.

Certain experts had certified that the scream was not human, which meant it had to come from some large, unidentified animal. Bigfoot, wolves, mountain lions…all were bandied about as possible suspects. But what Scott the semi-driver saw did not scream at all. In fact, no Manwolf eyewitness has ever reported seeing and hearing it scream or howl, so it's impossible to say there is any certain relationship. And what Scott saw was frightening enough without any sound effects.

The creature was like a man but with a "huge dog head," said Scott, who never gave his last name, on the *Coast to Coast* broadcast. He added that it was "all black," and was kneeling by the side of the road, eating a deer. (This is immediately reminiscent of Lori Endrizzi's 1987 Bray Road "kneeling roadkill-eater.") He had pulled up to a stoplight, he said, when he saw something moving ahead of him under the almost-full moon. It was very late at night, and he was driving along a two-lane country road. "As I came around the corner," he said, "my headlights hit this thing." It just sat there staring at him, he said. It had pointy ears and a long muzzle. And the body, he said, looked like the body of the werewolf in the 2005 movie *Van Helsing*.

"I don't want to call it a werewolf," he said on air, "but being twenty feet away from it, yeah, that's a werewolf. I'd swear on a stack of Bibles that's what it is."

Scott was perplexed by his observation of the way the creature was feeding itself. "I know dogs don't have hands," he said, "but this thing was reaching toward its mouth with its hand." The creature sat in a sort of crouched position, Scott added, the same way a person would crouch to "pick something off the ground." It had the "same backward legs like a dog leg," he said, and it didn't make a sound. As soon as Scott had passed the creature, he looked back in his rearview mirror, and it was gone.

The next morning he went back to see whether he could find any traces of it, and the deer carcass was still in place. "The deer was lay-ing there torn open with pieces missing," he said. And it was still fresh. "My theory is it's eating deer instead of people," said Scott. "It's smart, so no one ever sees them."

Scott ended his story by saying that if he could "unsee" it, he would. And he had noted earlier that seeing this creature has affected his entire life because of how scared it made him.

And no wonder it made him scared, if it indeed had the "body of the *Van Helsing* werewolf." Anyone who saw that movie knows that the Wolf Man was a hulking, muscular brute, perfectly capable of ripping apart a deer. This echoes many other witnesses who have described a formidable musculature, particularly in the upper body and thighs. Muscular thighs combined with relatively slender lower legs, by the way, are the biological mark of a biped. Anything that walks on its hind legs needs bulky upper leg muscles to handle the added stress on the hind limbs, as they support the entire torso and provide all the power for locomotion. Even chimpanzees, which are closely related to humans but are not true bipeds, have approximately the same amount of muscle mass in their upper and lower hind limbs.

And yet, said Scott, the legs were "bent back" like a dog's legs. We've heard that before. And of course, a dog's legs aren't actually bent back at all, they only look that way to us because they are actually walking on the balls of their feet and toes (the walking mode called digitigrade), while the joint that would correspond to a human heel sits about halfway up the leg, where we would expect to see a forward-facing knee in a human leg of the same length.

Scott also said in the course of the program that the head was different than the squat, big-necked head of the *Van Helsing* Wolf Man, because it was narrower. This again conforms to other Manwolf sightings.

Still, we have to ask whether it could have been a man in a *Van Helsing* costume…even though the movie was not new and on people's minds, and Halloween was months away. It would have to have been one hell of a costume, that's for sure. Beyond that, it's unlikely some human would be hunkered down on a lonely country road on a sweltering summer night dressed in a completely enclosed suit of fur, ripping apart and devouring a roadkill deer. I think not.

On the other hand, the little town of Liberty is not far from Sycamore State Park, and the Twin and Miami Rivers run nearby. Not an unthinkable terrain for a hungry Manwolf to roam. Maybe Scott's creature did utter the famous scream, maybe it didn't. Either way, his sighting is not diminished. As we've shown already, anomalous things seem to happen in clusters. Looks like little Liberty, Ohio, is a notorious clump o'strange.

Tennessee Dog Man

Fortean Times is a magazine that documents all things begging explanation, and the "Tennessee Dog Man" fits those parameters perfectly. The March 2005 issue contains a letter from Patricia Law of Pikeville, Tennessee, who works the night shift at a factory in Dayton in the state's mountainous eastern sector. Law wrote that she often found herself driving alone over the mountain that stood between the factory and her house, normally in the very wee hours of the morning.

It was on one such lonely drive in the winter of 2003–2004 that Law found herself buzzing along the winding road, which was dimly lit by the occasional homes along the way. As she traversed one straight stretch, she noticed a man hiking alongside the highway, dressed in dark trousers and a light shirt or jacket. As she watched the man, she saw him purposefully hunch over and turn away from her. No doubt trying hard not to hit him accidentally with her car, Law continued to watch the oddly bent figure. As she finally caught up and overtook the traveler, the figure twisted back toward her in a nightmare moment straight out of some dark Stephen King novel to reveal that its head was that of a huge dog or wolf! Law said, "The 'thing' had a long snout and large teeth…and it was sort of grinning at me." After she passed it, she tried to have another look in her rearview mirror but it was nowhere to be seen.

My first thought was that the motion this person or creature made when it bent over and turned away may well have disguised a swift motion to don a Halloween werewolf mask. The fact that the figure wore clothing mitigates against it being a bona fide Wolfman. Human garb on Furries is highly unusual, although not unheard of. On the other hand, the fact that it immediately disappeared after being sighted and the description of its leering, almost grinning expression are both very consistent with other sightings.

But the situation is quite understandable from a possible hoaxer's point of view. A person walking alone on a mountain highway in midwinter after midnight would have to feel very vulnerable. What better way to ward off unwanted attention from strange motorists than carrying a monster mask to pop on whenever someone passed? Not to mention the thrill of getting a rise out of so many unsuspecting people. Although I have no doubt that the writer was sincere in what she saw, I have to put this one in my probable hoax category. And yet, the presence of clothing does not necessarily rule out the possibility of an actual sighting, as the next tale will reveal.

Virginia: Henrico County and Fredericksburg

Another contributor to the southern scare factor is the Werewolf of Henrico County, Virginia. Henrico County is just east of Richmond, and is bounded on the south by the James River. While I haven't received any directly reported encounters, various Web sites describe it as six feet tall with silvery hair. As in other Manwolf reports, it is capable of running either on its hind legs or as a quadruped, and features a wolflike head. Again, like typical Beast reports, it has chased people but never caught or injured them. Several witnesses have reported hearing a howling sound, and it is most often seen around the Confederate Hills Recreation Center. An old battlefield lies in this area, and Civil War battlefields are notorious for their ghosts. A silver werewolf doesn't seem too far out of line, then.

A writer on Cryptozoology.com also reported seeing a "bipedal wolf with gray/red hair" in Fredericksburg. The writer said the creature was "sprinting" across the road at the time of the sighting, but switched to all fours when it hit the brush on the other side of the road. Sounds like a Manwolf to me.

Dates were not given for the above sightings but it was implied that they happened within the past several years.

Missouri: Show Me State Dire Wolves?

This e-mail came to me at the end of January 2004 from a doctor's son and professional firefighter. In his words:

> I live in the Ozarks southeast of Springfield, Missouri. My father is a local doctor and treats mostly rural farmers. He hears lots of stories about mountain lions and bear, but every so often he hears about a hyena-like animal roaming the woods.
>
> The latest one is about two coon hunters, who were following their dogs in the night. Suddenly the dogs ran back past them with their tails between their legs, ending up under the truck. The dogs would not budge, whimpering. The younger hunter decided to stay with the dogs,

while the older man decided to see what had spooked them. He was then chased up a tree by a "hyena-like animal," where he stayed for some time after the animal had left.

This was not spoken about for some time, but eventually was leaked to one of my father's patients. My mother years ago saw a pack of 'wolf-like creatures, muddy brown and black with weird heads and stove-pipe long necks' in a cohesive attack on a herd of cattle on our land. She broke up the attack by firing into the group, but could not hit one because at even 175 yards, they ran too fast for her to keep up with in the rifle's scope.

I have heard several stories over the years about these creatures here locally. I know that something is there, but I was hoping you could help me with what this could be?

The man added that he was a husband and father, "not a crackpot or an attention seeker," and he signed his full name.

Of course, what immediately comes to mind is the *Amphicyon* or dire wolf described in earlier chapters. Prehistoric beasts, surviving in the Ozarks? I guess the Ozarks could be as likely a place for something to remain hidden as anywhere else. Because these were not obviously Canidmen or Bigfoot, it might even seem superfluous to include them in the book at all, until we remember that if one anomalous creature is possible, so are others.

Feral hogs are one other possibility. They are certainly ferocious, and a female wouldn't have tusks. But surely, experienced woodmen would know a hog when they saw one, especially at such close range. And it's hard to imagine hogs attacking cattle in a pack.

Of course, if the present day Ozarks were medieval France, the appearance of any very large wolfish thing with a special bent toward aggression would signify a werewolf or *loup-garou*, for sure. Remember, they were usually considered otherwise indistinguishable from natural animals except for their ferocity and taste for farm animals and humans. Some poor schmuck of an Ozarkian would have been tortured into confessing that he had transformed into one of these creatures, and consequently doused in moonshine and burned at the stake for his supposed crimes. It's a good thing we live in slightly more enlightened times. A little heckling at the local coffee shop is the worst people can expect these days, and the more people who come forward with their sightings, the less likely it is that even that much will happen.

Illinois: Up on the Housetop, Wolfman Paws

This eerie and astonishing tale came to me via e-mail, and with the writer's permission, I'm going to pass it on in his own words.

> A couple of summers ago, my parents shared with me their strange experience. They live in Decatur, Illinois. Their house backs up to a wooded area next to a large creek. On a late summer evening amidst the melody of the crickets and frog symphony one grows accustomed to in the Midwest, my parents were awakened, not by the sounds of the elements but the lack thereof. A strange and eerie hush had arose them from them slumber. My dad peered out of his window to see if perhaps an intruder was in the yard. To his amazement, he witnessed a surreal sight walking past the window on the street in front of the house…four dog-like creatures walking on their hind legs!
>
> The creatures had very pointed ears and long snouts. They walked with a slight bent-over motion, single file, down the road. My dad yelled to my mother to 'take a look at this!' They both watched in shock as these things proceeded to the end of the street and up to a house that sat atop a small hill about one hundred yards from them. The creatures began to look into the windows and one jumped up and on to the top of the house. They methodically walked around the outside of the house for a while, then slowly walked off to the west towards the golf course and woods.

It really shook them up. My mom even said she pinched herself to make sure they were not dreaming. We really never thought any more about it until I heard Art Bell's program last night. This was the first time I had heard about the Beast of Bray Road. I was blown away when I heard the discussion. I had always kind of passed off their experience as two old people exaggerating something unexplained in the middle of the night. But now I think that their experience was valid and what they saw has some connection to this creature.

—Scott Nicol

This is extremely spooky. Not only are there multiple creatures, they appear to have had clear intentions of swarming one particular house. I can't help but think of Mary Philippsen in Williams Bay hearing the creature run across her rooftop. By the way, as a footnote (no pun intended) to that story, she later told me that shortly before moving from that house, she discovered two worn places directly beneath her bathroom window, as if something often stood there looking in. This is also the second time four creatures were seen in one area (the first was Katie Zahn's incident in Avon), and by multiple witnesses each time.

I should mention that Decatur has been famous for years for its sightings of black panthers. The panthers never walk upright, however.

The little house set up on a hill by itself is also intriguing. Since biblical times and probably before that, "high places" have always been seen as places of spiritual power. The Israelites were always being warned not go to worship at the altars of Canaanite gods set in the "high places." Moses received the Ten Commandments on a mountain, the transfiguration of Jesus was on a high hill, and those are just a few examples from Judeo-Christian tradition. Every religion has similar beliefs. Remember the Pennsylvania witches riding stolen horses up to Stone Mountain for their Sabbaths?

What makes this story even eerier, however, is that we really cannot ascertain any reason the one small house was chosen, and that leaves everyone's house open as a possible candidate for werewolf inspection crews. Silent and stealthy as the Manwolves were, if the house was indeed occupied, odds are good the inhabitants never knew they were being surveyed. Equally mysterious is the fact that the creatures simply walked away after their task was completed. There is something compellingly otherworldly about this tale. But since I cannot draw any conclusions, I'll simply have to leave it as an effective nightmare generator.

Illinois Loper

A woman I met at a book signing told me about a strange sighting experienced by her sister-in-law from Des Plaines. Both women prefer to remain anonymous, so I will call them Deirdre and Pam. Deirdre told me that the event occurred in July, 1989, as Pam and her husband were driving home after a late-night visit to Deirdre's house just south of the Wisconsin/Illinois border. "They go down on 31 and 12, then right on 12 to Des Plaines," explained Deirdre. "There are long stretches with nothing on either side, although there are condos there now. The north branch of the Nippersink Creek crossed near there. In the space between the road and a wooded area, Pam saw a very large man walking, wearing what she thought must be a long fur coat. Both she and her husband said, 'What is that?' when they got closer. It was loping along, very shaggy, a little hunched over, with a gait more like lumbering. It was about six feet tall. The first thing they thought of at the time was Bigfoot.

"Years later, I showed her the *Beast of Bray Road* book," continued Deirdre, "and I told her about the Witchie Wolves (legendary guardian figures of Native American burial places near Omer Plains, Michigan) and her face went white, just drained of color. Then she told me of the time they saw it. She said she had just laughed it off at the time."

I was able to interview Pam by telephone, and she confirmed her sister's tale. It was late at night, on an 80-degree evening…much too warm for a fur coat on anyone. She didn't get a good look at its head shape because of the darkness, she said, "but I did see its face. It turned and looked at the car as if we startled it. It didn't look like an animal face. It looked almost human but Neandertal. Not a normal human face, though, because it was hair-covered. It had a muscular body. I'd estimate it weighed about 200 pounds."

The creature turned and ran off into the woods just after they passed it, said Pam, and they did not turn around to look for it on the off-chance that it might be a "crazy person."

The "Neandertal" face makes this sound like our short Bigfoot, much like the one spotted on White Pigeon Road or the Bluff Monster of the Palmyra area. The sighting occurred about fifteen miles directly south of the White Pigeon Road sighting, although sixteen years earlier. The lumbering gait and the initial impression of a human walking along the road both sound like Bigfoot traits, as well. Not a Manwolf, probably, for lack of a muzzle or other identifying characteristics. But still a puzzling Big Furry in its own right.

The Freeport Furry

While it's frustrating to think of all the stories that are out there and never reported, it's even more vexing when someone makes half a report and then doesn't respond to further questions. I received this tantalizing e-mail on April 6, 2005:

> Yes I am from northern Illinois, me and three others have seen this thing at three different places and times, we don't tell anyone anymore because people just don't think you know what you're talking about. It was not a wolf, way too big and I saw it in the daytime, very large and confused-acting, I never saw anything like it. It really didn't look like anything I ever saw before. I saw it in 2003 as did my mother but my sister-in-law saw it just a couple of months back, signed Beck.

However, a few weeks before my book deadline, Beck surfaced again to my great delight when her daughter sent me another e-mail, apparently unaware her mother had written earlier. I was able to interview Beck and her sister-in-law by phone about these sightings that happened only about fifteen miles south of the four-creature Avon Bottoms incident.

The most unusual thing about this sightings cluster around Freeport is that it involves four family members who saw the creature in three different incidents at separate times and locations. It reminded me of Dennis Hasting and his sister, respectively stalked near Bray Road and chased through downtown Lake Geneva. Does the ability to see werewolves run in families?

In the Freeport case, Beck, who asked me to withhold their last names, was the first to see it in the summer of 2002. It ran out in front of her car as she drove south from Cedarville into Freeport along Highway 26, near a marshy area. "When I saw whatever it was," she said, "it was daylight, and it was running across a four-lane highway on four legs. It was dodging all these cars and looked sort of bewildered or confused."

Beck said the creature she saw had a wolflike head, but the size and shaggy brown fur of a llama. The legs were long but doglike, she said. "What I saw was related to a wolf but too big to be a wolf. It was a dirty, brownish color. I'm an animal person, I have three dogs and I know animals, and this thing had a wolf head but it was way too big and strange-acting to be a wolf."

About a week later, Beck said she was talking to her elderly mother, who lives about fives miles east of Freeport near the Pecatonica River. "She said there was something strange standing in her yard," said Beck, "and I asked her to describe it."

What Beck's mother was looking out the window at sounded exactly like what Beck had seen on Highway 26. "She's in her eighties and has lived in the country all her life," said Beck, "but she had never seen anything like this before."

Although Beck and her mother continued to watch for the creature, neither of them saw it again. But Beck's sister-in-law and niece did. "Glo" and her daughter "Angel" were driving east into Cedarville on Red Oak Road in the last week of January 2003, the day before Angel's sixteenth birthday. They were just crossing a small bridge when ahead to the right, in an area of brush, they both saw something very startling.

"It wasn't dark yet," said Glo in a phone interview, "just a little bit toward dusk but I had my headlights on. I think the headlights are what caught its attention. It looked at the headlights, then at me, and it made this full, unyielding eye contact. I was only going thirty miles an hour, but I was locked into the eye contact so it was hard to notice its other features. I was drawn to it, it was drawn to me."

Glo did have a few moments to check out the rest of the creature before it turned to look at her. It was crouching on its hind legs with its back toward the road, she said, and it turned from the waist up as her car approached. "It looked like it may have been eating something," she said. "It had dark, wiry fur. I didn't notice a tail. Its head was fur-covered, it had a muzzle, I don't remember the ears. I was totally, 100 percent into the eye contact by then. But I'd say if it stood up it would have been slightly under six feet tall. I had the feeling it could have walked on two feet or all four."

The creature was neither skinny nor heavy, said Glo, and its arms and head were covered in dark fur like that on the body. "There was something about the eye shape and color," she added, "but I can't describe the color, other than as yellowish. It's hard to even explain. The color was different than what you would see on a dog or a deer."

Its legs were definitely doglike, she said, although she was positive this was not a dog. The brush hid its feet from her view. Glo said she exclaimed, "What was that?" and her daughter replied that it looked like a werewolf.

"Neither my daughter or I was frightened," she noted. "I feel almost lucky. I'd love to see it again, but probably in a vehicle with a camera. We don't go walking by ourselves anymore, though."

I also talked to Angel. "The best thing I can think of to describe it is the werewolf in *Buffy the Vampire Slayer* TV show," she said. "It was on its hind legs, and when it looked over at us its eyes glared; they looked yellow-goldish. I was like, 'Whoa, what was that?' I'm glad we were in the van. It had a protruding snout, it was long," she added.

Glo waited a few days, then told Beck about what she and Angel had seen. The women found copies of *The Beast of Bray Road* and separately all chose my drawing of the Indigenous Dogman as the creature they had seen.

"I've never seen ghosts," said Glo, "I don't really believe in ghosts. In 1976, we thought we saw some UFOs, but they were just lights. But I feel privileged to have seen this creature."

The four women were not the only area people to see strange creatures, however. The June 10, 2005, *Freeport Journal Standard* ran a story by Diana Thome-Roemer entitled "Some Strange Sightings." Dakota resident Dennis Wells was quoted as saying he saw some kind of shaggy "lion." I was able to contact Wells and ask him myself, and he confirmed that on May 25, he was in his field on a tractor at about 8:30 AM when he saw a large animal lying near the fence line. He drove closer and turned off his tractor. "When it got up I knew it was something I never saw before," he saw. The animal turned sideways, and Wells knew it was some kind of large, tawny cat. "My first impression was that it was an African lion," he said, "because it had more fur, slightly darker, like a mane on the back of its head." The lion moved unhurriedly away as Wells watched in awe. He said he learned later that cougars, or mountain lions, shed their winter coats at about that time, and that the fur on the back of the head is the last part to be shed. In all, he feels fairly certain that what he saw was indeed a cougar.

What Wells saw sounds very different in color, looks, and behavior from what the four women saw. His sighting was two years later than Glo's, too. Cougars do seem out of place yet in northern Illinois, but there was probably nothing supernatural about Wells' sighting. We cannot say the same with any certainty about the creature spotted by Beck, her mother, Glo, and Angel.

And for the record, Illinois also seems to have its Bigfoot, but not the smaller, "Neandertal man" variety we find in Wisconsin. The little town of Seneca, approximately seventy miles southwest of Chicago, was recently featured in a *Chicago Tribune* story for its Bigfoot flap in the summer of 2005, and these were the eight-foot, highly aromatic variety. The Bigfoot Researchers Organization Web site reported two incidents in detail, occurring on June 2 and 10. Witnesses saw two fur-covered creatures near a woods on private land. Their descriptions and drawings depict classic Sasquatch features.

According to the story, sightings of the giant Furries go back forty years, when it became known as the DuPont Monster, named after DuPont Road that winds along the Illinois River. The river is studded with state parks and natural areas along most of its length between Joliet and Moline, providing great habitat for Bigfoot. I wouldn't be surprised to find a few Manwolves here, too, given the other locations where they have recently shown up.

Quebec, Canada: One Giant Leap for Wolfkind?

I learned of this story during the experience of being interviewed by the Canadian Global TV Network show, *Northern Mysteries*. Of course, Quebec is a part of Canada, and most assuredly not an American state, but I pray they will forgive being lumped into this chapter given the fact that they do border us, and that the New York state sighting was quite close to—if not spot on the border between—the two countries.

The Canadians were producing a show about a sighting in Quebec Province near Blue Sea Lake, and the producer was kind enough to send me the script so that I could get an accurate account of the incident. Of course, the script was in French, which might just as well have been Martian to me. Luckily, my good friend Julie Von Bergen nimbly translated the whole thing. And the story, told by a couple whose identities were known by the show's production staff but kept confidential for the airing, was nothing less than astonishing. The show called the couple William and Angie.

The time frame was the early 1990s, and the pair lived in a cottage in the woods near Blue Sea Lake in Quebec. About twelve miles away was an Indian reservation and wildlife area, perfect living space for all manner of creatures.

One night, William and Angie were returning from a late night visit at a friend's, driving at normal speed in calm weather through a thickly forested area. Suddenly, Angie screamed, "What is that?" There in the headlights stood what they described as an enormous wolf nearly seven feet tall. Emphasis on "stood." The hulking form was less than one hundred feet away. Startled, the creature squatted, then sprang into the air. The story added that it glared at William and Angie ferociously before landing a good thirty feet away on the other side of the ditch and disappearing into the dense vegetation. The couple was dumbfounded.

Not only had they just seen a giant, bipedal wolf make a leap that would only seem possible on the moon, the giant jumper was wearing a plaid shirt! The shirt hung carelessly open (buttons would be very hard to manage with paws) and William noticed that the hind paws were much too large for the creature to walk like a "real wolf" on all fours. Angie's observation was that the creature seemed enraged at them, as if it did not want to be seen.

Unable to let the unsettling event go, William returned to the scene of the amazing leap the next day by himself to look for tracks or any other evidence. He and Angie noticed that the creature had long claws and they thought there might have been scratch marks or perhaps even a patch of fur left as evidence. William found nothing. But he and Angie both knew what they had seen.

Other than the questionable Tennessee Dog Man, this is the only sighting I've found that included an article of clothing. Interestingly, John Keel noted in *The Complete Guide to Mysterious Beings* that plaid or checkered clothing is a popular fashion choice of ghosts and anomalous creatures.

And given the obvious difficulty a creature with canid limbs and paws would have in dressing himself, it's very tempting to suppose that perhaps the shirt was on the creature before it became a "creature." Evidence of true werewolfery? Well, there is certainly nothing ironclad here, but it's the closest indication of that explanation I've yet come across. I really don't know which thought is scarier—true werewolves that don't quite get fully naked, or an unknown species of bipedal canids raiding farmyard clotheslines to go styling through the woods.

Other Glimpses

I've collected a number of anecdotal incidents from several other states. I'm aware of others, as well, but I'll just give a sampling here. Richard Hendricks passed on a Texas legend called "The Converse Carnivore," which was reprinted from the *San Antonio Express-News Sunday Magazine*, October 29, 1989.

It was in the 1960s that a half-wolf, half-human creature killed a thirteen-year old boy at Skull's Crossing. The lad had been sent on a hunting mission by his macho father, told to stay out until he had shot his first animal. As the boy timidly walked through a wooded area, he found himself being stalked by what sounds just like a Manwolf. Terrified, he ran back to his father only to be scoffed at and sent back to the woods. Of course, the boy never returned, and when a search party was finally sent out, the horsemen encountered the wolfen creature devouring the boy's remains.

Louisiana has more than a few connections with *loup-garou*, too. One e-mail I received that bridged the Wisconsin–Louisiana gap read, "As a former resident of the Southern Kettle Moraine, there was no question that there was something out there. Not only did I see it several times, I knew several others that had seen it as well. It was not until I began to spend time in Louisiana that I realized our Bray Road Beast was very similar to the Cajun *loup-garou*."

Another person wrote,

> I am from Franklinton, a town in S.E. Louisiana. In the summer of 2000, I began hearing strange howling/screaming noises coming from the woods around my house. I have a pit bull who would take on a chainsaw and he was cowering in his doghouse. I hear the noise from time to time, at least once a month. It is the most horrid sound I have ever heard.
>
> Sometimes it sounds like it's in the backyard. I hope that I never see it. My mother, neighbors, and several friends have also heard it. I have a friend who lived in the same area as me who heard the same sounds and also saw its eyes. He described them as an orangish-green color. No one has looked for tracks.

The writer also told me that a neighbor's golden lab was found "completely torn to shreds" and that many other small animals in the neighborhood had been killed or had disappeared. As in Wisconsin, a horse was attacked but not killed.

I've had other correspondence; a wolf shadow creature in California, various Swamp Ape reports from Florida, and a few others not quite related enough to the topic to warrant inclusion. Overall, however, I think the reports gathered here are enough to show that Manwolves are not an isolated phenomenon. They show up in Wisconsin and track eastward to Michigan, Ohio, Pennsylvania, Virginia, and New York, and southward to Illinois, Missouri, Tennessee, and Georgia. By no means do I feel I've even scratched the surface in these other states. I also think that many Manwolf sightings are misreported as Bigfoot, since that is the most popular modern model for Big Furry Bipeds, or misunderstood as strange dogs or farm animals.

I have no idea whether the creatures have always lived in these locales, or whether they are spreading. And I do think it curious that I have no reports from Minnesota with all their lakes and woods, or from Iowa, land of the eternal cornfield. I have a feeling, however, that my third book on this topic will overflow with sightings from other states, once the awareness level rises and people are able to figure out what they are seeing or have seen. I hope to hear from every one of them.

CHAPTER FIFTEEN
CONFESSIONS OF A LYCANTHROPE

"The man as can form an ackerate judgment of an animal, can form an ackerate judgment of anythin'."
—Charles Dickens, *Pickwick Papers*

"Do you believe in werewolves?" Although my face went azure long ago from trying to explain that most people only use the term "werewolf" because it's the best descriptive phrase they can come up with, it's still probably the question I'm asked most often. That question does not mean, "Do you believe people are seeing something that looks like a furry, upright canid?" If it did, I'd have no problem saying yes. But what people are actually asking is, "Do you believe that human beings can grow shaggy fur, a muzzle, fangs, claws, whiskers, pointed ears that shift to the tops of their heads, unibrows, smaller brains, tails, wet dog-odor, and a canine skeletal configuration by literally transforming their flesh, blood, and bones—including their fore and aft soft tissue structures? When the moon is full?"

My answer is…nah-uh. The reader certainly may believe. I just don't. Even knowing that according to quantum mechanics, the world is never quite as we assume it to be, I still stand by my statement in the first book that I'll believe a bodily transformation when I witness it. It would help to even see a good video of someone changing from man to wolf or vice versa, although these days with the array of editing software available it would be hard to film anything that isn't suspect in some way. But there are people who believe that they do transform, and one of them claims to have made a video of himself doing so.

He told about it on an Internet message board (Cryptozoology.com), and kindly gave me permission to print his explanation of his self-professed lycanthropy, at least in the way he understands it. In fact, he wrote, "I do not mind at all and am actually rather relieved. It is good to know that there are those out there who are willing to contact me further and not simply slam me on a message board. You may use my story if you truly think it is worth publishing. There are some on the site who believe I am nothing more than an invention of [girlfriend's name] simply because I said she could use some quotes in her fan fiction. She's still laughing actually."

I like to respect everyone's opinion, and believe that people have the right to see themselves as they will. And yet, as you'll notice, this young man does not offer to mail his transformation video to anyone as proof. But before I analyze his tale any further, I would like you to read what he has to say about his condition in his own words. (One note: The "Therians" he refers to, short for therianthropes, are people who believe that they are spiritually part wolf, and do not necessarily undergo bodily transformation.) I'm going to change his girlfriend's name to Randi for her privacy, and I should also explain that in previous posts, he had talked about being chained in the basement every full moon. And I want to add that I do respect him for spilling his guts to the world…if he isn't putting us on. But I'll let you judge that for yourself.

Werewolf Confession

I'm going to start off by saying that a pretty big chunk of me wants to walk away from the computer right now. I've never been a very good writer of anything really. Thanks to the computer gods for spell and grammar check!!

I've never allowed myself to be this open before. What is a routine interview to you guys is a bare ham examination to me. For those who haven't figured it out by now, I'm the Brian some of you have been hearing about for a couple months now.

Also… I have no computer. I'm working off of either one at the Library or Randi's computer. (Most often hers cause I'm not really a people person, unless she's decided to take this one out back and shoot it like she did with the last one.) As I've said, I've never done anything like this before.

I don't think any werewolf has. Randi doesn't ask questions either so some of this is going to be new to her too.

I guess I should get down to it… I'll tell you what happened the night I became a werewolf. I know it sounds like a bad B-Movie plot, but this is my life.

Grandpa Willie took my family camping around the Redwood Forests area in celebration of his first grandson (me). I had lasted just long enough to hear the first of the scary stories when I fell asleep. I woke up sometime afterwards and climbed out of the tent cause I needed to go to the bathroom. So on the other side of the bush this monster dog (well I remember it as monster but when you're five, a poodle in the forest at night is a 20-foot flesh eating beast.) (I used poodle as an example. I have no idea what kind of dog it was) jumps up out of nowhere and I'm bitten.

Camping trip over, 12 rabies injections, and an entire box of lollipops to myself later and Grandpa Willie is telling everyone he knows that he's got a werewolf for a grandson. (Kids will believe anything these days) I can't remember when it stopped being a joke. Randi says that it's something like intellectual honesty, the truth is what you believe and all that. I can't tell you anything about that.

Do I grow fur? Yes—or at least I SEE fur growing. I can't tell you if I actually do because I'm too afraid to watch the tape of my last moon. If I touch my arm while I am transformed I feel fur. It's a coarse gray color and is normally about an inch long.

Can I remember what happens? Sometimes—I remember bits and pieces of the nights I transform, but not everything. There are gaps. Like I'll hear a scream and only in the morning realize it was me who was screaming. Or I'll see Randi coming down the steps and wonder whether or not I've killed her in the morning.

What's it like to transform? That's a tough one. The closest I can come to describing it is … Ya know that scene in Van Helsing where the guy rips all his skin off? Feels something like that. And you can't get use to it either.

Do I transform for three nights or for one night? One—I don't know how it is with other werewolves but I only transform for the one night.

Can I transform whenever I choose? No—I cannot force the change and nor would I ever want to. No one who has ever gone through something like that would ever want to force the change. And it's an easy way to spot the fakes. People running around claiming to be werewolves...

What's it like to be a werewolf? It stinks. For one you go through a hell of a lot of shaving blades. And the fleas are murder! I'm kidding. Ahhhmmm...... fear, loneness, pain, freedom, belonging, hunger, rage, containment, darkness, despair.

Fear of the transformations. Fear of hurting someone, most of all the people you care about.

Loneliness because you are too afraid to let anyone get close to you. Being the only werewolf in your area means there are no support groups you can go to. No one to talk to.

Pain in the actual transformation is incredible. You feel like your blood is boiling, your skin is on fire. You can't think. You can't stop it. You can only scream.

There is a deep sense of freedom as well. Something inside that only you can feel. I feel it most while I am outside wandering around. Something that is easily taken away.

To feel like the trees can speak to you. Telling you that it's ok. It's not all pain. To feel like you're a part of the grass, that the wind could pick you up and carry you away. To be both a part of the sky and a part of the dirt. That's to know that you belong.

Hunger is not meant in a literal sense. In fact, as far as food goes, a couple meals a day and you're good. I suppose you could use longing but that really wouldn't be enough.

You long for the latest CD or that new pair of shoes in the store window. But to need something so badly to feel yourself dying without it… What could I possible need that badly? Friendship. Acceptance. Things I can't have. To know that it's ok to be what I am. To not have to worry that there's some yahoo out there with a shotgun and a thing for the Lone Ranger. To not have to live in constant fear of the next Full Moon.

There is also rage. At yourself for not being able to keep control. At the thing that made you what you are. At God, if there is one, for not helping you. For leaving me the way I am.

To have to spend the night in a locked room chained to pipe does things to your mind. You start to feel that that's the only way. You know that you're in trouble when you start to need the chains. Not only physically. There are times when I am so afraid of transforming during the day that I bottle everything up. Forcing myself to not show emotion. Any emotion.

There is something dark about what I am. Some people can see it while I walk down the street. You fear the night, therefore you become the night. I had to take out and seal up the lights in the basement for fear I might zap myself. Barbeque werewolf, anyone? Extra Crispy!!

You lose hope after a while. Of ever finding a cure. Of the humanity walking around you. People who would rather see me dead out number people like Randi twenty to one. The more you lose hope the more you don't really care if you get out.

Drugs don't work. You name it, I've tried it. There was even this one (I'm pretty sure it was an animal tranquilizer) what would put a normal person into a coma. (They could have a stare down with the wall. And they'd win.)

Locking me up won't work. I've tried that. Twice actually. (You think High School was traumatic, try having a stay in a mental hospital on your record on the same time.) It's the fatal flaw of my kind. Just by walking down the street wandering around with a light breeze does more to calm me than anything. I'm going to tell you what I told Randi. If we (werewolves) are not free to wander, if we are denied the smell of the trees, the feel of the sun on our faces, if we cannot hear the whispers in the wind nor the voices in the rain, then we will gradually lose ourselves into the beast within until there is nothing left of who we were. Becoming only the animal.

If locking me up doesn't work, why do I chain myself to a pole? Cause Randi's there with key.

Have I hurt anyone? No—But I have caused some damage. Even attacking Randi a couple times. (No matter how often or insistent I tell her not to she's got to come downstairs.) I am terrified that I've come close to hurting her though. You can't dodge them all kid. And if I bite you, I don't even want to think about that. Well, there was that thing with the security guard the first time I was institutionalized. Yes, mace works on werewolves…

What's this damage I've caused? You asked—when I'm transformed and can't get out, I'll kick my own ass. I've also gone through a wall and 3 doors. Broken 4 pipes. Dented the shit out the water heater. Bent several pipes, broken out that little window at least a dozen times.

You mentioned a Tape—You caught that? Damn. I set up a video camera to record one of my transformations. Haven't looked at it yet. Too scared. If I can't watch it what makes you think you're going to get a copy? Sorry. I don't mean to snap.

Why am I talking to you guys? I don't know. Randi is the one who's smart on the whole honor thing. I could care less what you say or think about me. Why am I willing to relive the worst nights of my life for a bunch of strangers who don't believe in what I am saying any way? Maybe talking about it will help me. Or help some other poor fool out there. I don't know. I think Jellyroll's comment about having me hunted down had a lot to do with it. For someone who's never been through that, who's never had the realization that you are in the sights of someone's gun, you sure can talk.

Have I ever met another werewolf? I've met Therians, but 90 % of them are all wannabes who don't know what the hell they're talking about. What are the senses like? Normal I guess. No I can't hear a bird 3 blocks down… but I can smell a cheeseburger like no one!

Do I have enhanced strength and all that? Nope. You whack a pole with another pole several times and you're going to build up some big ass dents.

Am I allergic to silver? It won't kill me but it does turn my skin green over time, but that's a mild sensitive skin thing.

What do I eat? Burgers, fries and a Coke. Milk Bones when I'm meeting someone new just to be funny. The beef flavored ones are pretty good actually. Steaks are normally medium with a thick coating of babies blood. **That's what's called satire.**

Do I drink? A couple shots of Jack or Jose, maybe a beer, but that's it. Would you want to tango with a drunk werewolf? Neither would I. Well, I guess that about does it, cause I cant think of anything else I should add. Feel free to ask what ever you will. I promise not to bite.

HavingFunHowling

There you have it. A much more eloquent soliloquy than the short diatribe I printed from another Lycan in my first book, something about werewolves not standing out in the town square for everyone to see although that is doubtlessly true.

So is this guy for real? That's a good and valid question, but one I have no way to answer. He has a pretty smart way with prose for someone averse to computers. And he's very honest about his convictions. He is careful only to avow, when asked whether he grows fur, that he sees fur growing on himself. Seeing the fur, of course, is his perception. And I think that therein may lie the key. He doesn't say that Randi also sees the fur. He doesn't claim to have super strength, or even an abnormal appetite for bloody tidbits. But he perceives that he changes…that he is different from other humans…and for him, that is reality. Our perception of Brian, if we saw him chained to that pole in his basement, might conceivably be quite different. I have a feeling he wouldn't look at all like Warren Zevon's Werewolf of London, whose "hair was perfect."

Brake for the Wolfman

As I mentioned in *The Beast of Bray Road*, the condition known as clinical lycanthropy, wherein a person entertains delusions of animal transformation, is considered a type of psychosis by medical professionals. I personally believe that's why many people inclined to feel lupine now refer to themselves as Therians rather than Lycans. By falling in the Therian camp, they acknowledge that they don't actually grow a fur tuxedo, and so avoid people strongly recommending medication for them. (By the way, I'm sure any Therians reading Brian's essay would disagree vehemently with Brian's general assessment of them, and probably with mine, too. I'm not giving them equal time here, however, simply because since they admit they do not transform, they are not a possible explanation for the creature sightings and therefore not part of the scope of this book.) People who call themselves Lycans, however, don't generally believe they are brain-disordered. Most of them probably aren't, at least not to the extent of requiring clinical diagnosis and treatment. But there does remain the case of a fellow who, several years ago, came to believe that he was actually the Beast of Bray Road.

He lived in Elkhorn in the early 1990s, and had drug and alcohol issues along with a personality disorder that required medication. When he remained on his prescriptions, he was fine. When he did not take his meds, he would revert to his Beast character. This involved his roaming nude around Bray Road in the dark and jumping naked onto the hood of any car passing by slowly enough to be overtaken by a running human. He was known to plaster himself against the windshield of at least one horrified family's vehicle like a demented Garfield suction cup toy.

To those who would immediately seize upon this fellow's delusional acts as the explanation for the Beast phenomenon, I have a ready answer. True, the horrified family called 911, but they did not report seeing a werewolf; they reported seeing a crazed, naked man clawing at their windshield. There was simply no resemblance to a Manwolf, other than the fearful stare, perhaps. Besides, the man developed the Beast persona after the fact. He only began identifying himself as a werewolf and foisting himself au naturel upon innocent passersby long after the hoopla of all the sightings on that road occurred.

I happen to know one of this man's caseworkers personally, and she assured me that he did get back on his meds, is taking them as of this writing, and no longer believes that he is a wolfen creature of the night. In fact, he has moved out of the state. I wonder, if the Beast of Bray Road had never happened, what his fantasy character choice might have been. Godzilla? Bigfoot? Carrot Top? His particular disorder meant that he needed to become something different and more powerful than his own human self, and probably the Beast persona seemed the handiest to assume. I'm just glad he's okay. Naked car surfing at midnight with strangers is an unhealthy behavior in many, many ways.

I'm not necessarily assuming, however, that our friend Brian shares anything like this man's disorder. If Brian's story is on the level, only a medical professional could make that diagnosis—even with all the auto-butt-kicking going on down in his basement every full moon. What I do assume is that, like our Bray Road car frog, Brian does not look enough like a wolf even at the height of his "transformation" to cause anyone who sees him to report a furry, bipedal, wolf-headed creature running down the road. They are more likely to state, as did the gobsmacked family on Bray Road, that they have seen a human behaving oddly. By the way, I've also had an e-mailed report of another man who lived in a group home in that area taking on the Beast persona, running away at night and being found trying to eat a piece of roadkill. But again, this was after the Beast was publicized, it was merely a human, and in no way can account for the many witnessed sightings.

So until the alleged physical shape shifters somehow prove to the world that they can become true Big Furries, I leave the Lycans and Therians of the world to work out their own lives in the ways that seem best to them. Their views of reality are their own and probably prompt them to do many things the rest of us wouldn't understand. (Although you can Google "Therian" or "Lycan" and get a fairly good idea.) They might even have the ability to frighten bystanders, when in full moon mode, by their appearance and behavior. And I can't help fearing for Randi's safety should Brian's chains ever shake loose. But as a possible explanation for Manwolf sightings, I think this group is no more likely than an average college fraternity pledge group. Maybe less.

Got Ergot?

One other medical explanation that turns up frequently in relation to lycanthropy is the ergot equation. A fungus that affects rye, but sometimes also wheat and barley, ergot is now widely regarded as a possible cause of the bestial madness visited upon otherwise ordinary citizens of the seventeenth to nineteenth centuries. According to this theory, it was not demonic influence but the ingestion of *Claviceps purpurea* (which contains a compound similar to LSD), which led to the demented behavior and thus, executions, of many alleged witches, werewolves, and vampires. The victims were mostly of the peasant class, which depended on rye bread for their staple food. All it took was a cold winter in a particularly wet or low-lying area, and entire fields would be infected with the ergot fungus. With no good way to separate infected stems, the poison made its way into working class larders. Symptoms, confirmed by an outbreak as recent as the 1950s in France, include delusions of turning into hairy monsters, night terrors, a sense of alienation from one's own body, frantic motion and convulsions, paranoia, and even death.

Every Web site devoted to werewolves, and there are many, expounds at length upon ergot. I have absolutely no doubt that this grain contaminant did in fact cause many an "outbreak" of werewolfism and witchcraft in Medieval Europe, and that it probably plays a small but unrecognized part in some cases today. All of this is well and good, except that even the most rampant case of ergot poisoning still does not cause a human being to look like a Manwolf. So while ergot may play an important part in the history of werewolf lore, it doesn't explain our modern sightings of a wolflike biped.

I'd like to mention that my somewhat light treatment of these topics does not mean I am unsympathetic to people who feel they are part animal either in body or spirit, for whatever reason. Many of these cases are very complex medically, psychologically, and environmentally, and it's not my intention to judge any individual. Every human being drags some sort of luggage around on this planet, after all. No, the sole reason for this chapter is to consider these certain conditions that skeptics will often bat around as "explanations" for sightings of Big Furries. Well, I've considered them, and find them sorely wanting in terms of explaining wolfheads and doglegs. I have a feeling if we ever do find out what a "real" werewolf is, the answer may be as unwelcome as it is unexpected.

CHAPTER SIXTEEN

LIGHTS! BIGFOOT! ACTION!
THE PHENOMENA MATRIX

"With Warwoolfs and wild cates thy weird be to wander..."
—Alexander Montgomerie,
Flyting of Montgomerie and Polwart (1582)

Campfire Frights: Eyes and Orbs

I am from Racine. Here's the thing—I dunno if it was a werewolf I experienced or not. It was a number of years ago. I know it was in SE WI, although I cannot remember for the life of me what the name of the Scout camp where the retreat was held.

One evening, after supper, we were able to light a bonfire in the fire pit behind the mess hall. We straggled down to it well after dark, and many had already dispersed to bed. I was seated near my fiance on a log, with our backs to a set of two particularly tall pine trees that were a bit of the ways up the grassy bowl. The choir director and a chaperone, along with a couple of night owls much like ourselves sat opposite us on another log.

I couldn't help (as I sat watching the fire blaze tall into the night sky with its six-plus foot flames) but feel something was watching me. You know the feeling. The hairs on the back of your neck stand up and you expect to feel someone tap you on your shoulder any minute... or jump out and grab you as a prank. So I spin around expecting to see a classmate up to no good. Instead I see nothing at first, but as I stare into the night (expecting that they are crouched down somewhere trying to hide) I catch something out of the corner of my eye. (Now any of you that

HUNTING THE AMERICAN WEREWOLF

have a dog or cat and have seen light catch their eyes at night know the glow I am about to describe.) A glint of light, off two globe-like things back in the trees. Staring directly at me.

By this time I was on edge. Practically leaving nail marks in my fiance's arm as I attempted to see what was watching me. Throughout the next hour or two (I am not sure how long it was exactly), I would swing my head back toward the woods every so often to keep an eye on the eyes that were watching me. I noticed if it was a longer time since I had swung back, the thing appeared closer to where we were. But when I was checking more frequently it seemed to slink back toward the woods more.

Finally, as my eyes began to adjust to the darkness, I intentionally did not swing my head back for a bit, and then turned around to look in the direction of this stalker of the night. I could make out an outline. It appeared to be a wolf-style head…very furry, with those tell-tale trademark, fat, triangular ears. The color was darker than the night sky but provided almost no contrast to the surrounding it was in, at least in the low light of the fire.

When I was finally ready to retire for the night, I had my fiance escort me back to the mess hall so I could find another girl that was headed back to the girls cabin. When she and I found each other, we bolted out the mess hall doors and RAN back to our cabin.

The following morning, I awoke early, to a bright sun kissing the landscape. One of the first people up, I opted to go for a walk. (I am not sure why it seemed like a good idea, but I guess curiosity had finally gotten the best of me, and with no night to cloak the unknown, I must have figured I was safe. That or I was just a stupid teen.)

And wouldn't you know…the first place I stopped was the mess hall, although an awful smell permeated my nose long before I ever made it there. Some say it was mushrooms, some say it was a backed-up grease trap...but it looked like loose piles of unhealthy grayish brown scat. And it stank to high heaven!!!

I approached the two pines by which I had seen the "Thing" the night before. To my shock, the wood chips at the base of the trees had been pressed into the earth like something had definitely been there for a prolonged period of time. But there was also a bush directly behind the trees, so how did the thing move back and forth without making any noise? Ok, well, that did it, I was outta there! I headed down a path between the trees (again—I must not have been thinking), and ended up on the path that ran along the boys' cabin.

As I dilly-dallied trying to see if anyone was awake yet to see if my fiance was up and at 'em (lazy bum was still asleep), I finally got bored and headed in a direction I believe was east along the footpath...when I froze in my tracks. Up ahead of me was a bright, glowing red sphere (some might call it an orb), it was darkest/densest in the center (although still a bright cherry red), and faded to a pinkish color along its perimeter. It was roughly a little smaller than a soccer ball perhaps. It was floating at about eye level and was not steady really...more of a slow glide from spot to spot when it was in one area. It had come out of the hill up ahead (guess which one? I didn't realize until after I had passed it....yep! The one with the storage shed). It paused for only a brief moment when it began to move in an easterly direction along the path. Rising and falling somewhat as it went but by no more than an inch or two. It was almost like it sensed me at one point, cause it stopped (yes—I was following it). I froze in my tracks trying to not even breathe. After a moment, it resumed its course. And when the foot path T-sectioned, with our part dead ending, it continued on into the trees and dissipated rather quickly, just disappearing into the brush. I walked up to the trees and bushes trying to look for it, to see it somewhere.... (Surely this is a joke right?) I didn't see anything. And couldn't wander in, as things were too dense, and the area was littered with sticker bushes (young Hawthorn saplings they may have been).

After a few more laps along the trails, my fiancé woke up and we enjoyed a bit to eat for breakfast and one last stroll before things got nuts. But while on our walk, I noticed something lying in the underbrush. Long and black in color. I couldn't tell if it was an old tree trunk that had fallen, an animal, etc... I couldn't even tell if it was dreaming or dead. Whatever it was, it was tall, just like the thing I had seen the night previous. And the black lacked just as much detail. I just know I wasn't sticking around to find out what I was looking at!

Anyhow shortly after, things resumed their hectic pace as we resumed readying ourselves for parents night. I never did find out what all I encountered. Part of me wants to return for a more in-depth look, especially since my delving into the better ways of psychic self-defense, shielding, and the like. But since I can't remember the name...I guess I am S.O.L. I wouldn't go out at night by myself for weeks after this encounter. And when I did finally venture out, it was only with a baseball bat in hand, and only so I could be out there to defend my dog should something like it show up near my own house. I know it was a stupid worry, as it was a good few hours away, but that isn't what crosses your mind after you've seen something like that.

—Ahoaltuwi Mowichleu

This letter was sent to me by a Wiccan who preferred that I use her "craft" name (which I'll shorten to A.M.), although I do have her given name on file. Unfortunately, even between the two of us, we were unable to figure out exactly which camp she had visited. It was in southeastern Wisconsin; my guess was outside of East Troy, but there's no way to know for sure. Nonetheless, I found her story interesting because, although it isn't exactly a sighting, it has certain features of a sighting and it also involves one of those mysterious globes of light known generically as "orbs." Orbs are considered, variously, to represent earth spirits, spirits of the dead, electromagnetic phenomena, UFO "feelers," swamp gas, or hallucinations from serious eye disease. As I've mentioned earlier in this book, black panthers or other "mystery" cats and strange light phenomena have been connected by some researchers with sightings of tall, furry hominids. Are they also connected with tall, furry canids?

In this case, if A.M. was indeed feeling the eyes of a Manwolf upon her at that campfire, it would seem there might indeed be some connection, since she ran into the orb the very next morning in the same location as the sighting. Admittedly, searching for links to orbs and other unsure attractions will take us away from the "undiscovered natural animal" explanation from the get-go. "Accompanied by floating lights" is not part of the description you'll find of any mammal in any zoological field guide. And I think I've also mentioned that in just about every other sighting I've collected, no one else has reported seeing an orb or a UFO or any other strange light emanation at the same time as the sighting. The closest was the Lima Center sighting of a huge quadruped and a UFO in the same area, but the two were not seen together. Nor have I been able to discover any area in which "marsh lights" or UFOs frequently occur that is also a real hot spot for Manwolf sightings. Again, the only one I've come up with is the sighting on White Pigeon Road, and there the "swamp angels" are still a mile or so away, and the creature was probably not a Manwolf. But people keep trying to make this connection; I receive questions about it at almost every conference I speak at, and it's been treated at length by other researchers. Therefore, any possible local correlations need to be examined, in case Manwolves also belong in the orb/panther/UFO club.

Here is what I find ironic about these connections. Bigfoot is believed to be a possible flesh-and-blood inhabitant of our continent by far more people than those who will accept the possibility that

Manwolves walk among us. But why is Bigfoot, with his *Gigantop-ithecus* pedigree and his trademark footprints left all over the place, connected to woo-woo lights and black panthers, while the less bio-logically certain entity of the Manwolf seems to go it alone, phenom-ena-wise? Shouldn't the stranger creature possess the stranger com-panions? Perhaps eventually a story like the following Bigfoot flap will come forth involving a Manwolf.

Marshfield Bigfoot: Dancing in the Lights?

"Bigfoot, big cats, UFO reports often appear in waves and are much more common than people think," said New York sociologist Robert Bartholomew in a 2004 *Chicago Tribune* article about cougars spot-ted in Lake County. Indeed, a 1991 Marshfield incident chronicled in the August 1 Marshfield *News Herald* of that year, forwarded to me by Richard Heiden, was a perfect example of Bartholomew's observation. According to the *Herald*, Rita Massman of rural Colby reported not only that she had seen the Bigfoot at least four times near her home, but mentioned that she thought it might have something to do with a UFO spotted by neighboring teen, Robert Kocian, about the same time the Bigfoot sightings began. Kocian was in a field, cultivating corn, in the wee morning hours when he spied a "large object" about a quarter mile away from him in the sky. He said it reminded him of a helicopter, except it had "headlights." The craft made no noise, and after Kocian had watched it closely with his tractor shut off for a few minutes, it zoomed away.

I'd be·more convinced of the UFO/Bigfoot tie if Kocian had actually witnessed a Big Furry beaming down from the UFO and scampering off into the cornfield, but it does seem an interesting coincidence that both events occurred at the same time in such a small area, with witnesses from separate families. And Rob Riggs in his book about similar phenomena in Texas, *In the Big Thicket; On the Trail of the Texas Wildman*, says, "The association of light-form producing energies and ape-like creature sightings is reported again and again by independent researchers like Persinger, Keel, Devereaux and Coleman from remote places all over the world." He adds that black pantherlike creatures have been seen in the same vicinities as UFOs and marsh or spook lights.

Kansasville Mystery Animal

Southeastern Wisconsin does have its share of mystery cat tales, in case anyone has been privately decrying the severe canid bias of this book. In Racine County, home to several Manwolf sightings, is a large tract of marshland known as the Bong State Recreation Area, named after the famous World War II fighter pilot, Richard Bong. Eight miles south of Burlington on State Highway 142, the area encompasses 4,515 acres criss-crossed with trails. A large lake lies in the middle. Between Bong and the state line, the land is virtually stippled with lakes and nature areas. And it was very near the Bong area that Kansasville author Steve Sullivan and his wife, Kifflie Scott, each gaped at a black mystery creature on separate occasions.

Both sightings took place between highways J and 75, said Sullivan. He was driving the couple's two children home from a baseball game in Burlington on July 14, 2004, when a pitch-black creature appeared in the edge of his headlights. "There was no light reflecting from it at all," said Sullivan. "And it was FAST." Almost as soon as the creature's presence had registered in Sullivan's mind, it was gone. "I just got a glimpse of the back legs and tail as it disappeared into the brush," he said. "And it moved so quickly that I couldn't say exactly what it was, or even how furry it was...despite this, I felt that I'd never seen anything like it before." It moved south toward State Highway142, he noted.

The creature's tail was as long as the hind legs, he said, and he had the impression that it was about the size of an average German shepherd. "It could have been dog, or cat, or wolf, or coyote—but it definitely seemed odd." Both of Sullivan's children also saw the enigmatic beast.

Kifflie's sighting occurred five nights later, on July 19. She was also driving the children home after a baseball game, but they were both looking the other way at the moment "the thing darted across the road from south to north, moving from 142 toward B." Kifflie didn't see the creature's front end, either, but according to Sullivan, "she said it moved very fast, and that it turned slightly so that she could see its rump and sleek, thin tail as it went. She got a definite impression of a well-defined butt and tail. She thought it could have been a panther, though it might have been a dog or something else, too....

"She said that it seemed eerie...totally black, 'like a hellhound.' That's what I thought, too, like a shadow that moved. Her estimate of the size was the same as mine. But in a way, neither of us thought it was a dog, we both had the impression it was a wild animal. Do coyotes get wolf-sized and come in black?"

The utter blackness of the animal sounds very much like what A.M. saw staring at her in the Scout camp woods, although she was able to discern a canid face and ears.

To add to the unsettling ambience, as Steve and Kifflie taxied their children back and forth to baseball and softball events during this time frame, they began noticing a "strange jogger" along the same roads the creature appeared on. "He jogs with a black knit cap on all the time, including in today's ninety-degree heat," said Steve. "He's always jogging in that same area, sometimes coming, sometimes going. Usually, he wears black, plus the hat. Is he the black werewolf, prowling his territory during the day?"

The Black Monks

Actually, the jogger reminded me of a phenomenon known as "the Black Monk," a mysterious figure usually dressed all in black (sometimes in gray or white). Paul Devereaux, in his book *Haunted Land*, considers the Black Monk a type of "landscape spirit," connected to landscapes where land and river (i.e., a giant marsh with a lake in the middle like Bong) meet. (This reminds me of Todd Roll's comment about land spirits in Chapter 3, as well.) Devereaux described a road in West Sussex, England, where a figure dressed in black was often seen, sometimes even walking into traffic and then vanishing. Usually Black Monks are garbed in hoods and capes, but it's not a far leap to imagine the American equivalent as a black knit cap and jogging attire...equally out of place on a humid, sweltering summer day.

Closer to home, on the southern shore of Geneva Lake and about twenty miles to the west of Bong Recreation Area, some very creepy and perhaps related things were going on in the Township of Linn back in the early nineties. As I noted in the first book, Jon Fredrickson, who was Walworth County's animal control officer, reported that he received an anonymous call around that time from someone driving near the south shore of Geneva Lake on Highway 120. Fredrickson told me in a recent interview that someone witnessed a person in a black cape riding on a black horse, followed by a large dog, emerging from the woods.

This was just after several dog carcasses had been discovered in that area, one with its chest cut open and the heart missing. Its legs were bound with baling twine. Cats and even a turtle were also found in the carcass pile. Fredrickson was investigating reports of alleged cult activity taking place in several areas around the county at the time and could not say for sure whether the rider and the carcasses were related. He just thought the two incidents seemed oddly coincidental. And again, the black-caped figure fairly reeks with Black Monk symbolism. And this was right about the same time the two college co-eds were chased by a dark, furred creature down one of Lake Geneva's main highways (Chapter 5).

There is also a famous legend of a Black Monk haunting an Episcopal seminary in Nashotah, near Delafield. The hooded figure in black robes roams the institution's cemetery by night, of course, and is the subject of innumerable legends.

Another reference to strange, black-robed creatures turned up in a 2002 issue of *Filer's Files*, #46, when an Oregon woman wrote to say that her daughter saw a Grim Reaper figure outside her front door. Filer replied that he had received many reports about black-robed figures, usually with red eyes. He noted they are usually associated with either UFOs or demonic activity.

We might add Manwolves to that short list.

Mystery Cats from the UK to Waukesha

Getting back to Steve Sullivan's black mystery creature, however, could it have been a panther? It reminds me very much of a sighting reported on the *FarShores* UK Web site, which does a good job of keeping up with Great Britain's almost ludicrously high number of black panther incidents. A woman who worked for the local government almost hit what appeared to be a black panther with her car on September 2, 2002, in Northamptonshire. She was driving near Sywell when the creature jumped into the road and then bounced over a hedge and out of sight. She mentioned the animal's long legs and tail and jet-black fur, exactly what both Sullivan and his wife noticed. She thought it had come from a nearby reservoir—again, a watery area.

Several others had seen a similar animal near there in past weeks, and in South Wales, police actually sealed off an area in attempt to catch a black panther spotted by a landowner there.

But you don't have to cross the ocean to find examples of black panthers on the loose, according to the *Illinois Times* Web site. A man from rural Patterson in Green County, north of St. Louis and not far from the Mississippi River, said he was working outside his home one day when a "big cat" came slinking out of a creek bed and then jumped over his fence and ran into the woods. The animal was three times the size of a housecat. "It had a really muscular rear end and a long tail like a cougar," said the man. Again, sounding very much like the Bong critter.

The same site, by the way, notes many mystery cat sightings, including discoveries of at least two dead cougars…incontrovertible proof that cougars, also called pumas, mountain lions, or panthers, have roamed as far south as mid-Illinois. Of course, the Patterson man may have seen an escaped exotic animal, such as a jaguar. Although zoos and private owners always deny it, this sort of thing does happen. A California community about twenty-five miles northwest of Los Angeles endured rumors of a creature called the Moorpark Mangler for almost a decade. Pets were found shredded in their yards, occasionally with huge feline footprints surrounding the carcasses. Or more accurately, the heads, which were usually all that was left of the animal victims.

Imaginations ran wild, with everything from crazed serial pet killers to Satanic cults accused of the atrocities. But in February 2005, a Bengal tiger was finally shot and killed in the area and the mayhem stopped. The regal animal's origin was never found, but it's a sure bet it escaped from someone's private menagerie. And it managed to roam for years in a very populated area without being seen or caught.

Even in Wisconsin, a cougar was spotted and confirmed in Minooka Park in Waukesha, near Milwaukee, in July 2005. It begins to seem that if big cats are being positively identified in Illinois, California, Great Britain, and Waukesha,

Are black panthers responsible for mystery cat sightings?

the thought of one creeping through the Bong Recreation Area is not so strange, after all.

Black Ghost Dogs

Of course, Sullivan wasn't sure that what he saw was a panther. But even if it was a feral black dog (which seems a bit unlikely, given the length of the tail), it still fits into the strange matrix of Bigfoot, black panther, unknown light, and Black Dog sightings that seem to go together like rock stars and Hollywood starlets. I devoted a whole chapter to Black Dogs in *The Beast of Bray Road,* so I'm not going to make an exhaustive list of them here, but they often appear mysteriously and are understood to be phantoms. The "hellhounds" mentioned by Kifflie Scott would fall into this category, usually identified by their inky coats and glowing red eyes.

One rather classic American Black Shuck or ghost dog story came to me from John, in California. He wrote that he and his girlfriend came home one night around Christmas in 2002 and noticed some bushes rustling as they walked to the door. They were sitting in their living room, about four or five feet from the main window, when they both saw a very large black dog standing there in front of it. It was as close as it could get without actually touching the glass, John said, but there was no breath fog visible on the window despite very cold temperatures outside. Most upsetting were the creature's eyes, which glowed red as from some internal source. The dog would have had to stand five feet high on all fours in order to have been seen at that height, and it lasted for fifteen to twenty seconds before disappearing before the horrified couples' eyes. When John finally leaped up to open the door, there was no dog in sight.

Author Paul Devereaux connects the Black Dog to "stretches of certain roads and paths, with parish boundaries and other borderline or liminal locations like bridges and coastal areas, with death (often as a portent) and sometimes with the devil and with witchcraft." In the Kansasville and Linn Road incidents, the animals were not only sighted along roads (as Manwolves so often are), but near marshy areas, close to lakes (ditto the Manwolves, again). The Town of Linn sighting also smacks of cult activities. And we've already established the assignment of the Black Dog as guide to the underworld in the story of the Great Lakes Naval Station Manwolf, which reminded one of the witnesses of Anubis.

Not all phantom dogs are sinister. One Italian saint, St. John Bosco, who died in 1888, was often accompanied by a huge, gray dog of mysterious origin. The dog usually appeared when the saint was in danger, acting as a sort of canine bodyguard. The saint named the dog Grigio, which is Italian for "gray," and even wrote about it in his journal. He said that its attitude was not threatening, and that it treated him as its master. Whenever the saint had to make a trip through dangerous territory, Grigio would simply show up somewhere on the road. The dog refused food offered to it (very unusual behavior as any dog owner will agree) and evidently lived three times a dog's normal lifespan. Some people thought the dog a type of guardian angel, but the saint would give it no higher title than "my friend."

Dogs are not the only animals that show up as black phantoms. Black cats, rabbits, horses, and other fauna show up with great regularity in folklore of every nation. My personal favorite is the story of a black phantom pig in Wales. The pig had a habit of waddling from some old ruins toward passersby on a country lane near Pentrefoelas.

People who tried to beat it away with a stick would find themselves swatting at thin air. There was also a tale of a church in Gwynedd which, as the result of an exorcism gone wrong, became harassed by a demon pig. The satanic porker allegedly threw a second exorcist, along with the horse he rode, into the air and over the church roof before finally being subdued and banished from holy grounds. Another church was unofficially named Church of the Pig's Head because during its construction, a monstrous swine noggin would materialize and wreak havoc on the day's building progress. All of these stories were found in a column by Richard Holland called "Wales of the Unexpected" on *NorthWales.co.uk*.

All of these tales obviously concern creatures from some other "side" than our own three-dimensional world. In an interesting story on the Black Dog phenomenon in the June 1990 issue of *FATE*, author Gordon Stein comments, "The one thing which does seem clear is that the Black Dog of British folklore seems to live *outside the concept of human time*. It appears and disappears from human sight by its own contrivance (italics mine)." If this is true of Manwolves, it could shed considerable light on the creature's ability to seemingly vanish almost before the startled eyes of many witnesses.

And yet, interesting as all these sightings are on their own merit, and while we may infer certain connections, there still is no definitive, concrete tie between Black Dogs, marsh lights, UFOs, Bigfoot, and the Manwolf. Researcher Loren Coleman, in his book *Curious Encounters*, confesses some of the responsibility for these things all being linked in the first place from some of his earlier writings, particularly in the case of Bigfoot and UFOs. While he doesn't rule out the possibility entirely, he does take some giant steps back from his original position on their relatedness. Others, of course, still believe the connections are there, but that opinion is far from unanimous these days.

I did find one far-flung case from the year 1904–05 in Northumberland, England, concerning UFO-like lights and a mysterious wolf. According to Charles Fort in *Lo!*, a strange, wolfish-looking creature in that area was widely hunted by the best sharpshooters but couldn't be tracked even by champion bloodhounds. At the same time, a fervent

HUNTING THE AMERICAN WEREWOLF

religious revival was sweeping the countryside, complete with "deliri-
ous torchlight processions" and people emoting rabidly on the streets.
And on top of these headline-making stories was the report that "lumi-
nous" or "shining" things or beings filled the skies over Wales. One person described seeing something like a "ball of fire," which sounds suspiciously like an orb. As Fort so eloquently summed up the case, "A
wolf and a light and a screech."

In the case of the Beast of Bray Road or the Manwolf, however, I
doubt that even the few dubious connections to UFOs or black dogs
that I've pointed out would ever have been made if the expectation
for these patterns did not already exist. And since so few observations
of Manwolves appearing with other phenomena have been reported,
coincidence seems the likeliest conclusion by far in the Wisconsin
cases. If we do ever start finding a huge amalgam of black dog and panther sightings occurring near crop circles, UFO landings, and sites of
ancient worship here as they do in Great Britain, I'll have to take
another look.

I don't find that absence of Manwolf/phenomena connections disappointing at all. Spook lights, after all, often turn out to be only
swamp gas. And experts have established that even the famed
Paulding Light in Watersmeet, Michigan, is caused by headlights of
approaching vehicles on a nearby highway hill. Even panthers and
cougars are not supernatural, just out-of-place animals. Bigfoot may
keep his coterie of bizarre hangers-on, as far as I'm concerned. The
Manwolf is quite strange enough all by himself, thank you very much.
There's a reason, after all, for the phrase, "lone wolf."

CHAPTER SEVENTEEN
LIZARD MEN AND OTHER ANOMALOUS BIPEDS

"I have come to believe that the whole world is an enigma, a harmless enigma that is made terrible by our own mad attempt to interpret it as though it had an underlying truth."
—Umberto Eco

For Love of Monsters, Mythic or Extinct

There must be something inherently appealing about monsters; otherwise, why would every culture throughout history include so many of them in their lore, art, and religions? Of course, most of the fantastic beasts—griffins, fire-breathing dragons, even Wisconsin's Rhinelander Hodag—fall clearly into the realm of the mythic. But some monsters make even the dubious think twice. One example is the famed Nessie of Loch Ness, Scotland. The long-necked cryptid is said to bear a distinct resemblance to the supposedly extinct Plesiosaur, an animal documented by fossil remains. The existence of an extinct natural animal somehow seems much likelier than the existence of a creature that's not biologically possible. Never mind that Loch Ness isn't big enough to support a family of dino-sized aquatics. The fact that plesiosaurs once did swim Earth's waters is enough to satisfy Nessie believers.

The Manwolf, of course, has no known counterpart in zoological history. This unfortunate fact makes us look elsewhere for his *raison d'etre*, and that inevitably brings us back to the mythic Land of Unbelievables. But while we haven't been able to make any hard and fast connections between the Manwolf and UFOs or electromagnetic phenomena, there are indications he may share his turf with a tremendously varied monster posse. I've already noted that a smaller Bigfoot creature, for one, stomps the same cornfields and marshes as the Man-wolf, but there are other things prowling our roads and riverways right alongside the two of them, if witnesses are to be believed.

While so far I've only covered landlubber furries, there also exists a history of water and sky beasts that I feel compelled to touch on for various reasons. First, some of the creatures with gills and/or wings are also bipeds. That observation begs the only slightly tongue-in-cheek question, how tough could it really be to learn to walk on two legs, if any old vertebrate can master the trick?

Another purpose concerns laying the foundation for the discussion of some Native American legends I'll get to in the next chapter. And finally, does anyone ever really need a reason to tell a few good monster tales?

LaCrosse Lizard Man

One of the state's best-watered communities has to be the city of LaCrosse in far western Wisconsin, spread along the banks of the Mississippi River with a partial dollop of city spooned onto a river island. LaCrosse is also well-watered in terms of liquid refreshment, with the World's Largest Six-Pack decorating the City Brewery building and a giant statue of King Gambrinus, patron saint of beer, dominating the brewery district.

The French Island part of LaCrosse, named for its first settlers in 1849, started as a farming and logging community. It is now graced by a major generating plant that burns wood waste and processed municipal solid waste to produce electricity. The plant was built in the 1940s as a coal-fired generator and has occasionally been the target of several "green" groups for alleged pollution problems.

Just across from French Island, in a neighborhood bordering the Mississippi, a dog ran away from its owners one summer evening in 1993 or '94. The owner and his eighteen-year-old son grabbed a flashlight and went to hunt for the animal along the riverbank, peering into dense underbrush off the beaten path and calling the animal's name. Suddenly, a movement near a tree caught their attention and they trained the flashlight in that direction, hoping to find the runaway hound. Instead, they were astonished to find themselves looking at a creature standing on two legs in front of the tree, something taller than a man and covered with mud-colored scales. Its eyes were yellow and slitted, they said, and it stood its ground fearlessly and looked straight at them until they finally backed gingerly away and fled.

They did eventually locate the pooch.

The story was told to me by the man's ex-wife, who clearly remembers the night the pair came home and excitedly told her the story. "He said it was one of the weirdest things he'd ever seen in his life," said the woman, who prefers her name not be made public. "His son was traumatized. If it had just been his dad who saw it, I might not have believed him."

The family lived on St. Andrews Street at the time, on the north side of LaCrosse. There is a Hardee's restaurant near the riverbank where the incident occurred. The woman tried to persuade her ex and his son to talk to me about the incident, but they refused, probably still feeling spooked. Some people just don't have a very high comfort level when it comes to confessing they've seen Lizard Men. She did mention that she had also heard something about an elderly couple seeing the same creature from their car, but I wasn't able to confirm this or track down anything else about it.

Interestingly, the other big thing keeping LaCrosse in the newspaper headlines in the past several years is the high rate of young men who seem to drown in the Mississippi there, especially after a night at the downtown bars. Twenty-one-year old Jared Dion, for example, was one of a series of young men who have drowned in that river since 1997. His body was found April 15, 2004, after he'd been missing five days. There is no discernible reason for any of the drowning victims to have been in the vicinity of the river. Public meetings have been held in LaCrosse to calm fears of a serial killer.

The fact that a Lizard Man should appear in the city known for so many tragic and unexplainable drownings, of course, seems like an opportunity tailor-made for speculation of the supernatural kind. However, the riverbank sighting happened three or four years before the drownings began, so there isn't really anything to connect it with

The LaCrosse Lizard Man.

the incidents other than location. Unless, perhaps, you think of the Lizard Man as a watery herald of doom, in the same way that phantom black dogs are sometimes seen as portents of death.

The American Kelpie

Or maybe it was something else entirely. Scotland has a type of water spirit called a "Kelpie" that's outlined very well in Nick Redfern's hilarious and informative *Three Men Seeking Monsters*, about his quest for traces of legendary creatures throughout the UK. Although the Kelpie is known popularly as the "water horse" for its habit of appearing in the guise of a magnificent stallion, ready for a weary traveler to saddle up (albeit to his or her doom), the Kelpie is essentially a shape shifter, able to take whatever form seems most appropriate to attract the victim at hand. "But most intriguing of all," Redfern adds, "was the startling fact that the male Kelpie could transform itself into a *large and hair-covered man* (italics mine) that would hide in the vegetation of the Scottish waterways and leap out to attack the unwary. The females, when in human form, were always spectacularly beautiful."

Of course, the LaCrosse Lizard Man sported scales, not hair, but if we are talking about some sort of shape shifter, a la the Kelpie or even Paul Devereaux's landscape spirit from the last chapter, a little hair-to-scales morphing should pose no problem. Notice, also, that the Kelpie's preferred habitat is the vegetation of waterways, just like the Manwolf, as we've established in every sighting. Perhaps there is only one bipedal creature after all, but many transformational disguises. We have Manwolf, Bearwolf, maxi- and mini-Bigfoot, Lizard Man, and assorted sea monsters all hanging around our ponds, lakes, rivers, and marshes. If you think about it, this monster potpourri makes for a very crowded zoo of hidden creatures. How much tidier to believe there is only one actual entity, with the ability to "dress" to suit each particular occasion.

The Kelpie, however, has the unique habit of pulling people into the water once it has entranced them. We don't have eyewitness reports of this behavior regarding any of the other creatures mentioned above, but then drowning victims are notoriously difficult to interview. And if a shape shifting land spirit can exist in Europe, why not in the Americas as well? It could explain a lot.

Interestingly, there is a Native American legend that parallels the Kelpie lore and also pinpoints the Mississippi River. Published in *Wisconsin Indian Folk Legends*, the story is entitled the "Terror of the Rock," or "Rock River Myth." It was told around 1936 by a member of the Winnebago, or Ho-Chunk, nation, who often noted that when they used to camp with the Potawatomi on the Rock River, they needed to beware a "huge and terrible water monster." It was described as long-tailed, with horns, large jaws, claws, and a serpentine body. Moreover, it roamed freely along the river and even into Lake Koshkonong. Deer and people alike were dragged in and swallowed whole, and river crossings were considered especially dangerous. The water around it would "churn and boil," signaling its presence to the watchful. According to the story, some believed there was more than one water monster. The monsters left when the white people came and the Ho-Chunk no longer camped along the Rock River's shores. And the final sentence reads, "Some Indians thought that they established dens in the Mississippi River where they are today."

The Mississippi, of course, defines the western border of Wisconsin and flows right through LaCrosse, where the drownings occur. And while this story doesn't mention any shape shifting on the part of the monster, perhaps the morphing is something only its victims see. There are many animal effigy mounds in the shape of at least one type of water spirit, as we've already mentioned. But more on that later. The LaCrosse Lizard Man sighting wasn't the only instance in area history when something scaly this way came.

The Medford Reptile Man

Farther north from LaCrosse, near the town of Medford, a warden from the Department of Natural Resources was driving down a usually unremarkable stretch of Highway 13 south of Medford one day in the mid-1990s. The warden spied something in the road ahead of him, an occurrence that wasn't in itself out of the ordinary, but he couldn't tell if the figure was animal or human. He slowed down both to avoid hitting it and to satisfy his curiosity, and there, according to a story in *Weird Wisconsin: Your Travel Guide to Wisconsin's Local Legends and Best Kept Secrets*, stood "a shiny, green-scaled, man-sized figure—a reptile man."

Is there any difference between a Reptile Man and a Lizard Man? In this case, there appeared to be one biggie, as the *Weird Wisconsin* authors (one of whom is this author) continued: "As he got within several yards, wings suddenly snapped out from behind the creature's back. It went vertical, zooming straight up and over the vehicle, landing on the road behind him."

Wings lend a whole new aspect to the concept of Reptile Man and Lizard Man, making them seem almost like human dragons and/or Bat People, pulling us even further into the camp of the mythological. Of course, the LaCrosse creature may merely have kept his wings folded, since they weren't readily apparent on the Medford figure at first, either. And, outrageously bizarre as the wing-snapping aspect of this story appears, it's still hard to dismiss the sighting because the warden was not the only witness.

Not long after the warden's sighting, several highway workers were trucking south from Medford, also along Highway 13, when they, too, noticed something odd in the road that they hadn't put there. It was a creature that looked exactly like what the warden saw. It had the same green scales and performed the identical trick of unfolding its wings and rocketing skyward before it dove into a clump of trees. The workers were left scratching their furrowed brows over whether they should erect a "Slow, Monster Crossing" sign.

Inspecting the LaCrosse and Medford sightings for similarities, the time frame matches well, along with the scaly, human form. But there is another, less obvious connection. Checking a map of Wisconsin, I discovered that the Black River runs straight up from LaCrosse, where it diverges from the Mississippi, to Medford. It crosses Highway 13 just south of Medford, in fact, exactly where Reptile Man was seen. The creature could have enjoyed a lovely water highway journey between the two points. And just north of Medford is the vast Chequamegon National Forest, which could hide a multitude of strange bipeds.

Another Wing-Thing

Human-sized, bipedal winged things may be more common than we realize. A woman from Jefferson, Wisconsin, wrote a somewhat dis-traught-sounding letter to the *Weird Wisconsin* Web site's Yahoo group on July 4, 2005, about a truly odd being she and her boyfriend saw near Paradise Road on State Highway 18, east of Jefferson, the year before. Paradise Road, by the way, is a winding country lane that borders the Jefferson Marsh and is the subject of numerous teen urban legends. But the creature they saw standing next to the road as they drove past looked like something out of a comic book, said the woman. It was dark-colored, and the figure was "humanlike," but very tall with wings. "Huge, huge wings," she said. As is typical in many weird creature sight-ings, the couple became so frightened that they just kept on driving and didn't tell anyone but her mother what they had seen.

It's no wonder they were scared. The creature had glowing red eyes, said the woman, and she described its visage as "not a human-ish face by any means." But the wings were not batlike, she noted. "They looked feathery and full." She added that the face seemed "demonic" to her. She described herself and her boyfriend as Chris-tians who did not believe in evil beings…until now.

Astute readers may remember another creature sighted just outside of Jefferson that was described as "demonic," the werewolfish hairy biped caught digging in the Indian Mound behind St. Coletta Institute in 1936. Mark Schackelman, the night watchman who encountered the being on two successive nights, called it a "demon straight from hell." I've also been told by a longtime resident that many exorcisms were performed in that same rural area back in those years, a lead that I'm still investigating.

The Jefferson Square of Weirdness

It's quite a confluence we have in this little area near Jefferson…a haunted road, a bipedal hairy entity, exorcisms, a tall, winged creature with a human shape and demonic face, and a marsh. Moreover, to complete the picture, Fromader Road, the site of the Hurd Bigfoot incident, lies only about three miles south of Paradise Road. Three miles southeast of Fromader lies that spawning-bed of strangeness, the Kettle Moraine State Forest. Just north of Jefferson, moreover, is the ancient and mysterious ruin called Aztalan, a Misssissippian stockade village with the remains of several pyramid structures. It lies very near Rock Lake, reputed to shelter pyramidal, underwater structures and a lake monster named "Rocky." All of this in an area that makes an almost perfect square, 13 miles on each side with Rock Lake as its northwest corner and the end of Fromader Road as its southeast. The center of Jefferson, the intersection of state highways 18 and 26, sits almost at dead center.

All very circumstantial, certainly, but what strange circumstances! If ever there was a "window area" where things can creep in from other

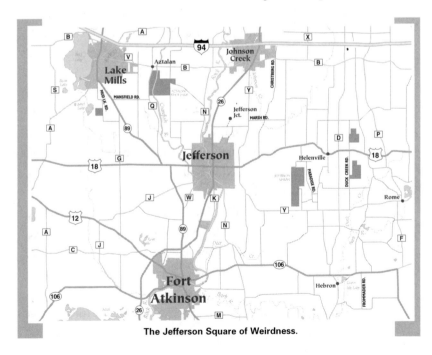

The Jefferson Square of Weirdness.

dimensions as John Keel and others have posited, this Square of Weirdness should certainly qualify…and it's a window that appears to be stuck wide open.

Other Winged Things

Others have seen giant winged things, too. *Weird Wisconsin* tells of several. There was the Brookfield Thunderbird, a black, flying form "bigger than a full-sized pick-up truck," seen by twenty-five-year-old Kevin W. from a window of Elmbrook Memorial Hospital. The creature, with an estimated wingspan of twelve to fifteen feet, glided instead of flapping its wings, and appeared to make eye contact with the startled young man. Its head reminded him of a pterodactyl. Then there was the Mauston Birdman, spotted in 1980 on a bluff five miles west of Mauston by a grandmother looking out her window. She said it was six feet tall, had yellow feathers and a long beak. But its body was like a man's, she said, and had arms and legs rather than wings. The head was birdlike, as were the feet. Sounds a lot like Big Bird, of *Sesame Street*, and as a matter of fact, the family's youngest member insisted that Big Bird had visited her one night and even took her outside.

More sightings occurred from 1990–94 in Stangelville, a tiny town at the base of the Door Peninsula where several people saw a huge, gliding thing that tore the deltoid muscles from an elderly man's shoulder.

Lizard Men and giant winged creatures are not unique to Wisconsin, of course. The Associated Press ran a story in 1988 about a monster seen near Bishopville, South Carolina, which did a great deal to popularize the notion of amphibious or reptilian bipeds. Like the Jefferson winged thing, it stood seven feet tall and stared with glowing red eyes. Its scales were black-green, somewhere between the mud green and bright green of the two Wisconsin reptilians, and it featured three digits on each hand and foot, plus four-inch claws. This creature was a little scarier than its Wisconsin cousins, because it actually charged and attacked seventeen-year-old Christopher Davis just as he finished changing a blown tire—in a swamp area, of course. The teen saw the creature come sprinting out of an adjacent bean field just in time to leap back in his car and slam the door. The young man tried to flee in his car, but the thing hopped on the roof and then held on in a virtuoso performance of car-surfing until Davis finally swerved and threw it from the vehicle. Reportedly, the Lizard Man left scratches on the car and almost twisted the side mirror from the vehicle. (This is reminiscent of Doris Gipson's Beast of Bray Road sighting where the Manwolf charged her car and left scratches, though it didn't hang on. It also allegedly scratched witness Tom Brichta's car.)

Typically for local authorities, the South Carolina community's sheriff's department claimed the thing that attacked Davis had to be a bear, no matter how un-bearlike in size, description, and behavior Davis' description had been. The sheriff's other ludicrous and lame theory? The attacker was only a person stopping for water by an artesian well located nearby. Perhaps the well-seeker mistook the young man's car for a water jug. The absurdities authorities will resort to in order to "explain" anomalous experiences never fail to amaze me.

Later, however, three-toed prints were found around the area, and other residents claimed to see the Lizard Man. A media frenzy ensued, not unlike the one that surrounded the Beast of Bray Road revelation in early 1992.

This creature didn't have wings, evidently, or if it did, it kept them folded up. Humanoid reptiles have been spotted in British Columbia, New Jersey, California, and Loveland, Ohio, to name some of the most prominent locations. Most recently, in late March 2005, the Russian news organization *Pravda* reported an "amphibious man" seen swimming with teeming shoals of fish in the Caspian Sea near Iran and Azerbaijan. The article said residents had been spotting him for two years, sometimes swimming alongside fishing trawlers. This guy had four fingers rather than three, with "moonlight" colored skin and hair on his head...not at all like the American reptoids. He sounds much more like a Fish Man than a Reptile Man, in fact.

Sightings of New Jersey's Jersey Devil and West Virginia's Mothman have been so well-covered elsewhere I won't go into them here.

But as far as the American reptoid sightings go, I reluctantly must conclude that they don't behave much like Kelpies. No beautiful horses or enticing ladies to beckon weary or lustful travelers...just hideous monsters with no apparent fear of man and very little subtlety of approach. But there is another type of water monster to consider, the traditional, long-necked lake serpent. These have been spotted all over the country and world, including Wisconsin Manwolf territory. Some of the more famous are in Madison's Lakes Mendota (1917) and Monona (1897), Elkhart Lake (1890s), Lake Michigan (1990s), McFarland's Lake Waubesa (1920s), Stoughton's Lake Kegonsa (1920s), Pewaukee Lake (undated), Cambridge's Red Cedar Lake (1891), and Lake Mills' Rock Lake (1882). One more noteworthy and fairly well-documented report is of a monster reported to dwell in a lake that has been at the center of a number of Manwolf sightings, Geneva Lake in Walworth County. Might we find a Kelpie who can double as a Big Furry at work here?

Jenny, Geneva Lake's Serpent

Geneva Lake, a popular watering hole poured handily for Illinois tourists into southern Walworth County, is Wisconsin's second-deepest lake. It's a 142-foot plunge to the bottom, and its waters are kept toe-numbingly cold by many underground springs, considered by Native Americans to be doorways to the spirit world. The lake is also crystalline—the Potawatomi called it *Kish-wau-ke-toe* or "clear water"—making it an unlikely hiding place for creatures not listed in local guides to marine life. And yet, from prehistoric times into the early twentieth century, something long, serpentine, and frisky has been spotted gamboling over its eight-and-a-half-square mile surface.

In September 1902, the *Milwaukee Sentinel* reported as fact that "a sea serpent actually appeared in Geneva Lake Wednesday afternoon." The writer referred to the creature as "his snakeship," noting that he not only burst onto the lake surface in broad daylight but was witnessed by at least six people.

The first to see it were two women camping at Reid's Park. They watched the creature "coiling and rolling about in the water not far from shore," while two young men rowed out to get a better look. That spooked the reptile, which "dove down into the water and went out of sight like a shot." The group estimated the creature to be as long as the Steamship Aurora, or sixty-five feet. The Reverend M.N. Clark of

Delavan also reported an encounter with the creature that year, and the minister's reputation for honesty won over many skeptics.

The Reid's Park group was not the first to be involved in a sea serpent scare on this lake; the *Chicago Tribune* reported in July of 1892 that two boys and a man named Ed Fay (see the Name Matrix in Chapter 19) saw a fearsome reptile while fishing from a boat. The three were about to pull in their lines when a huge head suddenly popped up and its jaws opened wide, revealing spiky rows of needle-sharp teeth. To the men's horror, the massive head continued to rise until it bobbed 10 feet above the water. The creature was covered with scales ranging from light green at the belly to dark brown at the tail, and the group estimated the serpent's body to be 100 feet long and three feet in diameter.

The trio became even more frightened when they began rowing away and the creature followed them! However, as the men frantically pumped the oars, the emerald beast finally turned back and headed slowly for Kaye's Park, a resort next to the Black Point mansion, making "bizarre sounds" as it swam.

Thousands of people flocked to the lakeshore in the following days, hoping to catch their own glimpses of the monster. It's unknown whether any were successful, but one local newspaper declared the whole thing a hoax, accusing Chicago newspapers of trying to make a buck on the sensational story. Still, many of those who have lived around Lake Geneva all their lives have kept the faith. They refer to their lake's denizen as Jenny and believe that she particularly frequented the central portion of the lake known as "The Narrows," the shortest point of passage between the north and south shores and the scene of several major boat mishaps.

Some have guessed that Jenny was actually a surviving plesiosaur, a forty- to fifty-foot-long sea reptile that lived in the Cretaceous period, but naysayers join Loch Ness skeptics in their insistence that these lakes aren't large enough to support a breeding population of such a large animal. Others have linked Jenny to old Native American legends. These stories may date back to the mysterious builders of the animal effigy mounds, since a huge lizard mound representing the water spirit was found by settlers at the water's edge on the lake's north shore.

The mound is now gone, cleared away in the early development of the City of Lake Geneva. The mound builders, however, were not the last indigenous people to inhabit these shores. Historian Paul B. Jenkins, in *History and Indian Remains of Lake Geneva and Lake Como*, related that the Potawatomi who lived in three villages around the shore at the time of the settlers also insisted the lake hid a monster serpent "much like an eel in appearance." The Potawatomi avoided taking their canoes out on the lake on stormy days, the monster's preferred weather.

As if the lake could get any scarier, the same indigenous people also believed the lake contained *Nampe-shiu,* the great horned water panther, probably the same creature mentioned in the Ho-Chunk Rock River story. Jenkins was told, "There is an evil power in the water, who possesses the ability to pass through the earth as well as its natural element." The panther was believed to drown hapless people, whose mode of death could be proven by the fact that they would be found with mud or clay in their mouth, eyes, and ears.

The water panther was said to be at constant war with another member of the effigy pantheon, an aerial creature called the "Thunderbird," which some might say corresponds to our Wing Things. This giant being could make thunder by flapping its wings, and it liked to touch down on a jutting peninsula of the lake's northwestern shore known as "Conference Point." This spot happens to lie just off the lake's deepest area and was not only the site of a *Beast of Bray Road* encounter (Jessica Anderson, 1998) but was featured in a book called *Darkness is Light Enough* by Gerald Lishka, who detailed a transcendental experience with a mystical light being that rose up out of the water just off the shore.

Although modern times have brought such a horde of summer boat traffic that it's hard to imagine a serpent so much as poking a fin above water without being mowed down by Jet-Skiers, hard-core sea serpent fans like to believe that perhaps Jenny still lives somewhere in the depths, possibly entering and exiting the lake bottom by means of the supernatural doorways in the ever-bubbling springs. Admittedly, she hasn't been spotted recently. But it's almost enough just to know that she used to show up now and then.

Pioneer Monster

The chief disappointment of most of the lake monster tales, including that of Jenny, is their antiquity. Most of these greenies haven't been seen since the 1920s or earlier, with the exception of the Lake Michigan sighting. However, the 1920s is exactly when most of the lake frontage around the southern half of the state began to be snapped up by developers and vacation-bound Illinoisians, greatly increasing traffic on all lakes and rendering them sea-monster-unfriendly. Lake Michigan in its deep vastness would be a different story, though, and it makes sense that if any monsters were still cavorting in state waters, the Great Lakes are where they would be found.

As for Kelpie correlations, there are not many records of Big Furries being sighted in the same time period as those lake monsters. A possible exception comes from an old newspaper report passed on by Richard Hendricks. It was found in a book called *Pioneering the Upper Midwest: Books from Michigan, Minnesota, and Wisconsin, ca. 1820.* It's a story about some very early settlers in the Oshkosh region who were "besieged" one day by an animal described as "long, black, fierce, and rough-haired." It completely intimidated the family dog, and "sat" in front of the cabin door occasionally as it prowled about. The man of the family insisted it was not a bear, wolf, catamount or lynx, and in fact he couldn't identify it at all.

Some have interpreted this as a Bigfoot story, but the description as "long" rather than "tall" and the absence of any mention of bipedalism makes me think this creature was on four feet rather than two, as Manwolves are sometimes wont to appear. Oshkosh is located on Lake Winnebago, which is the site of another Native American water monster story concerning a creature that looked like a giant sturgeon. And again, we find that effigy mounds once were located in this region.

Overall, it's hard to know what to make of all these different creatures. Thinking of them as different aspects of a land spirit simplifies everything but will probably not fly with the flesh-and-blood crowd. Regardless, after studying all I could find on area Native American lore, I made a few more interesting discoveries regarding Manwolf sightings and those quixotic animal effigy mounds. I think it is time to have a respectful look at them.

CHAPTER EIGHTEEN
THE NATIVE LANDSCAPE

"I only repeated what the spirits said to me. I heard their
voices. The top of the lodge was full of them, and before
me the sky and wide lands lay expanded."
—Johann George Kohl's account of the words of a
dying Ojibwe medicine man, in *Kitchi-Gami: Life*
Among the Lake Superior Ojibway

The Effigy Mound Enigma

The United States is a relatively young nation, compared with most other countries in the world. Suffice it to say that if this country harbors land spirits, if it shelters unknown, hidden animals, if it contains remnant populations of creatures thought by modern science to be extinct, they were all likely here before the Declaration of Independence was signed in 1776. Unless, of course, they are or were planted by aliens from outer space, which some people believe (see Chapter 20).

Contrary to some people's general notions of what this country was like before Europeans arrived and took over, this continent was not a vast wasteland or giant, uninterrupted forest. North and South America hosted populations of many "nations" of people with some surprisingly large population centers, especially in the cities of the Mississippian, Mayan, and Aztec cultures. Early settlers were amazed to find forests that looked like well-groomed parks, thanks to industrious management by controlled fires and other means practiced by the indigenous peoples who lived here. Settlers also found cultivated fields and organized villages.

But what amazed early explorers the most, particularly in southern Wisconsin, was the staggeringly large numbers of precisely formed earth mounds that graced the landscape; some 20,000 or more in at

253

least 3,000 locations. Some were round or lozenge-shaped, whereas others formed enigmatic, abstract symbols. But many of the mounds were in the shape of stylized animals of recognizable species. Bears, deer, birds, turtles, and long-tailed water spirit forms (*Nampe-shiu*, mentioned in the last chapter), misinterpreted as lizards, were some of the most prevalent, along with some human shapes. Other than for the few that extended over the border into Iowa, Illinois, and Minnesota and the giant Serpent Mound in Ohio, these animal effigy mounds of southern Wisconsin were unique in all the world. What could have inspired the ancient woodland-dwellers to even conceive of these artistic masterpieces, and why do they exist in just this area?

Some of them were used as burial mounds, but many, as artifact-hungry Europeans with no respect for Native American traditions soon learned, were not. The more numerous conical mounds seemed to serve that purpose. So what were the effigy mounds for, exactly? The amount of planning, effort, and design that went into their construction and orientation on the earth meant these were not casual or meaningless piles of dirt.

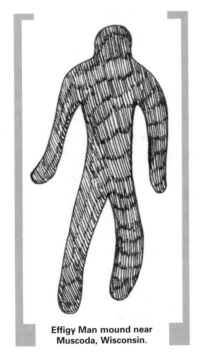

Effigy Man mound near Muscoda, Wisconsin.

The tribes who were here at the time the mounds were "discovered"—the Winnebago (or Ho-Chunk), the Chippewa (or Ojibwe), the Potawatomi, Ottawa, Sauk, and Fox—told early researchers that the mounds were very old, and they were not sure of their use. (Of course, that may simply have been their way of protecting their private heritage.) And some of the information given by the Ho-Chunk to early researchers such as state historian Charles E. Brown was ignored by those who later wrote about the mounds.

Most of the mounds are estimated by anthropologists to have been constructed between 800 and 2,800 years ago. And it is generally agreed, on the basis of which populations were known to have been in this area at the time, that the distant ancestors of today's Ho-Chunk were probably the creators of the effigy mounds. Different speculations on mound purposes have included use as low-lying fortifications, tribal totem markers for individual clans, and ceremonial centers.

The animal species represented do correspond to the totem animals of various clans of the Ho-Chunk. And it's almost a given that something so impor-

Effigy Man mound near Muscoda, Wisconsin, which features horns—or wolflike ears.

tant to the ancients, especially since many do contain burials, would have been sacred and therefore the focus of ritual and ceremony. But most anthropologists suspect there is more to the mounds than that. So do some Ho-Chunk, and so do I.

Water Spirits and Manwolves

We've already discussed the fearsome water panther or water spirit. I was looking at a map in Birmingham and Eisenberg's *Indian Mounds of Wisconsin* one day when a few dozen lightbulbs went off in my head. It almost hurt. Their map of Wisconsin shows major groupings of animal effigy mounds, with different types represented by tiny symbols. It suddenly occurred to me that the placement of the symbols, especially symbols of the water spirit or panther, corresponded very closely to a map I had made showing the main concentrations of Manwolf sightings around the state!

I made a transparency of my map, sized to fit the one in the book and *voila*, the connection was undeniable. I couldn't place sightings

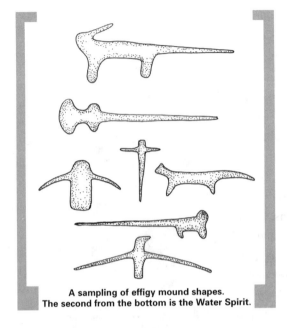

A sampling of effigy mound shapes.
The second from the bottom is the Water Spirit.

to *exact* locations of the mounds, say within a few feet or yards, in every instance, but the distribution of the two phenomena was very much the same. The water spirit mounds are found predominantly in the mid- to eastern part of the southern half of the state, with the exception of one near LaCrosse (where tradition says the Rock River water monster now abides). The western part of the state seems to be Thunderbird (sometimes called eagle) mound territory, with effigies in the shape of four-legged animals mixed in between. These are just general patterns, of course, since most of the effigy mound groupings contain at least a few examples of all three of these categories.

I should note that some discrepancies should be expected, since the mounds are stationary but the creatures seem to have free ability to roam. Even taking that into consideration, I still think the way the two maps coincide is remarkable. It seems more than mere coincidence, in fact.

I did come up with a few more theories and ideas about my discovery. The guardian spirit model was the first that came to mind. In *The Beast of Bray Road*, I discussed the Witchie Wolves of Michigan's Omer Plains. These were said to be phantom wolves set up to guard sacred grounds such as burial sites. Years later, they were still around to spook exploring teenagers.

Big Furry humanoids would do the job just as well. Again, consider the fearsome Manwolf that was seen digging on the burial mound (since graded over) in Jefferson in 1936. It could have been anywhere else on the expansive acreage, but there it was, scratching away at the one ancient Amerindian feature on the grounds. As the realtors like to say, "Location, location, location."

My suspicions of a long-standing knowledge of the Manwolf by the ancient Ho-Chunk (and probably other tribes who came here later) were deepened when I received a call from a young man who said he was a member of that nation, and that he remembered his grandfather telling stories of a creature that sounded very much like the Beast of Bray Road. He promised to ask more about it, but I never heard back from him. Most likely, his elders felt he had divulged too much already.

My next step was to seek an interview with a tribal elder. This was easier thought of than accomplished. It took a long time to figure out whom I should be contacting, and then an equally long time to per-suade anyone to talk to me, but permission was finally given after I shared what I had figured out about the sighting and effigy mound connection. I was permitted to interview a highly esteemed elder woman who was also a retired anthropologist with a keen interest in the effigy mounds, on the condition that I not publish her name.

And so it happened that I found myself traveling with my hus-band to Black River Falls one crisp autumn day in 2004, headed for the casino where we were to meet. It worked out nicely since the hub was able to occupy himself in the popular gaming establishment while I sat and chatted with my interviewee. In lieu of the traditional tobacco usually offered as a gift of respect when seeking advice from a respected tribal member, I gave her copies of *The Beast of Bray Road* and my earlier book, *The Poison Widow*. We had a great time and a very fruitful discussion.

During the course of our talk, she shared some things that I am not permitted to divulge, including her own sketch of a little-known petroglyph of the water spirit located on land that is not generally accessible to the public, which she did not want me to copy since it is sacred to her people. All I can say is that it appeared possibly bipedal.

Interestingly, Birmingham and Eisenberg's *Indian Mounds* relates that in 1911, a historian named Arlow B. Stout interviewed some

Ho-Chunk in Wisconsin Dells about the mounds, and one told him that their elders identified the long-tailed mounds as representations of a spirit being. The creature was said to live in the water and emerge at night. The identification of lizard or panther mounds with the Ho-Chunk water spirit was confirmed a second time in *Indian Mounds* when the authors cite archaeologist Robert Hall as pointing out that correlation. A picture begins to emerge, then, of a bipedal creature that would always be seen near water and at night. Other than for a handful of afternoon sightings, that picture fits our Manwolf pretty well.

My new Ho-Chunk acquaintance agreed that it would be all right to tell about the connection I had made between the sightings and the water spirit mounds. And I think it is also permitted to give her people's general view of creatures such as Bigfoot and the Manwolf, although she asked me not to tell the sacred story that is used as a basis for the belief. (I have found versions of that story in some published works of Wisconsin tribal beliefs but I am going to honor her wishes and allow readers to search for themselves.)

The gist of it is that both of these creatures exist in a sort of limbo between the spirit world and ours. There is a human component to their background, and they are able to go back and forth between the two worlds. When in this world, they are mostly corporeal and must eat to sustain themselves, and can leave footprints, fur, and other evidence. It is because of their human part that they are forbidden to hurt or kill people. And their ability to pop back into the spirit world explains the ability of Manwolf, Bigfoot, and other humanoid creatures to seemingly vanish when pursued. A later phone interview with another tribal member confirmed this view.

The man-shaped effigy mounds are also interesting. There are two main types; one usually features a round head set on broad shoulders with no neck, and disproportionately long arms. The other is more proportionately human but has two projections on either side of the head. These are usually interpreted to be horns, and the figure is thus meant to portray a shaman wearing a horned mask. However, as I often like to show with transparency overlays at conferences, the "horns" could also be ears, and this mound outline matches almost exactly the witness sketch of the Manwolf drawn by artist Marv Kirschnik (Chapter 5).

The other, neckless man-type mound matches the Bluff Monster sketches by Judy Wallerman and David Pagliaroni. Since all the other mounds, with perhaps the exception of the water spirit, represent particular animals, might not these two types also represent the Manwolf and Bigfoot? If the two creatures were seen around southeastern Wisconsin woods then as they are today, the effigy mound builders would have been familiar with them, half-spirit beings or not, and it's hard to imagine that the Big Furries would have been left out of something so sacred as the effigy mound system. In fact, these two "man" mounds were selected for the cover of a pamphlet for the mounds group near Muscoda, suggesting that even today they are recognized as having some special significance.

The Lake Superior Ojibwe have a story about an abandoned brother who transforms into a wolf on the shore of a lake, told in Henry Schoolcraft's *Ojibwa Lodge Stories*. The child was left to fend for himself in a wilderness area and was forced to scavenge for the remains of wolf kills in order to survive. By the time his older brother returned for him, the boy was already beginning to howl. The older brother paddled furiously across the lake as the boy cried, "My brother, my brother, I am now turning into a wolf! I am turning into a wolf!" The lad grew fur and ears before his brother's amazed eyes and ran from the lakeshore into the woods.

This is a much-simplified version of the story, and I'm sure it has more layers of meaning than I am aware of, but again the symbolism of water, transformation, and the human–wolf connection is very striking. I can't help but note the similarity of those elements to the connections I have found between water areas, water spirit effigies found near those areas, and the sightings of Manwolves.

I know that hard-core cryptozoologists, still hoping for a flesh-and-blood creature, won't like this explanation any more than the Kelpie theory. But the idea of a multi-dimensional shape shifter, similar, as I noted in the first book, to John Keel's idea of inhuman creatures he calls "mimics," makes a lot more sense than the idea that all these large creatures are actually running around the countrysides of various American states.

Of course, Native Americans have other traditions regarding shape shifters, too. I've already mentioned the *Yenaldlooshi*, or Navajo creature. There are many others, probably one for every tribe. These differ from the Ho-Chunk explanation for Bigfoot and Manwolves, however, in that they are intentionally produced by shamans or witches, who control the entities for their own purposes. The same would go for the kinds of beings described in modern-day books on creating magical entities that we touched on in the very first chapter. They are not unlike Tibetan *tulpas*, creatures that some religious disciples there are reputed to bring into existence from their own "thought forms." (Although according to some accounts, *tulpas* can get out of hand and get away from their creators.) Kelpies, landscape spirits, or the version explained by my Ho-Chunk friends, on the other hand, all seem to be free agents.

Before anyone gets too excited about heading for the hinterlands and calling up a Kelpie or even looking for a Manwolf, I'd like to echo a precautionary note from the Bords' *Alien Animals* book. They explain that people who go out expecting and hoping to see such creatures open themselves to manipulation by the entities, who may be actually feeding on human energy emitted by shock and surprise. Take that as you like.

There is another way of explaining this same direction of ideas that doesn't involve independent entities or even magical creatures, necessarily. Some people have theorized that the natural electromagnetic fields of the earth, which are concentrated in certain areas according to the composition of rock layers and water aquifers below the soil, may combine with all the man-made sources of electromagnetic energy we keep erecting all over the place. Together, these energies create a fluid and unseen force capable of displaying both enigmatic "lights" in the atmosphere and causing false impressions or hallucinations in people.

The Bords, in *Alien Animals*, note: "R. Martin Wolf reminds us that UFOs, BHMs (Big Hairy Monsters) and other paranormal phenomena occur near to 'microwave towers, high-tension power lines, nuclear power installations, hydro-electric dams, bodies of water, missile silos, railroad tracks, and even mobile homes; most of these having some association with electromagnetic energy."

That leaves a lot of territory wide open for anomalous entity appearances. I can't say that I've been able to correlate Manwolf sightings with nuke plants, missile silos, or mobile homes. And, as in the case of the Eau Claire fuzzy home invader, why the "hallucinations" should be of big, hairy animals is a very interesting question. Also, why, in cases with multiple witnesses, would everyone see exactly the same hallucination?

But I have to think about the Bluff Monster weaving and bobbing through the shadows of the giant Christmas star on Young Hill. Not far away from that point, on Tower Road, is a massive electrical tower. Combine that with the megawatts coming off the huge electric star, poise them over a bluff area known to Native Americans as a sacred point, probably because of the unique rock structure beneath it, and there we have a Big Furry appearing visible to all sorts of people. Sounds like a logical recipe.

Nevertheless, I think that even if the Bluff Monster and other Big Furries are created by some poorly understood combination of human mental process and electromagnetic wave bombardment, the creatures could still be said to be "real" in a very authentic sense. They move, eat, interact, and exist for all practical purposes on our plane. Who's to say they don't have somewhere else to go, another dimension perhaps, when their time is up in Walworth County or the Shenango Valley? I think perhaps the Ho-Chunk lore may strike very close to the truth of the matter.

The Genie in the Lamp

Here is another, wilder theory, on uses of the mounds, however, that is completely my own. And it didn't hurt my brain nearly as much as the map correlation epiphany. It started with the thought that, if these sightings truly have been going on for centuries, since before the industrialization of the world, man-made electrical fields are not always necessary to bring these creatures around. My admittedly strange idea is that perhaps the mounds, especially those of the water spirit and Thunderbird, particularly since they were often empty, may have been some sort of spirit containers.

If the ancients wanted guardian spirits to guard their burial places, either conjured by shamans or hired from the Landscape Spirit Employment Service, it makes sense that some sort of base for them would be needed, both to ground them to the area and keep them in check. When the mounds were cut open, plowed under and otherwise desecrated by settlers, the guardians may have been set free. That would explain the proximity of these creatures to the mound areas, as well as why it was so important to place mounds everywhere and go to such lengths in their construction and design. Perhaps the reason the Manwolves seem to stick so close to water is their past association with the water spirits contained in those mounds.

There is some basis for the idea of Native American water monsters as hairy rather than scaly. The Navajo water monster is furred like an otter and has horns, which signify that he is a powerful being. The Arapaho legend of Hairy Face describes an infant water monster as spotted with a long tail, hooved feet, a dog's face (!), and strangely, a complete lack of eyes. The Paiyuk, water monster of the Ute of the far western states, resembles a fuzzy elk.

Jim Brandon in *The Rebirth of Pan* lends some support to my notion, I think, when he notes that in the U.K., raised earthworks were traditionally believed to be "decorous figures concealing formidable processes of what we might as well call natural sorcery." He adds, "Ancient Chinese landscape science likewise believed that elevations and disruptions of the ground denoted places where nature's breath pulsed forth."

Again, this concept of the effigy mounds as conjured spirit containers is purely my speculation, perhaps born of a day when I drank too much English breakfast tea while taking decongestants. I'm sure that those who don't believe in a spirit world or other dimensions beyond our own, or that electromagnetic forces or spirits can play with human heads and vice versa, will probably not get too excited about it. I rather like the idea of all those mounds designed as giant, elegant Aladdin's lamps, though. And if you recall that Arabian legend about Aladdin, things never work out too well for the people who disturb the genie.

Dogrib Nation

Nationally, many other Native American connections can be made to the Manwolf and other Big Furries. In the first book, I covered Skin-changers, Skin Walkers, Windigo or Wendigo, and even Carlos Castaneda's *nagual* as to their relation or non-relation to Beast of Bray Road-type sightings. We've already talked about the upper Midwestern counterpart, Bearwalkers, in Chapter 3 of this book and also touched on the Navajo *Yenaldlooshi* or Skinchanger. The *Waheela*, a native term for what some think may have been a remnant population of extinct dire wolves, was also discussed in Chapter 3.

But I keep running into one other Native American connection with the canine world that appears unique, and that is the people of the northern Canadian Nation who refer to themselves as the Dogrib. According to their creation stories, they are descended from Copper Woman, the first female, who marries a dog that transformed into a man for their union. The Aleuts also believe the male ancestor of their tribe was a dog that fell from heaven, and Eskimos share a similar belief. According to Patricia Dale-Green's *Lore of the Dog*, even Italian folklore contains a legend explaining that a dog was used to carry the rib from Adam, from which Eve was then created.

Like the legends of werewolves, these stories show a very deep-seated connection between human and canine, and seem to express that, on some level, people and wolves or dogs are one. Perhaps the Manwolf is only an outer manifestation of this ancient, subconscious attachment.

Despite this wealth of native lore and legend, as I concluded in the first book's chapter on the topic, the shape shifters and the spirit guardians or land spirits still seem like the best match to the Manwolf. And I also still believe that southern Wisconsin's animal effigy mounds have more than a casual connection to this phenomenon.

Birmingham and Eisenberg believe that the many studies made of the mounds and their meaning lead to the conclusion that "the ideological concerns of the effigy mound people were directed at maintaining balance and harmony between human beings and the natural world through spiritual forces."

The images of those forces are evident to us now. The Thunderbirds, or air spirits, depicted by eaglelike shapes, were always at war with the water spirits. The earth animals such as bears and deer played intermediary roles. These ongoing battles between spiritual forces, perhaps focused and even extended by the animal effigy mounds, kept the earth harmonious and balanced in the eyes of the effigy mound builders.

But decades after modern society destroyed most of these mounds, we find ourselves with Manwolves, Bigfoot, Lizard Men, and even Thunderbirds apparently running amok in physical or at least visible form. And the state of the earth, obviously, is anything but harmonious. Perhaps something was destroyed other than the bones of ancient Native Americans when the effigy mounds were desecrated and razed.

CHAPTER NINETEEN

HOAXERS, THE NAME MATRIX, AND WEREWOLVES HEARD BUT NOT SEEN

"Sometimes a scream is better than a thesis."
—Ralph Waldo Emerson, *Journals, 1836*

Hoax or Cold Feet?

It was one of those stories that seemed too good to be true. A man had asked Richard Hendricks to forward his letter to me, and it was one of the best I had seen yet. The man said that while living on a lake in the eastern part of Walworth County in 1991, he was driving home very late one night after a barbecue. When he pulled into his driveway, he was dismayed to see a tall figure walking away from the house where his daughter and wife were asleep. Since the figure appeared furry, the man said he thought it must be someone in a Halloween costume, and stuck his head out of the car and yelled to the figure that he was trespassing. The creature, which he estimated to be six and a half feet tall with red, glowing eyes and a nasty skunklike stink, turned and looked at him. He described it as having a long snout, long hands with nails "like Freddy Krueger's," and legs like a dog's. Its ears were like a German shepherd's, he said, "much more of a canine than it would be an ape." The fur was short and brown, and the creature walked with a "gait."

The strangest part of the story was what happened next. After staring at the man in his car for a few moments, the creature "morphed" down onto all fours, and then quickly made its way into some dense underbrush. The man hunted all over his yard but could find no trace of it. And he told me he was now coming forward because, after seeing newspaper articles about my book, he realized others had seen the same thing and he wanted to share his story. That's a very typical statement from witnesses, by the way.

Of course, I called him, since he had asked me to get in touch with him, and he said on the phone that this creature was the scariest thing he ever saw. He added that he could tell it was "mad" at him. The man, who was thirty-five at the time of the occurrence, said he had not been drinking, had not ever had any other paranormal experiences or seen a UFO, but that he felt this thing might be "demonic." He was sure it wasn't a human in a costume, he said, because the face was too real to be a mask. And when it morphed, it did "a little dance or something" before dropping down on all fours. He said it reminded him of trick photography, like what you would see on the SCI FI Channel. The moon was almost full, the man remembered, so the night was very bright.

The man seemed quite believable. He offered to show me the place where he saw the creature, and he brought his wife and children along and videotaped the whole scene. He offered to speak at a public appearance I was making the next week, which is a little unusual, but again he brought his family along and seemed very sincere. He also brought along a cartoonlike sketch he had made of what he saw, and gave it to me that night. He purchased a copy of the book, promising to read it right away.

Within a few days, he wrote me saying he had made the whole thing up and that he didn't want me to print anything about him. "I have to protect my family," he said.

So I did not include his story in the regular sightings, although I did paraphrase the incident here from my own notes. Of course, I don't like having my time wasted, if he was indeed playing a prank or looking for attention. But his statement about protecting his family left me wondering, did he really make up the whole thing, or did he just get cold feet after reading about how some of the early Bray Road witnesses were teased by people they knew?

He did seem more eager than most witnesses to tell his story in public. And he had heard about the Beast of Bray Road phenomenon, both when it first hit the papers around New Years of 1992 and, more recently, when my book came out. His "witness sketch" looks more like a copied cartoon than a drawing of a memory. But he did mention a lot of things that are discussed in this book, such as the characteristic long snout and the "morphing," that hadn't been emphasized or even mentioned in the stories that were publicly known at the time.

Also, while he was showing me the place where the sighting allegedly took place, his former landlord happened to stop by, and while he obviously knew nothing about what was going on, the landlord did confirm that the man had lived there when he said he did. And I have a very long videotape of the man telling about the incident from every possible angle in the yard. And in all of that, he never wavered from his story.

In the end, though, I took him at his second word, returned the sketch, and omitted what could have been an important sighting from the official archives. The incident still could go either way, truth or hoax, in my mind, but it's included here for whatever it still may be worth.

The Bogeyman Farmer

People frequently ask whether someone on Bray Road in a costume might have been the real Beast. As I mentioned in the first book, I know a couple of boys who lived on that road who donned Halloween masks on a couple of evenings, but this was after the initial reports came out. But I learned that someone else on the road also played furry masquerader right about the time the story broke.

The man who told me this (and he wasn't anonymous; I have his name and phone number), said that he was at a wedding reception about ten years ago and was talking to a man who said he lived on Bray Road with his father. The dad was renting some farmland and was not one of the Bray family members. The guy started acting "a little goofy," my informant said, and confessed that his dad was "involved" in the Bray Road sightings because he had worn a gorilla costume a couple of times to scare away kids who were parking on the property. He soon stopped, however, because of the other people cruising the road with rifles after the Bray Road sightings story broke.

I have no doubt this farmer may have indeed put on a costume and scared a few teens out of their wits. However, the sightings that were reported in those first stories in the newspaper had happened one to three years earlier, and the witnesses were not teenaged, parking couples. And, of course, one farmer in a gorilla suit can't explain the greater number of sightings that happened in other places before and since then. The farmer, who later moved, is really lucky that he didn't end up with a few silver bullet holes in him. And I'd love to hear the stories of the teens who encountered the creepy guy in the mask peering into the steamy car windows at them.

And people wonder how all those urban legends about monsters and necking teens get started.

The Great Red Rock Werewolf Hoax

Werewolves are evidently considered fair game for hoaxers around the country, even as far west as Colorado. In a place that is coincidentally named Jefferson County…strange what's in a name, but we will get to that later…a couple of Denver police officers thought they had discovered a gruesome crime scene one August in the early 1970s, almost two decades before the Beast of Bray Road was ever heard of.

There was blood, shredded women's lingerie, and muddy tracks of something that appeared to be "part man and part beast."

But the blood was made from Karo syrup and food coloring, the underwear came from another policeman's wife, and the prints were made by a barefoot deputy who artfully added clawmarks with a stick. Everything was designed to spoof one deputy, Ron Pierson, who had come to believe in werewolves while on a military tour of duty in Germany.

I found that fact interesting in itself. Partly because of Germany's longstanding history of werewolf lore, and partly because I'd discovered that Hitler was also a big werewolf fan. He had an entire, elite guerilla fighter division named *Werwolf*, designed to spearhead a German resistance after Allied occupation. The emblem on their red flag was a symbol called the *Wolfsangel*, which is claimed by some to be an ancient Nordic rune, although it doesn't appear in any ancient runic alphabets. It means "wolf's hook." It was also used for several other Nazi tank and infantry divisions. Moreover, I've had several secondhand reports from people who told me that family members who served in Europe during World

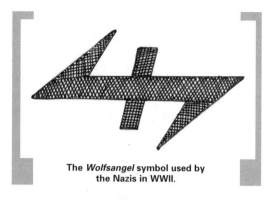

The *Wolfsangel* symbol used by the Nazis in WWII.

War II reported seeing werewolflike creatures in those countries.

But in Red Rock, what Pierson's fellow deputies set up for him to find confirmed his worst fears, and he quickly called in to headquarters to report that he'd discovered a murder perpetrated by a werewolf. Right about that time, the pranksters revealed themselves and the joke was ended. Or it would have been, if any of them had thought to clean up the torn undies smeared with red syrup. Others found the "crime scene" and called the media. All hell broke loose at the station. And guess what the irate sheriff's name was? Harold Bray. (The name of the late owner of the first farm you see after turning onto Bray Road was Howard Bray.)

"Red Rock" is a classic werewolf hoax story, and I have to thank Richard Hendricks for finding the *Evergreen Papers* article about it for me. But I'm really more impressed by the name coincidences than the hoax itself, especially since the prank was explained so easily.

More High Strangeness...The Name Matrix

The linkage of certain names with weird events and circumstances has been documented by several writers, most notably in two 1983 books, *Mysterious America* by Loren Coleman and *The Rebirth of Pan* by Jim Brandon. Coleman refers to the phenomenon as the "Name Game," Brandon the "Name Network." Brandon speculates that perhaps there are certain "names of power" such as those contained in old magical texts that somehow spark strange happenings around them. He concentrates on one particular name, LaFayette, from Revolutionary War hero the Marquis de LaFayette, and notes that names of U.S. presidents also seem highly represented in areas of quirky events. For instance, in the Red Rock story above, the werewolf hoax occurred in Jefferson County. And you'll remember my Jefferson "Square of Weirdness" in Jefferson County, Wisconsin, with the city of Jefferson squarely in the center. On top of that, the annual Texas Bigfoot Conference is held in the city of Jefferson, Texas.

I also noted in the Red Rock story that the name of the sheriff in the incident, Harold Bray, is almost identical to Howard Bray, the name of the farmer for whose ancestors Bray Road, and therefore also our "werewolf," were named. But let's get back to LaFayette.

Both Brandon and Coleman cite numerous examples of LaFayette weirdness. In 1970, in LaFayette County, Wisconsin, a white Bigfoot was spotted. Another was seen in Fayette County, Pennsylvania, in 1973. In 1976 in Fayetteville, Tennessee, a boy was kidnapped by a Bigfoot. LaFayette and Big Furries just seem to go together, for whatever reason. Many more LaFayette connections are described in both books.

I had some interesting e-mail correspondence with Loren Coleman over a few other name synchronicities, but I was most anxious to tell him of one in particular that I'd found. Believe it or not, Bray Road is located in LaFayette Township. A nearby crossroads community named Peck Station was originally known as Fayetteville. "Fay" in old French, meant "little enchantment" or fairy. Its Old English equivalent, "fey," means fated to die or doomed. Brandon wonders in *Rebirth* if this root word is some sort of "triggering factor" for anomalous phenomena.

Even things associated with LaFayette seem interwoven with unusual associations. The Marquis de LaFayette's summer home, for instance, was named LaGrange. LaGrange Township in Walworth County is the site of several Manwolf sightings and a major crossroads between sightings areas, including the Bluff Monster.

There seem to be associations between Godfrey and Bray, too, besides my own obvious connection as investigator and author. To name just a couple of them, a house my husband and I used to own in Elkhorn was once occupied by the town librarian, Mary Bray. And a few weeks before this writing, one of my sons, Nathan Godfrey, found himself lost on a busy street corner in Chicago. He stopped a young lady hurrying past him to ask directions, and of all the people in the world who might have been walking around Chicago that day, it turned out to be the granddaughter of Howard Bray. There are others involving churchyards in Virginia and genealogy that I won't take time to get into, and I'm sure that if I looked at all the Manwolf and Big Furry sightings in other states, those same old monikers would continue to emerge in Michigan, Pennsylvania, and everywhere else. Perhaps I'll save that for another book.

What does all this mean in the grand scope of things for the Manwolf? Until we can decode the symbolism involved, not much, probably. The main thing we can walk away with here is that we have still another mystery emphasizing that Manwolf territory is an area of high weirdness that appears *specifically* related to patterns of wild and wacky stuff.

Hearings: Encounters of Another Kind

Over the past two years, I've been both gratified and amazed at the number of people who have written to share experiences. Many who have contacted me haven't exactly seen the creature, but feel they heard it. Since one of my aims is to tie together as many threads of evidence as possible, I'm going to include some of these letters and e-mails here. Unearthly screams emanating from a dark woods, pet dogs going zonkers over red eyes in a bramble patch, young paintballers stalked in the Kettle Moraine…all fodder for monstrous consideration. In a way, the things we don't see, but simply hear and feel, are even scarier than the things that fully present themselves to our eyes. Imagination is fear's best friend.

A Bray Road Howling: October 15, 2005

Hi Ms. Godfrey,

This past August my girlfriend M. and I took the first of what I hope will be an annual Summertime "supernatural road trip." The idea was to use weird points of interest as an excuse to hit the road and drive. (A desire to encounter something weird is wrapped up in there, too).

Bray Road was not one of our initial destinations. But early in the trip, we caught the second half of a Travel Channel segment on the dog man. It freaked me out. I am—as you will see—easily freaked out. A few nights later, while scanning the Weird US book, we realized that Bray Road was right in the very same state that we were exploring. Such synchronicity. We had no choice but to head down to Southern Wisconsin.

It was a sunny weekday afternoon when we finally got there. Having spent the previous night in a creepy Delavan Hotel (and being from Detroit, Michigan), Bray Road didn't look all that scary. We drove its length once back and forth, and didn't see anything strange or frightening.

M. said the way to really do this would be to get a hotel in town, and stay a couple nights, ask around about the thing, drink some beers at the local bar and do some actual investigating. And come back to the road itself after dark. That sounded scary, and like a lot of work, and we were anxious to get on to Spring Green.

On our way off of Bray I stopped at an intersection and suggested we snap each other in front of the Bray Road street sign. As we performed the camera hand-off, an awful shrieking echoed across the field from a nearby forest. We froze. Then, even more terrifying wailing. Before you could say "Lon Chaney, Jr." I was back in the Oldsmobile, fired up and ready to flee. I told M. to get back in the car. The noises continued.

"Give me the tape recorder," she said. (I brought a mini tape recorder with us. Big Twin Peaks fan.) "Get in the car," I said. "We should go." She reached through the window and grabbed the tape recorder, flicked it on. Of course, just then the noises stopped. I'm not joking and I'm not making this up. M. stood by the roadside with the tape recorder held up. There had been so many consecutive shrieks that it seemed reasonable to think they'd start up again. No such luck. It was silent then, except for the car and my repeated insistence that we get the hell out of there. After a few minutes M. got in and we drove away. M.'s a lot more reasonable than I am. She's more skeptical, too. (Also: gutsier). But we both agreed: Those were very unusual noises, like nothing either of us had ever heard.

We have four solid theories about what it might have been:

1. An animal being slaughtered
2. A mischievous local with a loud stereo system and a CD of weird noises
3. One of those Owls that kind of shriek (as seen in the film, *My Cousin Vinnie*)
4. The Beast of Bray Road

In retrospect I feel like 2 and 3 are our safest bets. Nevertheless, in the moment, I was highly unnerved. The noise itself was very intense, very feral, kind of high pitched and pained. It was really, really weird, and after finding your site today I thought I should put this out there. Best,

—J., Detroit, Michigan

It's fascinating that J. would have heard this sound on Bray Road, particularly when the Manwolf hasn't been reported there in almost a decade. But the Bluff Monster creature has been getting around not so far away, and the high-pitched sound would fit better with that creature than with the Manwolf. It's hard to say for sure without hearing the sound. Rabbits can sound strangely like a screaming woman when caught by an owl at night; I've heard that mournful screech myself. Still, because of the place, and because area residents also reported strange screams and howls at the time of the sightings around 1990, I think this incident is definitely worth keeping in mind. They say the criminal always returns to the scene of the crime; perhaps the same goes for Manwolves.

A Brush with the Bluff Monster: November 28, 2003

Wow! You write of weird coincidences, well I have some for you. I am a college student and have lived in Whitewater for about four and a half years. I have never heard anything about the Beast of Bray Road or any other strange animal stories since I've been here. I recently moved to a more rural address and my mom seemed concerned for my safety. I wasn't, I love being outdoors and have spent a lot of time hiking in the kettles in the area. My new landlord told me he thought there was a coyote in the area; his cat had come home the week before minus a leg. On quite a few nights we could hear dogs and coyotes howling in the distance, but we were never concerned about it.

Well, one night a few months ago my roommate and I had been in Waukesha and were driving back on Hwy. 59. It was about 11:00 PM or so, a clear night, and the moon hadn't risen yet. We pulled off the highway and took some back roads and ended up near LaGrange. We pulled over right across from a log cabin. There's a farm with some horses right across the street and we love looking at these horses, and we also wanted to look for meteors. So we got out of the car and we thought it was cool because some coyotes were howling. Then I heard (honestly) the second strangest noise I've ever heard. (The most strange was back home in Glenbeulah Cemetery, but that's another ball of wax.)

The noise was like a combination of a dog-like howling and a scream. Like a human-in-pain type of scream. I don't know. It was really weird and totally freaked me out. We waited, but we didn't hear it again. The coyotes stopped, too. The sound had come from northeast of where we stood [Author note: that would be toward the Kettle Moraine State Forest]. I realized the road was narrow, it was really dark, and I didn't want to be there anymore. I got back in the car to wait for my roommate, who was down the road a bit and my cell phone rang, scaring the crap out of me. It was my mom, wanting to tell me about this book she bought that day for me…it was *The Beast of Bray Road*! Weird, eh?

—Mandy

Chalk another one up for the Name Game and LaGrange. Mandy and her friend had to be very near Young Hill, in the area of Bluff Monster sightings, and also not far from a Manwolf sighting on County Highway H north of LaGrange listed in the first book. Very hard telling what they heard, although, as noted after the previous letter, screaming sounds are usually associated with Bigfoot.

Stalked by the Bluff Monster? 2002

Hello, about 3 years back me and a few friends were out messing around with paintball guns in a field during the middle of the night. This was in a field surrounded by woods on Kettle Moraine Drive, Whitewater. We were driving the truck around while two guys hid out in the woods. About 15 minutes later the two guys ran terrified towards the truck. We were having a good time but these guys looked like they were being hunted by something. We asked them what was wrong and they said they heard the weirdest noise they've ever heard, it was like a deep warbling noise and they said it sounded like it was circling them then moving in closer and when they ran towards the truck they said that it followed them and was getting faster and closer.

They jumped in the back of the truck and closed the topper, while we rolled down the windows to see if we could hear the noise. We did—it was like I said, the strange warbling noise. To this day I've never heard anything else like that. I recently called my friend back and he said this werewolf business has been going on. His little brother in the same field that we were in did the same thing with paintball guns and the exact same thing happened to him. Some could say it was a coyote, but I've heard coyotes and it's not at all the same. Recently we moved to Arkansas and heard the noise that deer make during their mating season, and it wasn't anything like this, that noise we heard was the single most terrifying noise I've ever heard.

Kettle Moraine Drive runs along Whitewater Lake and through the Kettle Moraine State Forest. That circling and stalking maneuver reminded me of what Dennis Hasting and his hunting companion experienced in the woods near Bray Road. A warbling sound could be attributed to either Bigfoot or Manwolf, but Bigfoot is more likely. Either way, the young men were probably wise to make a hasty retreat. I doubt that paintballs would have done anything to either creature except make it angry and colorful.

Elm Grove Predator: May 1, 2005

Last night some friends mentioned a story in the newspaper about sightings of a creature with a wolfish face in SE Wisconsin. I had not seen the story, but about five nights ago, my dogs were on a rope in the backyard when they started a tremendous racket. I hauled them in and saw the reflected eyes of an animal in the backyard at the treeline (we have a woods in the back). I live in Elm Grove, a suburb of Milwaukee, and deer are frequent visitors. However, these were not the round eyes of a deer, but the slanted eyes of a predator, set in the front of the head. I at first thought it was a coyote, but was surprised to realize they were six feet off the ground! The next day, they captured a small black bear about a mile from our house, and I originally thought it may have been that. Now I am not so sure. They certainly appeared "wolfish" to me at first.

— Russ

I know Elm Grove, and find it hard to believe a black bear could have lumbered around without being sighted at all. The bear Russ refers to was a small one found in a tree in another suburb. It made all the evening newscasts after being shot with tranquilizers and dropping like a rock from the tree. Black bears do stand up momentarily for various purposes, but they are usually frightened away by barking dogs. And their eyes are very different from those of wolves, and set farther apart due to the larger skull. Manwolves have been seen around other parts of Milwaukee, so perhaps one visited Elm Grove on May Day Eve, a traditional night for sorcery, as well.

The Edgerton Growler, or Ginger Snaps: June 8, 2005

I live in Edgerton and have a story to tell you. Saturday, June 4, 2005, at 11:55 PM, I got up to use the bathroom. When I was done, I looked out the back door to the south and noticed a lot of lightning. It wasn't raining yet so I decided to sit on my back deck steps to watch the storm come in. I have a golden retriever, Ginger. I called her to come outside with me but she'd have no part of it, which I thought was strange because she's never been afraid of storms. So I sat out there for about half an hour watching the lightning—mind you I turned off the floodlights so I could see the lightning.

At 12:30, I heard this growl/snarl to my left and it wasn't too far away. Five seconds later I heard it again and it was closer. I was sitting at the edge of the front of my garage, and my garage is twenty-four feet deep, so that's how far away whatever this was, was from me. Now, I am an experienced hunter and have never heard such a noise in my life. It scared the daylights out of me, and I booked it into the house.

Now what I don't get is this animal was downwind of me, so I know it smelled me. Why did it growl and come toward me? Anyway I turned the floodlights on but never seen it. Now, we live on the east side of Edgerton just off 59. We have coyotes come through our yard but I'm convinced this was not a coyote.

Now for the rest of the story. Ginger. Thirty minutes later I head to bed. Ginger always sleeps in the living room on the couch. I head for the bedroom door and Ginger IS coming in the bedroom with me come hell or high water. I say what the hell is wrong with you, you're not coming in my room. She has never tried to do that, ever. Something had that dog very scared.

Now I have never heard of the Beast of Bray Road until tonight, June 7. I was at work and was telling a friend what had happened. He looks at me and says I'll tell you exactly what it was, he goes in his locker and pulls out your book and hands it to me. At first I looked and laughed, but after I thumbed through it, it made sense to me. This wasn't the run of the mill animal I had contact with. It was something different.

—Jeff

Alert readers may have noticed yet another connection with State Highway 59 here, like the story before it and the March 2005 sighting of a bipedal Manwolf between Milton and Whitewater, the Lima Marsh Monster (Chapter 10). Also, Edgerton was the site of the second story in this book (Chapter 2), the materializing Manwolf glowering from between the two witch houses. Like Jeff says, makes sense to me.

The Canine from Hell: August 12, 2005

Linda, I watched the piece on the Travel Channel about werewolves in Wisconsin. It reminded me of a night I was coming home on Highway 22 from Madison to Pardeeville about 3:00 AM after work. I had seen many animals on the road but that night, I saw a canine that could only be described as the "canine from hell" defending a raccoon, its meal. I was so surprised at the sight that I turned around and went back to see what I saw. All I saw upon returning one quarter mile was...nothing. I know I saw "it" and it was like no dog, wolf, or coyote I have ever seen but definitely canine and large. I often wonder why some people "see" things and others don't. I saw the ghost on the Chippewa Flowage and we had a ghost in our house near Pardeeville. Thanks,

—Pat

This was actually a sighting. So why didn't I include it in the sightings part? Lack of information, mostly. The writer did not get back to me with the date or more specifics on the creature, so I felt it was not definitive enough to list as a Manwolf, even though the creature sounds very canid. Other aspects such as dining on a dead raccoon, disappearing before the witness could come back, and even the "hellish" aspect sound very familiar, though, and I think it should be counted somewhere among very likely sightings. I rank it close, but no hand-rolled Cuban.

All of the above stories are rather like the Apocrypha, books of ancient scripture that didn't quite make it into the Bible for one reason or another. They are referred to by my own church's catechism, however, as "useful for instruction." Same goes for these stories. And I think it's perfectly reasonable that if there are strange creatures around our woods, you would find people who heard them but never were able to actually see them. It would seem odd if that were not the case, in fact. But we will always have to wonder—along with the earwitnesses—exactly what those unseen howlers and growlers may have been.

CHAPTER TWENTY

WEREWOLVES FROM THE FAR SIDE... AND THE VERY NEAR SIDE

"Mystery is underrated, understanding is overrated."
—Larry McMurtry, *Flim-Flam: Essays on Hollywood*

The reader can't claim lack of warning. In the introduction, I made it plain that we would be taking some extraordinary side trips on this journey through the watery, liminal land of marsh-striding Man-wolves. This chapter will provide a major excursion.

Over the years that I've been researching various strange phenomena, I've met or been contacted by any number of people who practice unconventional means of gathering information. I asked a couple of them for their interpretations of the Manwolf enigma and was contacted by another who heard me on a national radio show and e-mailed to say that he might be able to shed a new light on the phenomenon. A few phone calls and numerous e-mails later, I agreed—his light was new, all right. None of the three I interviewed had any knowledge of the others' contributions or views.

These ideas come from some very intelligent people and are certainly no stranger than many of the sightings we've detailed throughout the chapters of this book. Carl Sagan is often quoted as saying, "Extraordinary claims require extraordinary evidence." But his prelude to that statement was, "I believe that the extraordinary should be pursued." And I would add that if, in our pursuit, no extraordinary evidence turns up, we may as well entertain extraordinary theories about our extraordinary claims. The alternative is to shunt the monsters under the bed and try to forget that anyone saw them. And as every small child knows, monsters do not stay quietly under anyone's bed.

Here are a few of those extraordinary ideas from the myriad that are probably out there.

Time-Traveling Werewolves

Robert Beutlich is a practitioner of a dying art. Radionics, the main focus of a movement called Psychotronics, seeks to literally "tune in" to various facets of the spirit world. Psychotronics is the catchall name Beutlich and other members of the U.S. Psychotronics Association (USPA) apply to the interdisciplinary studies to which they've devoted their lives. That's "Psycho" for mind-consciousness, and "Tronics" for physics and instrumentation. By marrying the human mind to electronic instruments, they believe, mankind can extend its senses to realms beyond our physical world and achieve a more harmonious state of existence.

"We are not an 'experiencing' type of group," noted Beutlich when I visited him one day in his sunny living room filled with a cheerful clutter of books, stacks of papers, and scientific journals. He lives in a rural area north of Elkhorn, not far from my own home. "We don't do seances or New-Age-type retreats or things like that. We look at the technical side; it's hard nuts and bolts theory of how psychic phenomena work within alternate realities."

Some of those nuts and bolts theories have included time travel, and Beutlich told me he believes the Manwolf appearances occur during "time slips."

"You mean," I asked him, "that at one time there were wolf-people walking around here?"

"It's quite possible," he answered. "Time dislocation zones are part of the earth grid that is run off the pyramids. There are pyramids found all over the world—Egypt, Mexico, even Aztalan in Wisconsin. All these energy flow lines were set up by Lemurians or Atlanteans. And the time dislocation zones are also the teleportation zones."

Beutlich has a few other ideas about how the Manwolves could be created, too.

"Also, the human mind can create a gargoyle. It's like a Golem (a spirit creature from Jewish legend) or a *tulpa* (Tibetan thought form). It's somebody who is keeping that damn thing (the Manwolf) alive...it's an energy field. Christ said if you had the faith of a mustard seed you could move mountains. There are people who have faith all right, but it's faith in some screwball things."

Like Manwolves, presumably.

Beutlich continued, "People who see the Beast are falling into the *tulpa*-creator's paradigm. Or, it could be these are transported from other worlds. Travel vortices are turned on by planetary alignments. I've walked through some of these vortices, there's a big one by the crushed house (Rock in the House) by the Wisconsin River on Highway 51. There's a hell of a vortex there. All the trees are bent inward toward this point."

That area is in Fountain City, north of LaCrosse. And while I don't know of any Manwolf sightings reported there, I suppose the Lizard Man could have crawled out of the vortex in Fountain City and made his way south to LaCrosse.

I'm just happy Bob didn't get sucked off to some Planet of the Werewolves when he walked through these vortices. A human suddenly popping into a place like that would have about as much chance as a Snickers bar appearing in the middle of a classroom full of fifth-graders.

The Animal Whisperer's Vision

Rebecca Moravec is a gentle, soft-spoken woman who talks to animals, and hears what they say back to her. The conversations are not held in Horse-ese or Cat-ish; they are telepathic, using impressions and symbols of the universal language Moravec says is spoken by all living things. I heard about her from a friend who attended a luncheon at which Moravec was the main speaker. One of Moravec's abilities is to "link" with a subject that isn't even physically present. My friend had asked her to tune into her dog at home and find out why it didn't like to come into her kitchen anymore. Moravec closed her eyes and thought a minute, then said to my friend, "He's afraid of the pointy lights." My friend was astonished. We were standing in her kitchen at the time she told me this, and she pointed overhead. There on the ceiling was strung a row of triangular-shaped lights in various primary colors she had recently had installed. The lights did indeed look pointy.

It seemed logical that if Moravec could tune into an absent, unknown dog's mind so easily, perhaps she could also hone in on the Manwolf. Moravec has actually studied these techniques with an Australian Aborigine shaman. (Of course, some will wonder whether she picked the image of the lights from the brain of my friend, who probably was imagining her kitchen as she asked the question, but Moravec would still have to be telepathic to do that.) I asked her to try communing with the Beast at a small conference another friend and I were presenting in Milwaukee, and she agreed, using my drawing of the Indigenous Dogman as a focal point. "I suspect whatever this is, it is rather telepathic," she noted. "Wild animals aren't usually interested (in humans) so what is the connection between it and humans?"

An excellent question, I thought, and one I would really like answered. She concentrated while the room remained silent. Finally, she raised her head and told us she had made contact with a creature, something rather like a "master spirit" of the species.

Master spirits, as we discussed in Chapter 3, are well-known concepts in Native American lore. *The Dictionary of Native American Mythology* calls them the "Master/Mistress of Animals," and explains that the spirit can occur either as a super-sized member of the species or as a humanized version. Shamans can assure successful hunts by appealing to this chief of the animals ahead of time, and propitiating it afterward with offerings. Anthropologists feel many examples of cave art and petroglyphs were created for ceremonies involving the master animal spirits.

Moravec looked a bit startled as she spoke. "I was just told this is really, really old," she said. "I was told I wouldn't be able to speak to one of these individuals, but there's an 'oversoul.' He took me through yellow tunnels. These creatures are older than people, he said, and when we leave, they will still be here.

"At first I thought it was something demonic," she added, "but now I feel it's benign and intelligent. Before coming here today, I had no belief in it whatsoever."

That was all she was able to get from the Manwolf spokescanine. It impressed upon her somehow that this was all we would be allowed to know. The message was a little spooky, I thought, but makes odd sense in light of the story you will hear next, which I received about a year later. And I wondered if the "yellow tunnels" could be deep, subterranean caves winding from Wisconsin to New York State? Or perhaps they are Robert Beutlich's time/space travel vortices.

At any rate, I was glad to hear one opinion, at least, that Manwolves are benign. It's certainly true that they have never hurt a human, to my knowledge. At least, not any humans who have lived to tell the tale.

Interplanetary Wolfen Warriors

The *Coast to Coast AM* radio show started by Art Bell deals with all aspects of strangeness in and out of our world and is one of the nation's most listened-to talk shows. I was glad to be invited as an interview guest by host Ian Punnet over Labor Day weekend, 2005. Afterward, I received e-mails from all over the country, including one from a man who said he was a remote viewer. Remote viewing, or "RV" for short, is a highly disciplined method for retrieving information by use of the mind's psychic faculties. It was at least partially developed by the United States military as a means of spying on other nations during the Cold War and is now taught in books and videos offered over the Internet. Like any form of psychic practice, it is not always accurate, but most RVers are very confident they make more hits than misses.

The man did not want his name disclosed, so I will call him Noah. A middle-aged, married man with a Master's degree in biology, Noah had at one time lived in the Whitewater, Wisconsin area. He said he had used his RV techniques on the Beast of Bray Road and had come up with some surprising information.

"The Beast you speak of is not from our period of evolution," he told me in a phone interview. "The Indians say the earth has been terraformed three to four times completely." Noah explained that each time the surface of the earth was destroyed and rebuilt, different life forms would fight for possession of it. "During one of these periods," said Noah, "giant seven- to nine-and-a-half-feet-tall 'werewolves' came from space. They had armor and were like Berserkers, eating while they fought. They didn't win control of the planet but some were caught and 'left over.' They have a very, very long lifespan.

"These guys will have an extended snout area because of skills they had in battle," he continued. "With my remote viewing, I was able to go back and check out the story a Native American elder had told me about them. Great battles were fought between them and a Cyborg-type race; our planet is attractive because of its free water and magnetic fields that shift quickly. When I first viewed them, I said, 'Omigosh, they look like Anubis.' [We've heard that before, but Tobin did not have access to any of the stories in this book at that time.] These are not unintelligent beings, they are highly intelligent and evolved. They can be vicious, though. I wonder if these cats aren't coming back."

Noah also felt that the Manwolves are subterranean life-forms (similar to Moravec's vision of the tunnels, perhaps?), organized like a "pack culture," with a top leadership of alpha females. "There's a phosphorescence when the Wolfen move," he noted in a later e-mail. "They have a bacteria that lives in their fur that actually produces a shimmering light along the surface of their hair when they are in mating season, or enraged. It's kind of like a miniature *aurora borealis*, but usually quite faint. Kind of creepy, really…that's part of the source of the odor that people smell around them, as the bacteria release a hydrogen sulfide gas waste product."

When I read this, I immediately thought of several witnesses who had described a "silvery" aspect to the fur, as if it were white-tipped or multi-colored. I also dashed into a dark closet with my sample of "werewolf" fur to see if it glowed. It did not.

The Wolfen on this planet now are of the race's "scout" caste, said Noah, but there are also warriors, perhaps waiting to come, with bio-armor under their fur. "That's why the ones that are here scavenge to live...or they would be dining on us regularly," he said. "Scouts observe, record, exist off the land, and help provide surveillance for future actions. They are under direction to avoid contact or confrontation; that draws too much attention."

But why Wisconsin, Illinois, Michigan, Ohio, Pennsylvania, New York, and Georgia, I asked him. Why, in particular, southern Wisconsin? "These rascals are aware of the safe places to enter back onto this planet once all of these earth changes start cracking and whacking the coastlines," he answered. "These guys aren't as dumb as Napoleon and Hitler. They wouldn't try to invade Russia in the late fall."

Noah says he has seen a "built-in logging and tracking device" on the Wolfen scouts, something like an implanted microchip. And when they do travel, he added, they come out of "cones of darkness that just appear, they walk through, and that is it. If UFOs have been seen in their vicinity, it was because the inhabitants of the saucers were drawn to the space-time rifts, trying to find out who is using that technology. Something in the Wolfen forehead area, under the bone, allows them to open these portals at will."

The "cones of darkness," of course, immediately sound like Beutlich's time/space vortices. They would also explain the creature's uncanny ability to escape trained hog-hunting mastiffs and the few humans who haven't been too frightened to go looking for them. Perhaps the "cones of darkness" are the actual "windows" in the "window areas" talked about by researchers John Keel, Loren Coleman, and others.

Of course, there is no more tangible proof for Noah's claims than we have for the other theories. If the sample of fur we have is indeed from one of these creatures, its bioluminescence is no longer detectable. But the overall tale is strangely congruent in many ways with what Beutlich, Moravec, and even the Ho-Chunk have said.

I guess we will find out in thirty years or so.

Demons Straight from Hell: Theories from the Near Side

The view of many people I know, and that of some of the witnesses themselves, is that Manwolves are some literal spawn of Satan. Remember the words of Mark Schackelman at St. Coletta Institute in 1936? "I thought it was a demon straight from hell." At least one Lutheran pastor and his wife that I know agree with him. And they are certainly not the first people to link Big Furries with the cloven-hoofed one.

I've already noted that among Native Americans, Skinchangers, Skinwalkers, and Bearwalkers are associated with witches and sorcerers allied with evil spirits. Kelpies, the Scottish "water-horses," were considered supernatural agents of the devil, too. In *Three Men Seeking Monsters*, Redfern quotes from an 1823 article published as a warning against the diabolical shape shifters: "The Kelpie was an infernal agent, retained in the service and pay of Satan, who granted him a commission to execute such services as appeared profitable to his interest.... However, he had no authority to touch a human being of his own free accord, unless the latter was the aggressor."

Pacts with the Devil, Then and Now

During the European witch and werewolf hunts of the Middle Ages and beyond, it was routinely assumed that anyone even temporarily resembling another species had made a pact with the devil to receive that power. Sabine Baring-Gould's 1865 classic, *The Book of Werewolves*, discusses the famous French case of young Jean Grenier, self-admitted werewolf. According to Baring-Gould, one of the young girls in Grenier's village in southern France said Grenier had told her many times he had sold his soul to the devil. Grenier confessed to killing and eating several young children, and stated that even after he was imprisoned, the "Lord of the Forest" visited him twice. He was jailed rather than killed since it was determined by the court that the werewolf form was mostly in Grenier's head, "and that the change of shape existed only in the disorganized brain of the insane, consequently it was not a crime which could be punished." He died in prison at age twenty.

Another case Baring-Gould tells of happened in the early 1500s in France, when an accused werewolf named Pierre Bourgot told of meeting a black horseman in the woods who promised him safety for his flocks and money if he would swear allegiance to the devil. This the man did, and eventually found himself at a ceremony where he was turned into a werewolf. After this, he committed many cannibalistic murders.

Could it be...Satan?

Some old church authorities claim that Satan himself assumes the form of a wolf-headed creature. Baring-Gould includes part of a sermon from a prominent Strasbourg preacher, made in the year 1508, which describes seven causes for werewolfism. Under the sixth, the preacher says, "the injury comes of the Devil, who transforms himself, and takes on him the form of a wolf. So writes Vincentius in his *Speculum Historiale*. And he has taken it from Valerius Maximus in the Punic War. When the Romans fought against the men of Africa, when the captain lay asleep, there came a wolf and drew his sword and carried it off. That was the Devil in a wolf's form."

According to the Bible, Satan is able to appear as an "Angel of Light," so why not a Humanoid of Fur?

Some may take slight offense that I included the Satan hypothesis in the same chapter as the other theories described above. Part of my reason was that there was no other good place to insert it, and I didn't want to leave it out. But to a Bible-believing Christian, the idea that the devil prowls the earth in various guises, seeking souls to devour, may not be strange theory but theological truth. I have to say that as a Christian myself, I think they are right on that point. The question is whether Manwolves are manifestations of Satan, or of some lesser, earth-based spirit, or natural but unknown animals.

The Manwolf hardly seems angelic. Its snarling behavior toward people does not indicate that the creature is up to a whole lot of good where we are concerned. Even the Ho-Chunk and other First Nations do not see the Big Furries or water spirits as benign creatures, however, but as monsters that eat people or drown them. However, many people believe any sort of supernatural explanation is as extreme as the idea of alien wolf forms. Calling the Manwolf "Satan" would strike them as bizarre as anything else.

And yet, a certain number of witnesses couldn't help but wonder if those glowing eyes reflected hellfire rather than headlights. Those who believe Hell is a literal, subterranean chamber of flames where devils romp may share some strange accord with the visionaries who speak of yellow, underground tunnels or deep-earth caverns filled with space-wolf technology. It might behoove us all to be careful where we dig.

But all of that only applies if the Manwolf is a supernatural being and not some kind of hitherto-unrecognized species or even a fluke of nature. I'm going to look at a few of those natural flukes in the next chapter. It turns out that man is not the only creature that can walk erect, after all.

CHAPTER TWENTY-ONE

OF WOLVES AND MEN

*"In brief, we are all monsters, that is
a composition of man and beast."*
—Sir Thomas Brown, *Religio Medici*

No matter how many people have plainly witnessed the creature, the idea of a Manwolf still seems like a crazy notion, I grant you. And I made it plain in the first book that from a biologist's or zoologist's point of view, the idea of a bipedal canid is indeed absurd. It would take an entire volume written in darkest, deepest scientific jargon to fully detail all the reasons this is so.

But don't worry…I'm not a scientist. And I'm not foolish enough to attempt such a giant exposition, especially at this stage of my book.

Despite my lack of official biological expertise, however (unless an A in Biology 101 at University of Wisconsin-Whitewater counts), I do feel obliged to briefly show just how differently assembled are the canids from the great apes (which would include gorillas, humans, and ostensibly, Bigfoot, among a couple of others). Their apparent incompatibility, however, is a two-edged sword. On one hand, it makes it seem like the twain could never meet. In that case, we may as well throw all the bipedal canids back in the underwater springs from which my Native American friends say they sprang. They can't exist, then, pure and simple.

On the other anterior limb, it shows that when people describe a leg and foot as either "bent backwards like a dog's, with a dog-type foot" in contrast to "thick and humanlike, with a big flat foot," they are distinguishing between two very different animals. These are not simply variations of the same creature; hence, Manwolves are not just some strange variation of Bigfoot.

Why Humans Aren't Quadrupeds and Wolves Shouldn't Walk: A Bit of Comparative Anatomy

I'm going to skip over the differences between the two groups in head shape because they are quite obvious; you either have a flat-faced, round head with small ears positioned on the sides of the skull near the middle, or you have a muzzle-nosed, flattened skull with pointy ears that extend over the top of the skull. One is clearly hominoid, the other very canid. (For the sake of argument, we'll pretend those few cases that sound like Goat Men or Pig Men or Lizard Men don't exist. They're very rare, and I prefer to keep this discussion mano a lobo.)

So we will move on to the limbs. As I've mentioned before, the Manwolf is reported to walk with a "backwards bend" like a dog, on the digits and balls of its feet, or digitigrade. The Bigfoot and human species walk with a knee that bends forward, on the entire soles of their feet, or plantigrade. Check out the illustration to see how easily apparent this difference is. But there are other requirements for being bipedal.

In a book called *Human Ancestors* that is a compilation of *Scientific American* articles, Napier says, "In order to alter a bent-hip, bent-knee gait into a man's erect, striding walk, a number of anatomical changes must occur. These include an elongation of the hind limbs with respect to the forelimbs, a shortening and broadening of the pelvis, adjustments of the musculature of the hip (in order to stabilize the trunk during the act of walking upright), a straightening of both hip and knee and a considerable re-shaping of the foot."

It's obvious from observation of the Manwolf that very few of these changes have taken place in this creature. The leg is still "bent," the posture often described as "bent over," and the footprints show a foot that is not re-shaped from that of a dog or wolf, just considerably bigger. And yet, except for a certain tendency toward what looks to us like poor posture, the thing dances divinely. Moreover, it can run well on four or two feet.

Being able to move smoothly from biped to quadruped locomotion is the unlikeliest characteristic of all, because quadrupeds and bipeds are built very differently at the shoulder. The scapula or shoulder blades of humans are large and wide and our arms are oriented to the side so that we can swing them for balance or more easily grasp and carry things. Quadrupeds have tiny scapula, and their front legs aim forward so that the impact of the front limbs hitting the ground is absorbed by soft tissue and not just the skeletal frame. That's why when you see a squirrel or a dog or a bear sitting upright, the front limbs and paws are bent in front of the body and the animals appear to have no shoulders. Even chimpanzees and gorillas are built this way. And it's why adult humans find it very uncomfortable to move on all fours for any distance after infancy. Not only are our spines and necks aligned poorly for this posture, our shoulders aren't designed to bear the weight.

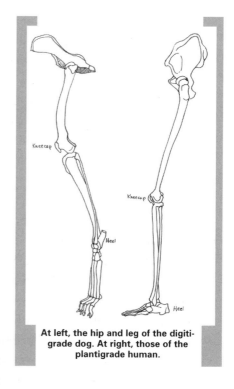

At left, the hip and leg of the digitigrade dog. At right, those of the plantigrade human.

How, then, is it possible for animals that appear to be canid in every other way to walk around on two legs with ease? Could there be some canid creature we don't know about that has adapted in a relatively short time?

Bipeds in the Fossils

The first thing I did was look to see whether I could find any extinct member of today's canid family that appeared to start out bipedal. I met only disappointment. Certain birds, like ostriches, and some lizards are bipedal, but anything identified as having branched off into the canid family stands squarely on four feet. Of course, not everything appears in the fossil record. The creature called an "aardwolf," for instance, appears nowhere in the fossil record, and yet it exists. It is a canid related to the hyena, but one that is specially adapted to eating termites to the extent that its teeth are mere vestiges. The aardwolf is an interesting-looking animal; it sports the spiky back hair a few people have reported seeing on Manwolves. But since it stands only about twenty inches high at the shoulder and measures about twenty-four inches in length, it could hardly be mistaken for a man-sized creature, much less induce adult humans to quake with fear. Besides, it is found only in southern and eastern Africa where there are large mounds of termites to eat.

Jerboas, Gerenuks, Sick Monkeys, and Other Upright Mammals

In *Human Ancestors*, Sherwood L. Washburn wrote, "The capacity for bipedal walking is primarily an adaptation for covering long distances.... According to skeletal evidence, fully developed walkers first appeared in the ancient men who inhabited the Old World from 500,000 years ago to the middle of the last glaciation."

Notice that the last sentence of that quote says "ancient *men*." Not ancient apes or ancient wolves. It seems apparent, then, that if the creature is a natural, flesh-and-blood animal, it has been around for a very long time but, like the aardwolf, somehow missed its turn when the evolution gods were handing out the fossil records. The only other explanation is that it has somehow recently adapted to an upright posture. Since these things are supposed to take eons, if the theory of evolution is correct, adaptation would have to be the result of one of several unlikely scenarios. These possibilities are:

1. A successful freak mutation in some wolf/hybrid cross that was able to be passed on (my "Indigenous Dogman" from *The Beast of Bray Road*);

2. Genetic engineering or some wildly outlandish selective breeding (*a la* the fiendish black-ops work supposedly going on in secret government labs); or

3. An origin in a biological system outside our known world (Chapter 20, Interplanetary Wolfen).

But ancient men were not the only creatures to develop the ability to "walk" upright.

Take the weird little jerboa, a mouselike creature with rabbit ears and a speed of up to forty miles an hour—on its hind legs. It's family name, *Dipodidae*, actually means bipedal. It's hind legs are so overdeveloped, in fact, that its front limbs are shrunken to puny stubs, leaving the jerboa to make it on two legs or not at all. Jerboas could hardly be taken for Manwolves, however. They range in size from two to eight inches long. Besides, they inhabit Old World deserts, not wetlands of the United States. Still, here is one creature we really can't call a quadruped, while most of its other close relatives clearly are.

Then there is the gerenuk, also called "Waller's Gazelle," a member of the antelope family you don't hear much about. Gerenuks spend much of their time standing around trees in their East African habitat. And I do mean standing. They have developed the ability to remain on their hind legs for remarkably long periods of time because much of their food, leaves of certain trees, is high off the ground. To accentuate this erect posture, gerenuks also feature very long necks and legs that appear much too long for the rest of their bodies. I can imagine that it would be a startling sight to come upon a band of grazing gerenuks. They would look much like a group of loitering, naked humans, except for the deerlike heads and "bent backwards" legs.

Of course, gerenuks, like jerboas, do not inhabit North America. White-tailed deer will sometimes feed upright; I've seen one standing at my own

The gerenuk can stand on its hind legs to feed.

bird feeder, holding itself in position with its front hooves on the feeder dish and slurping away at the available seeds. But when it was finished, it didn't walk away on its hind legs. It dropped rather heavily to four feet again and despoiled my lawn before ambling on.

Birds are another group of animals that get around land on their hind feet, the front limbs having totally converted to appendages for flying. Most of them hop, but many walk with a sort of rolling gait. Penguins waddle on flipper feet, and ratites, the flightless group that includes ostriches, emu, and rheas, walk, run, and kick extremely well with their only two usable limbs. Certain lizards, too, such as basilisks, run on their hind legs. The Latin American basilisk, in fact, is called the *Jesus Cristo* lizard because of its amazing ability to run on water surfaces. Strangely, Bird Men and Lizard Men as bipedal entities may be much more believable than Manwolves. At least there are already examples of their species that regularly locomote on two legs.

Deformed Deer and Sick Monkeys
There is one other category of possible mammalian bipeds, although their conditions are not hereditary and usually not conducive to surviving in the wild. There have been numerous instances of farm animals whose front limbs were either deformed at birth or damaged accidentally, who learn to hop about quite well on their hind limbs. One Dutch physician, according to *The Illustrated Encyclopedia of Animal Life*, wrote a paper in a scientific journal about a goat he owned that was born without forelegs, and learned to jump around on its hind legs. It did lean at a forty-five-degree angle, however, which makes me think of the "hunched over" description many witnesses give of the Manwolf. And yet, in all these cases, the creatures are hopping, not striding or truly walking as the Manwolves have been seen to do. Besides, the Manwolves still evidently have the capability of zooming off on all fours, which shows that their bipedalism is not a forced characteristic.

That leaves kangaroos, also hoppers rather than walkers, which are often cited as possible Manwolf explanations. I already talked about Wisconsin's recent flap in the western part of the state, which ended with the out-of-place 'roo captured and given to Vilas Park Zoo in Madison.

What was interesting to me, however, was that not once did anyone in those western counties report seeing a werewolf. Everyone who saw it phoned authorities to say they had seen a kangaroo. People, by and large, are not stupid. Of course, they were still scoffed at by many until the creature was caught.

We've also already been over Wisconsin's other big kangaroo flap, in the vicinity of Waukesha in 1978. This creature was seen by many, but disbelieved by many more. It was never captured, the puzzle never solved. However, I recently spoke to a Manwolf witness from that general area who said someone he knew was able to get very close to the "kangaroo," close enough to see that the creature was actually a deer with very deformed or injured forelimbs. Like the Dutch doctor's goat, it had learned to hop on its hind legs, and was probably hanging around the Waukesha backyards for access to bird feeders since it couldn't feed normally in the wild any more. It likely died a normal deer death, and anyone who saw the carcass, if it wasn't devoured immediately by predators, wouldn't have thought twice about seeing a dead deer with mangled limbs.

Primates, chimpanzees, gorillas, and the like aren't true bipeds either, as I've noted earlier in this book. They use their knuckles on the ground. Nor are monkeys, even baboons. But strangely, at least one monkey proved that his kind could walk fully upright with no genetic modification in July 2004. A black macaque named Natasha, an inmate of the zoo in Jerusalem, Israel, contracted a bad case of stomach flu that almost killed her. But once she was released from the zoo's clinic, Natasha did an astonishing thing. She began to walk upright, never again reverting to all fours. Most monkeys will walk around on their hind legs at times, but not all the time. Veterinarians speculated she may have suffered brain damage. But there she was on TV film clips shown all over the world, striding along like a miniature Bigfoot.

There has also been a famous walking chimpanzee, sort of. Known as Oliver the Humanzee, because he looked like a cross between a chimp and a human, the potty-trained male was exhibited widely during the seventies and touted as part human, but tests by the University of Chicago showed him to be all chimp. Still, Oliver could mix cocktails and perform other stupid human tricks, and he inspired a raft of other rumors, such as the supposed Chinese chimp impregnated with human sperm. The chimp and the scientist who experimented on it were both killed by superstitious villagers in the tradition of Frankenstein's monster, or so the legend goes.

But even if Natasha or Oliver or something like them did walk around upright, and against great odds managed to get lost in the Wisconsin woods and survive even one Wisconsin winter, they would still look like primates to people who might see them, and rather short ones, at that. Not Manwolves.

More interesting is the case that might be made that, if sick monkeys can walk upright, why not some type of wolf or wolf hybrid? It's a long shot that a wolf could even be infected by the same type of stomach virus that infected Natasha the macaque, but say that it did happen. Let's even say that the infected, suddenly upright wolf was living in the vicinity of Bray Road circa 1988 to 1990 and was seen by many people. That would explain one cluster of incidents, but not those that went before that time frame or the many after it, not to mention all those in other states. There would have to be a great number of sick wolves, they would all have to suffer the same kind of brain damage from the illness, and they would all have to recover well enough to survive many more years despite their brain damage and unnatural posture.

Besides, Natasha was said to always walk erect after her illness, while Manwolves have often been observed on all fours. It seems very unlikely, but I do think it's an explanation to keep in mind.

Hypertrichosis Strikes Again

Another topic I'll quickly revisit from the first book is that of hypertrichosis, or hairy humans. This is a rare genetic anomaly that strikes certain humans from time to time, people such as the now-famous Gomez brothers of Mexico or Jojo the Dogfaced boy of the Barnum & Bailey Brothers Circus; they may be covered with long hair over ninety-six to ninety-eight percent of their bodies. Another Mexican family currently being studied may have as many as thirty-two members with the condition. The disorder has nothing to do with the psychiatric diagnosis of lycanthropy, and the humans underneath all that hair are otherwise normal in every respect. No claw, fangs, muzzles, or tails. Some people also refer to the condition as a type of atavism, which means a return to a form from an earlier state.

The most recent person with this disorder to make the news is a young man from China who calls himself Hairboy and has said he wants to be the first completely hairy rock star. He plays the guitar and saxophone and performs at small venues for a living. But Yu Zhenhuan of Shanghai doesn't need tattoos or strange makeup to make himself stand out from the crowd; he is completely covered with black, furry-looking hair except for his palms and the soles of his feet. Growing up, he had to endure taunts of "caveman" from classmates at school, and at the age of twenty-six needed to have excess hair surgically removed from his ears to improve his ability to hear.

One medical site I visited noted that around fifty people with this condition have been described since the Middle Ages, with about thirty-four of them confirmed (evidently not including that Mexican family). They are very rare, and when they do show up, they cause a huge commotion. Again, although China's Hairboy has brought the idea of the Beast of Bray Road as hypertrichosis victim forward once more in the minds of a few people, I still think Wolfen warriors from another planet are more likely.

Having covered and re-covered all these arguments from the many people who are understandably searching for a rational explanation for the Manwolf sightings, I want to say that I wish one of the ideas did fill the bill. They just all have too many problems. I look very carefully at every suggestion people make as to what this creature might "really" be, but the truth is that so far nothing that covers all the bases has been presented.

Even my own fantasy of the Indigenous Dogman, some wolflike carnivore that may have survived from the recent Ice Ace and then quickly adapted to bipedal locomotion, is a stretch and quite improbable. Not completely impossible, I guess, but again it makes the space wolves look good.

The fog may come in on little cat feet, as poet Carl Sandburg once purred, but those who have seen the wolf-headed walker also know this; the Manwolf comes in on big dog feet. And we simply don't know why.

CHAPTER TWENTY-TWO

IMPLICATIONS

"There are more things in heaven and earth, Horatio,
than are dreamt of in your philosophy."
— Shakespeare, *Hamlet*

The Coming "Thing"

I was looking at the March 2005 issue of *FATE* magazine recently and came across a story called "UFOs and the Evolution of Man," by Scott Corrales, a very thorough researcher.

He tells about an incident in 1951 that occurred in the Pyrenees between France and Spain. A hotel owner and former meteorologist named Jaime Bordas Bley or Jacques Bordas found himself receiving a strange guest one day, a delicately built man with very long hands and platinum blonde hair, wearing iridescent clothing. Just to check how out of place that would have been, I looked up some old women's magazines from '51, and iridescent duds were definitely not the style. I'm not sure iridescent fabric was even being manufactured at that time. The odd guest requested milk and bread as daily fare. He and Bordas had conversations about mankind's future and the being said eerily apocalyptic things like:

"Man considers himself to be alone on the earth and is not aware that he is one of evolution's many elements. With his boundless pride and alleged wisdom, he does not know that there exists on Planet Earth AN ANIMAL THAT WILL REPLACE HIM IN THE FULLNESS OF TIME. He cannot imagine that SOMETHING that will surpass him is currently being prepared.

"Man has been given many extraordinary attributes to dominate a vast array of extraordinary forces, but he does not know this. If he misuses them, he will not only bring about his own holocaust, but also the APPEARANCE OF THIS THING WHICH SHALL COME AFTERWARDS. Man must wait. He must learn to mark time without burning stages futilely. Only then shall it be possible for Man to establish a link with that future THING."

Of course, the strange man never said what the future THING was. But the whole speech reminded me of Noah's remote-viewed Space Wolfen, waiting in the woodsy wings for their own curtain call, as well as Rebecca Moravec's enigmatic Manwolf Spirit Master, which intimated that his pack would survive humanity. UFO contactees seem to come up with similar messages on a regular basis. Vague predictions of future gloom for mankind seem to be on every other page on the Internet.

Personally, I think there are negative forces out there, corporeal and incorporeal, that would like humankind to think negatively about tomorrow. People who feel they haven't much to live for are much easier to control. Besides, most major world religions teach that the things of this present world should not be our utmost concern. So I'm not going to get too worked up over what seems to be a sort of paranormal consensus that Manwolves are here to take over the planet once we humans are somehow annihilated. We've evidently survived alongside them for eons, whatever they are, and they don't appear to be picking us off for lunch.

I do believe that the phenomenon of the Manwolf is real. People are seeing these things in droves, across the United States and Canada. And sightings seem to be on the increase, particularly when those in states other than Wisconsin are counted. That might only be due to the larger human population and more people living and playing in what used to be wilderness areas, of course, but it also could mean that these things have become more inclined to move among us in our populated areas. Where there are people, there are small animals, roadkill, and garbage. Supernatural or not, the Manwolves have been observed in the act of snacking too many times to believe they are not at least partially corporeal and in need of protein sustenance.

I still don't believe in werewolves, but I do believe there is such a creature as the Manwolf. I also believe there is much more to it than meets the terrified eye.

Shape Shifting

It can shape shift, apparently, for one thing. There are several possibilities as to how it might accomplish this mysterious feat. As we discussed in Chapter 1, the shifting body could be a projected thought form, from either a drug-enhanced shaman or a New Age magician or some combination of the two. Of course, in that case, given the number and spread of cases, there would have to be a country-wide raft of shamans and/or magick practitioners out there creating thought forms run amok. I just don't believe those harder-core occult practices have reached mass-entertainment levels yet.

For more of a classic horror approach, one might consider that morphing forms or different monster guises could originate from highly developed psi powers on the part of the creature itself (a shamanic animal?) whereby it is able to project its own version of reality on the unaware human mind. A number of witnesses have said they could feel almost a telepathic message coming from the animal, a "stay away" impression that ordinary fauna just do not emit. Many have sensed that it is intelligent, and human psychic ability is now a proven national asset in our military laboratories. Why couldn't an intelligent creature possess this type of ability as well as man?

Of course, if the creature is supernatural in origin, either a demon from the Christian concept of hell, or something from another dimensional world, it would not be bound to strict conformity to our ideas of matter. Shifting its shape would come as naturally to a Manwolf as swimming to a duck.

But we also know the creature leaves footprints, and can be heard when running on a hard surface or crunchy leaves. That means at least some of the time, it has body mass and weight. It can make a low, throaty growl, so it has a voicebox. If it eats, it has a stomach and presumably, intestines. It must then excrete scat, although perhaps it buries or covers its droppings as some other large predators do. It may even leave fur strands. It's more than a ghost, hallucination, or someone's imagination.

And although it probably has very sharp senses, it is not all-knowing, evidenced by the many people who have caught it unawares and startled it. It does in most cases seem much more intent on getting away from us than anything else. This urge to flee has been observed to border on panic when dogs or guns are present. It knows when to get out of Dodge. It is also adept at concealing itself, for the most part. I believe the reason we have so many sightings between August and October here is that the cornfields are tall and standing for most of this time. They grow just high enough to conceal a six-foot Furry and enable access to many places that would be much too open for safe travel the rest of the year. The cornfields are also filled with grazing deer and other game.

And yet, solid and hidebound as all these observations may be, it just seems very unlikely the Manwolf is physically running around along with the small Bigfoot and the Lizard Men and the other beasties all year long. There is still something very unreal, very quasi-matter, about the creature, beyond the fact that the great majority of the population, myself included, has never seen one.

Like Todd Roll, I enjoy the idea of the creature as a Protean earth spirit. Jim Brandon, in *Rebirth of Pan*, sees the earth spirit as an "incomplete mosaic, something like a paint-by-numbers dot pattern of an unknown image, in which we have only a portion of the necessary reference points." It is certainly true that our picture of Manwolf sightings and all the seemingly related phenomena is far from complete.

I think it safest to treat the Manwolf as an idea, for the time being. As soon as someone pins the beast down and pronounces it one absolute thing or another—a deformed wolf or a demon, an anorexic bear or an alien—discussion stops because the mind has closed. A particular "thing" is an open-shut, done deal. An idea, however, can be studied, dwelt upon, and adjusted to suit new facts as they arise.

That is not to say ideas don't exist as real things, or that the Manwolf doesn't exist. Both of them do, I think, in their own realms. But since the Manwolf's realm seems to be intersecting more and more with our own, it would probably behoove us to pay close attention to the *idea* of this creature and its true nature. A sharp, in-focus snapshot or video of it would also be nice. Of course, if my hog-hunting friend Andy in Georgia has his way, we may someday have a body to examine...if it is susceptible to bullets. Would that be murder? I don't know.

I'm also well aware of the part my investigations and publicity have played in the story and in the sightings expansion. As experiments in quantum mechanics have shown, the amazing truth is that mere human observance of tiny sub-atomic particles changes the behavior of those particles. If that truth plays out in the larger, visible world, perhaps the very act of all those witnesses viewing the creature some-how changes the Manwolf phenomenon in ways we don't understand. Perhaps it even changes us.

John Keel wrote in *The Complete Guide to Mysterious Beings*, "The mind is unquestionably involved in many UFO and psychic experi-ences, and, very probably, in a number of our most bizarre monster sightings. Thus we only see what the phenomenon wants us to see and we only remember what it wants us to remember." Think of Glo in northern Illinois, who could barely remember anything but the crea-ture's eyes. Again, it makes me wonder why certain people see the crea-ture, while others, driving through the same area at almost the same time, see nothing. I still don't know of anyone who's gone out monster-hunting and come home successful in sighting a Manwolf, including myself. Much as it hurts our egos to admit it, we do not seem to be in control of this phenomenon in any tangible way.

I've done my best to lay out in these pages all I have been able to discover about the Manwolf since the first book was published two years ago, including all the additional speculation that has come my way. There is still no definitive, handy answer to give a waiting public about this creature, but I think that with these further sightings, descriptions, and even evidence such as footprints, we have come much closer to gaining a true understanding of this furry Unbelievable.

As more incidents inevitably come to light, I hope that people will continue to contact me and report their experiences as fully as possi-ble. I don't think this creature is going anywhere (except, perhaps, more closely among us) anytime soon. We may as well come to grips with that and keep looking to the woods and the cornrows for that furry brow and fanged snarl. After all, it is looking at us.

CHRONOLOGY OF CREATURE INCIDENTS BY STATE

• Denotes listing from *The Beast of Bray Road: Tailing Wisconsin's Werewolf*
* Denotes listing from *Hunting the American Werewolf: Man Beasts in Wisconsin and Beyond*

Wisconsin Incidents

• **1929** — The Wild Man of LaGrange is reported, not a "werewolf" sighting per se but perhaps the source of some local legends.

• **1936** — Mark Schackelman sees creature on Indian mound behind St. Coletta Institute, Jefferson County, Wisconsin, standing upright, uttering "gadarrah."

* **1941, Fall** — Muscoda, Wisconsin, young men see bipedal furry creature standing on a hilly roadside.

* **1959, early July** — Pittsville, Wisconsin, farmer sees huge, unidentifiable quadruped canid.

• **1960s/1970s** — The Eddy, large hairy creature, is rumored to stalk rural East Troy.

• **1964** — Dennis F., rural Delavan in western Walworth County, says "Bigfoot" creature crossed road upright and hurdled fence on either side.

* **1964 or 65, Summer** — Linda Bladel's dog fights a large, unknown creature on Bowers Road, rural Elkhorn, Wisconsin.

* **1970** — Bluff Monster (Bigfootlike) seen on Young Hill by Judy Wallerman and Rochelle Klemp on several occasions.

• **1970s** — The Bluff Monster, large hairy creature, seen by campers around Bluff Road, near LaGrange.

* **1970s (early)** — Manwolf seen along Highway 13 near Glidden, Wisconsin, by Helen and Larry Woiak.

• **1972** — Jefferson County farm, creature slashed horse, left scratch marks on house seven feet above ground, investigated by Department of Natural Resources agent David Gjetson.

• **1972** — Milwaukee, Kim Del Rio saw upright, doglike creature on neighbor's lawn.

* **1972** — Edgerton, summer, six teens saw an upright wolf form materialize near Lake Koshkonong.

* **Late 1970s and early 1980s** — Todd Roll recorded Bearwolf sightings near Wausau, Wisconsin.

• **1980** — Ronald Nixon, early summer, observed bipedal hairy hominid on shores of Bark River north of Whitewater, Wisconsin.

• **1980** — Marv Kirschnik, Marinette County, Wisconsin, sees seven-foot-tall dark-colored biped with glowing yellow eyes from snowmobile trail in winter.

* **1981, September** — Marv Kirschnik sees Manwolf by side of Highway 11 near Bray Road.

*1982, Fall — Dousman, Wisconsin, Denise Benson and her brother see red eyes walking through a cornfield seven feet from ground.

*1983 or '84, Summer — Twin Lakes, Pete Peterson sees Manwolf on roadside.

*1984, October — West of Kenosha, Wisconsin, on Highway ML, Rick Renzulli sees two huge quadrupeds cross the road.

*1984 (est.) — Girl on farm on Highway 11 near Bray Road is "treed" by a Manwolf.

*1986, October — Diane Koenig sees Manwolf eating deer on Bray Road.

*1986 or '87, October — Tom from Palmyra sees likely Manwolf on Highway H near Bluff Road.

*1987 — Mineral Point, Wisconsin, alleged werewolf sighting by a crowd of people.

• 1989, Fall — Scott Bray sees creature by rockpile on Bray Road, on all fours, dog or coyotelike but larger.

• 1989, Fall — Lori Endrizzi sees creature kneeling by side of Bray Road, holding "roadkill."

*1989, November — Dennis Hasting and companion are stalked by bipedal creature on Highway 11 woods near Bray Road while coon hunting; another man sees hairy bipedal creature run on two legs after rising from all fours.

*1989, November — C. and her friend are chased down Wells Street in Lake Geneva by a furry, tall biped.

*Late 1980s, November — Joy Smage finds huge animal print in Bray Road field.

• 1990, late December — Heather Bowey, Russell Gest, and three young cousins see creature by creek near Loveland Road, Bray Road vicinity, both upright and on all fours.

• 1990, March — Mike Etten sees creature holding roadkill on Bray Road, sitting on haunches.

*1990, May or June — "Half-Pint" Manwolf seen on Larsen Trail between Oshkosh and Winneconne by two teen males.

*1990, July — Second sighting of Half-Pint creature on Larsen Trail by same teen males.

• 1991, Fall — Sharilyn Smage sees creature in cornfield on Bray Road, on all fours.

• 1991, October 31 — Doris Gipson sees creature near cornfield on Bray Road, running upright, lunging for car.

• 1991, November — Tracks of "Potsy" are seen in snow on Potter's Road near Simons Feed Mill, Bray Road vicinity.

• 1991, November — "Jennifer," twenty-year-old radio call-in guest, reports creature seen running across road on two legs by her and boyfriend, probably in Elkhorn vicinity.

• 1991, November 30, 10:00 AM — The Robert Bushmans see creature dash across road on all fours on Highway 11 between Elkhorn and Delavan.

• 1992, April — Martha Kerkman sees creature in New Munster, western Kenosha County, on four legs Easter morning. Friend also saw same animal next day.

• 1992, August — Tom Brichta, Chris Maxwell see creature near cornfield on Highway 106, Jefferson County, standing upright, lunging for car.

• **1992, October** — Tom Brichta, Scott Freimund see creature near cornfield on Highway 106, Jefferson County, walking upright.

• **1992–93** — Mitch and friend run over large creature on Highway A, north of Delavan; creature six to seven feet long stretched out on road, apparently dead.

* **1993, late August or early September** — Angie Beaudoin sees Manwolf on Highway 67 in Waukesha County.

* **1993, summer** — Andy Hurd sees Bigfoot in family barn near Hebron, Jefferson County. He and his mother see a strange, huge canid on all fours soon after.

* **1993 or '94, Summer** — Father and son, names withheld, see Lizard Man on riverbank in LaCrosse.

* **1993 or '94, late Summer** — Teenage girls see huge, black, doglike thing cross Highway 11 just west of Delavan.

* **1993 or '94** — Madison woman sees huge, fanged, large-headed quadrupeds at her garbage cans.

* **Mid-1990s** — Medford Reptile Man seen on Highway 13 by DNR warden and highway workers.

* **1994, January or February** — Richard Fanning sees huge, unidentifiable quadruped canine near Lima Center, Rock County.

* **1994, January or February** — Ed Mallonen sees Manwolf rise from all fours and run away on two legs on Highway 59 between Eagle and North Prairie.

* **1994, April** — Two young girls witness a creature change from wolf to bear in a field near Maribel.

* **1994, early Spring** — David and Mary Pagliaroni see Bigfoot jump bridge rail at Honey Lake, Walworth County.

• **1995, November** — C. Doe menaced by huge, doglike creature on four legs near east shore of Lauderdale Lakes at dusk.

• **1996, early February** — Glenn North sees very fast quadruped "taller than a dog" crossing Highway 12 between LaGrange and Whitewater in Walworth County.

* **1996 or '97, June** — Racine teacher sees probable Manwolf along Highway 38.

* **1997, October** — Hope Schwartz sees Manwolf eating small deer near Argyle, LaFayette County.

• **1998** — Jessica Anderson sees creature at her in-law's window in Williams Bay, near Geneva Lake.

* **1998, Spring–Summer** —Theobald sees a Bearwolf in Oconto County.

• **1999** — Young girls see huge, large-headed, wolflike animal in their yard near Marshfield, Wood County, Wisconsin.

* **2000, late December** — Three young women see a Manwolf on the I-94/Moorland Road interchange in Brookfield.

* **2003, May** — Young man in Eau Claire is visited by Manwolf phantom.

*2003, Summer — Katie Zahn and three companions see a total of four Manwolves near Avon Bottoms, Rock County.

*2003, Fall — Sheryl Cunzenheim sees likely Manwolf along Highway DM between Waunakee and Arlington.

*2004, January — Chuck Hampton sees "dire wolfish" dog in driveway in Honey Creek.

*2004, May — Madison book store clerk "Preston" sees a morphing dog/ape creature in Isthmus neighborhood in Madison.

*2004, early October — Renee Fritz sees Manwolf head and shoulders on Stateline Road three miles east of Sharon, near Illinois border.

*2005, January 1 — Erik Binnie and friend Andy see extremely large quadruped with glowing yellow eyes on Highway N near Jefferson.

*2005, March 9 — UW-Whitewater student sees Big Furry biped crossing Highway 59 near Lima Marsh.

*2005, March — Racine teen sees Manwolf by roadside between Racine and Kenosha.

*2005, April — Mary Philippsen, Williams Bay, hears a manlike creature run over her roof and jump off. It leaves large, round footprints in her flowerbed. A month later, there are more footprints and a hunk of unidentified dark fur is found on the lawn.

*2005, July 4 — Winged humanoid seen on Paradise Road near Jefferson by two people.

*2005, September 16 — Young man sees small Bigfoot creature at County Highway B and White Pigeon Road, Bloomfield Township in Walworth County.

Georgia Incidents

*2005, June–July — Manwolf and prints are sighted twice in southern swamp area of Georgia by hog hunter and companion.

Illinois Incidents

• 1964, Early Fall — Richard Moe sees large black creature with furry paws rocking car of parked couple in Wadsworth, Illinois (near Gurnee, not far south of Wisconsin border).

*1960s (est.), Summer — Married couple see four Manwolves walking on hind legs down street at night in Decatur.

*1989, July — Couple see Bigfoot creature on Highway 12, heading toward Des Plaines.

*1994, September — Manwolf seen by several guards at Great Lakes Naval Base north of Chicago.

*2002, Summer — Woman, Beck (last name withheld), sees huge, wolf-headed quadruped dodging cars on Highway 26 just north of Freeport.

*2002, Summer — Beck's mother sees same huge creature standing in her yard five miles southeast of Freeport, near Pecatonica River.

*2003, last week of January — Beck's sister-in-law and her daughter see same creature crouching by a bridge north of Freeport on Red Oak Road.

Michigan Incidents
*1700s–early 1800s — Legends of French werewolves told in Detroit.

• 1880s — Dog Man terrorizes lumber camp in Wexford County near Manistee River.

• 1938 — Doglike creature on two feet confronts Robert Fortney on the banks of the Muskegon River near Paris, Mecosta County.

*1955–1959 (est.) — Tall, furry creature seen in Byron Center by a child, including in her basement.

• 1987 — Dog Man blamed for attack on a cabin in Baldwin area.

*1989–1990 — Tammy Moss sees tall, furry, yellow-eyed creature in Woods in Acme Township, northeast of Traverse City.

*2005, August — Jeff Cornelius is charged by a growling Manwolf near Holly, on Fish Lake Road.

Missouri Incidents
*20th century, dates unknown — Hyena-like creatures seen in Ozarks east of Springfield.

New York Incidents
*2004, June — Carper brothers see two bipedal running Manwolves near Plattsburgh.

Ohio Incidents
*2004 — Fisherman sees "humanoid doglike creature."

*2005, August — Man sees "Mandog" near town of Liberty.

Pennsylvania Incidents
*Mid-1800s — Northumberland werewolf guards the flocks of shepherdess May Paul.

*1850s — In Clinton County, aunt of Peter Pentz is attacked by bipedal werewolf.

*1894 — A black wolf considered to be the devil frequents the grave of outlaw Cyrus Etlinger in Centre County.

*1972–1998 — R. Jason Van Hoose receives reports of Shenango Valley werewolf.

*1973 — Two Lancaster County farmers see Goat Man.

*2000 — Man and two friends see Albatwitch on Route 23 between Lancaster and Marietta.

*2002, February — Rick Fisher sees an Albatwitch walking alongside Route 23 between Lancaster and Marietta.

Tennessee Incidents
*2003–2004, Winter — Patricia Law sees "Dogman" between Pikeville and Dayton.

BIBLIOGRAPHY

Ball, John, ed. *From Beowulf to Modern British Writers.* New York: Odyssey Press, 1959.

Baring-Gould, Sabine. *The Book of Werewolves.* London: Senate (imprint of Studio Editions), 1995.

Birmingham, Robert A., and Eisenberg, Leslie E. *Indian Mounds of Wisconsin.* Madison: University of Wisconsin Press, 2000.

Bloom, Howard. *The Global Brain, Evolution of the Mass Mind from the Big Bang to the 21st Century.* Hoboken, NJ: Wiley, 2001.

Bord, Colin, and Bord, Janet. *Alien Animals: A Worldwide Investigation.* Harrisburg, PA: Stackpole, 1981.

Boyer, Dennis. *Giants in the Land: Folk Tales and Legends of Wisconsin.* Madison, WI: Prairie Oak, 1997.

Brandon, Jim. *The Rebirth of Pan: Hidden Faces of the American Earth Spirit.* Dunlap, IL: Firebird, 1983.

Coleman, Loren. *Bigfoot! The True Story of Apes in America.* New York: Paraview, 2003.

Coleman, Loren. *Mysterious Encounters: Phantom Trains, Spooky Spots and Other Mysterious Wonders.* Winchester, MA,: Faber & Faber, 1985.

Coleman, Loren, and Huyghe, Patrick. *The Field Guide to Bigfoot, Yeti, and Other Mystery Primates Worldwide.* New York: Avon, 1999.

Corrales, Scott. "UFOs and the Evolution of Man." *FATE Magazine*, March 2005: Vol..58,#3, Issue 659, pp.52–57.

Cruz, Joan Carroll. *Mysteries, Marvels, Miracles in the Lives of the Saints.* Rockford, IL: Tan, 1997.

Dale-Green, Patricia. *Lore of the Dog.* Boston: Houghton Mifflin, 1967.

Deveraux, Paul. *Haunted Land: Investigations into Ancient Mysteries and Modern Day Phenomena.* Bath, UK: Bath, 2001.

Dorson, Richard M. *Bloodstoppers and Bearwalkers: Folk Tales of Canadians, Lumberjacks and Indians.* Cambridge, MA: Harvard University Press, 1972.

Ferrol, Stuart. "The Hexham Wolf." *Fortean Times*, January 2005: archived online.

Fort, Charles. *The Book of the Damned.* New York: Ace, 1941.

Gard, Robert L., and Soren, L.G. *The Romance of Wisconsin Place Names.* New York: October House, 1968.

Gill, Sam D., and Sullivan, Irene F. *The Dictionary of Native American Mythology.* New York: Oxford University Press, 1992.

Godfrey, Linda S. *The Beast of Bray Road: Tailing Wisconsin's Werewolf.* Black Earth, WI: Prairie Oak Press, 2003.

INDEX

A
Acme Woods, MI, 169-170
Adams, Charlie, 186
Albatwitches, 183-186, 188, 191, 311
Allegan County, MI, 170-171
amphibious man, 248
Amphicyon, 27-29, 92, 96
Anderson, Jessica, 150, 309
animal-human communicator, 283-285
Anubis, 105, 110-111, 236, 286
Arlington, WI, 118-120, 310
Avon Bottoms, 125-131, 146, 310

B
baboons, 176-177
Backus, Joyce Sheard, 36
Baring-Gould, Sabine, 288-289
Bearwalkers, 24-25, 288
Bearwolf, 21-30
Beast of Bray Road, 7-8, 31, 34, 36, 40, 67, 170,
   220-221, 307-308
Beaudoin, Angie, 70-71, 185, 309
Belle Fontaine, MI, 173
Belle Isle, MI, 172-173
Bennett, Colin, 123
Benson, Denise, 47-49, 308
Beutlich, Robert, 282-283, 285, 287
Bigfoot, xi, xiii, 34, 38-39, 49, 74-79, 81, 87, 101,
   146, 162, 184, 185, 195-196, 291, 309, 310
Binnie, Erik, 133-134, 310
birds, giant, 247
black dogs, 189, 235-238, 242
Black Monks, 232-233
Black River Falls, WI, 31-32, 257
Black Shuck, 235
Bladel, Linda, 34-35, 307
Blue Sea Lake werewolf, Canada, 209-120
Bluff Monster, 36-37, 261, 274-276, 307
Bord, Colin and Janet, 260
Bordas, Jacques, 301-302
Brandon, Jim, 262, 269, 304
Bray, Earl and Olive Sheard, 36

Bray Road, 34-35, 51-52, 54-60, 67-70, 267-268,
   270, 271-273, 307-308
Brookfield, WI, 113-118, 247, 310
Bushman, Mr. and Mrs. Robert, 73-74, 308
Byron Center, MI, 171-172, 311

C
Canada, 209-210
Carper, George and John, 193-194, 311
cat people, 163
Cedarville, IL, 206
Champy, lake monster 193
Cherney Maribel Caves County Park, 19-21
Clinton County, PA, 188-191, 311
clothed creatures, 210
Coleman, Loren, 146-147, 163-164, 185, 237,
   269
convergence, in mammals, 130
Converse Carnivore, 210-211
Cook, Steve, 168
Cornelius, Jeff, 174-178, 311
Corrales, Scott, 300
cougar, 43, 49, 80, 148-151, 163, 190, 208, 234-
   235

D
Dale-Green, Patricia, 263
Decatur, IL, 202-204, 310
deformity as cause of bipedalism, 296-297
Delavan, WI, 40, 72-73, 117, 307, 308, 309
Del Rio, Kim, XIII, 93, 307
Des Plaines, IL, 204-205, 310
Detroit, MI, 172-173, 311
Devereaux, Paul, 102, 232, 236
DiFonzo, Carla, 183
dire wolf, 28, 133, 89-97, 200-201
Dogrib Nation, 263
Dorson, Richard, 24
Dousman, WI 47-49, 308
DuPont Monster, 209

E
earth spirits, 6, 11, 30, 242, 229
Eau Claire, WI, 120-124, 309

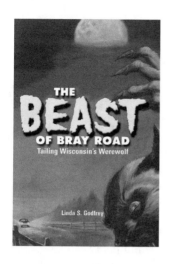

The Beast of Bray Road
Linda S. Godfrey

In the early 1990s, people in the small town of Elkhorn, Wisconsin, reported seeing strange, hairy, wolf-like creatures that could walk upright. Named after the rural back road where the sightings occurred, the Beast of Bray Road became an international sensation. Local reporter Linda Godfrey set out to understand what the terrified townsfolk were seeing—an unknown animal, a demonic apparition, or a real werewolf?

With its fascinating combination of solid research and wry humor, *The Beast of Bray Road* will convince even the most skeptical reader that someone . . . or something . . . *is* lurking on Bray Road.

"Move over, Bigfoot! Honest, sober Wisconsinites have for decades reported horrifying accounts of a man-beast at the boundaries of science. This fascinating book would be gripping science fiction—except that it's fact!"

—Jay Rath, author, *W-Files*

Softcover, 6" x 9"
216 Pages
$16.95
ISBN 1-879483-91-2

Trails Books & Prairie Oak Press
Madison, Wisconsin
www.trailsbooks.com

More Great Legends & Lore
From Trails Books
& Prairie Oak Press

Driftless Spirits: Ghosts of Southwest Wisconsin, *Dennis Boyer*
Haunted Wisconsin, *Michael Norman and Beth Scott*
The I-Files: True Reports of Unexplained Phenomena in Illinois, *Jay Rath*
The Eagle's Voice: Tales Told by Indian Effigy Mounds, *Gary J. Maier, M.D.*
The M-Files: True Reports of Minnesota's Unexplained Phenomena, *Jay Rath*
The Poison Widow: A True Story of Sin, Strychnine & Murder, *Linda S. Godfrey*
The W-Files: True Reports of Wisconsin's Unexplained Phenomena, *Jay Rath*

For a free catalog write or visit us online.

Trails Books
a division of Big Earth Publishing
923 Williamson Street
Madison, WI 53703
www.trailsbooks.com